GET MONEY DO GOOD

Get Money Do Good

A TRUE STORY HOW-TO

J.D. Vermaas, Ph.D.

AN IMPRINT OF VERMAAS, LLC.
HTTPS://WWW.GETMONEYDOGOOD.COM
Franklin, Tennessee

Get Money Do Good: A True Story How-To
Copyright © 2020 J.D. Vermaas. All Rights Reserved.

Publisher's Cataloging-in-Publication Data:

Names: Vermaas, Jodi D., author.
Title: Get money do good: a true story how-to / J.D. Vermaas, Ph.D.
Description: Includes bibliographical references. | Franklin, TN: Get Money Do
Good, an Imprint of Vermaas, LLC, 2020.
Identifiers: ISBN: 978-1-7353966-1-3 (Hardcover) | 978-1-7353966-0-6 (pbk.) |
978-1-7353966-2-0 (ebook) | LCCN: 2020913598
Subjects: LCSH Vermaas, Jodi D. | Vermaas, Garry. | Vermaas family. | Mothers—
   Biography. | Fathers—Biography. | Adoptive parents—Biography. | Intercountry
   adoption. | Older child adoption. | Parenting. | Parent and child. | Adoption—
   Moral and ethical aspects. | Adoption—Religious aspects—Christianity. |
   Social justice—Religious aspects—Christianity. | Parents of children with dis-
   abilities. | Parenting. | BISAC BIOGRAPHY & AUTOBIOGRAPHY / Personal
   Memoirs | BIOGRAPHY & AUTOBIOGRAPHY / Social Activists
Classification: LLC HV875.5. V47 2020 | DDC 248.8/45—dc23

Cover design: Klassic
Interior design and typesetting: Stewart A. Williams
Creative Consultant: Alee Anderson
First Editor: Elizabeth Bruce
Final Editor: Shauna Perez

This book is a memoir that reflects the author and her family's recollections of
their experiences, as well as ideas taken from adoption dossiers, medical records,
school reports, and newspaper clippings. As with all adoption stories, the children's experiences must be understood through a patchwork of borrowed memories, especially regarding their missing brothers and sisters whose voices had to be
recreated. Some names and characteristics have been changed, some events have
been condensed or filled in, and some dialogue has been recreated.

For more information on special discounts, group orders, or speaking events, contact us at our website www.getmoneydogood.com

To see the **PHOTO ALBUM** that accompanies this book, see our page at
www.getmoneydogood.com/photo-album

For Angel—and all who are lost.
We are coming for you.

TABLE OF CONTENTS

PART I

A NEW BEGINNING

Give Her a Name

ANGELA'S SISTER

5 February 2008

I am first daughter, and I have no name. When they talk about me, they call me *bata ni Evangeline*, Evangeline's kid. I call myself Angel because I'm not here. I exist—but only in the shadows, gone as soon as I am noticed. It's better that way and easier for you to go about your lives if my story remains untold. But before I go, let me explain the circumstances of my departure and introduce you to someone else's story—that of my sister and the unlikely family that would become her own.

I stand on a narrow dirt path, peering at my former home, a squatter's hut along the waterway near Barangay 275, District III in Binondo, Manila. Although technically Binondo, everything about my neighborhood is Tondo, the nearby district with the largest slum in Manila, bound by the dark canals from the main

Pasig River. I have heard that this river used to be full of life, but I've never seen anything alive in those gray waters. Staring across the garbage-filled waterway framed by the crossed clotheslines of the slum's inhabitants, I am glad they will never see me again.

I had planned my escape many times in my mind, but the details did not come together until recently. Several weeks ago, the skinny man with a tattoo of a spiderweb on his left elbow spotted me in the market. I had seen him before, but this time he approached me. I had been stealing rice, scooping it into a used plastic bottle that I had slashed into a cup and hid in my dress pocket. I knew he wasn't one of the bad men because they wore blue with a gold-colored badge. The man with the tattoo showed me a picture of another place far from here and said a girl so pretty could get a really good job there. I didn't know where *there* was, but I knew it wasn't *here*.

That day, I walked away from the man, not saying a word. For many days after, I couldn't help but wish to see him again. I had dreamed about leaving Binondo, where crowds of shoeless wanderers picked through heaps of garbage, looking for food and items to sell. They were the lucky ones. The unlucky ones were floating in the Pasig, dead from the drugs or the gang dealers or the bad men with badges. As soon as the bodies were dragged away, they were forgotten.

I had heard from some ladies in my district that important people needed cleaning ladies and nannies in Dubai and remembered the stories of girls becoming entertainers in Japan. These rumors captured my imagination. I spent hours staring at the posters on the market walls of the *Divisoria*, which showed uniformed women working at fancy hotels, and I tried to read their words.

For some time now, I had been seeing the man with the spiderweb tattoo, as I ducked around the rows of milkfish and open sacks of rice, near Lalang's oyster counter and right next to the chicken shop next door. Like me, the chicken shop also had no name, identified only by its purpose. From my station, I would wait for something to distract the old ladies selling rice, so I could shove my cup into the open bag just steps away from where I stood. As I waited for my moment, shooing away the flies from my sweaty cheeks, I would watch the man. He often approached other girls like me, girls who were too young to leave home, but old *enough*. Anyone older than five was old *enough*. Mama already had sent me to other men four times in exchange for money for Papa's medicines. I, too, was old *enough*.

On my long walk to the market a few months back, I spotted a miniature white bus in front of the sari-sari store, dirty and bent in on the driver's side from what must have been several motorbike accidents. I had seen this bus before but never parked in front of the sari-sari store.

The man with the spiderweb tattoo grabbed the hand of a small girl I knew from District III and led her onto the bus. She was younger than me, or at least smaller. I watched as the bus drove away, seeing her long, black ponytail blowing in the breeze from the open window. *She, too, is gone forever,* the thought came easily. And she was. No one talked about her or spoke of her disappearance. There was no commotion in the District the next day when her parents finally came home. Girls often left, whether by choice or quiet force. And here in Binondo, they never came back.

I used to fear being picked up by the minibuses, the old vans, and the trolling motorbikes, but I am no longer afraid of them. I fear nothing—not Mama, not her boyfriends, not the drunken visitors, or even the bad men. Night terrors left me long ago, along with other emotions that I recognize in the happy faces of the people on the posters at the *Divisoria*.

Gone are the sparks of hope that would sometimes rise in my chest when I was a younger girl and Papa would bring *lechon* on *Noche Buena*. No longer does my belly tighten when I hear the shrieks and screams in the darkness during the hot summer nights on the river. And the softness that used to fill my mind when I thought about my family has been absent since Papa got sick. In fact, I no longer feel anything at all. I think that's what *old enough* really means.

I knew Mama was going to give birth to her next child any day. She already had five boys other than me, and now they said she was having another, this time a girl. As her belly grew, I thought maybe I would feel excited, but I felt nothing—not joy, fear, hope, or love. I saw my soon-to-be sister's whole life and future before me without ever seeing her face. I am no Plaza Miranda psychic, but life in my neighborhood was predictable, if nothing else.

I refused to follow the ways of the *estero* and claimed my way out. I found the man with the tattoo on a cool Tuesday evening in January and planned my pickup. Then I waited for my day. I would sneak away and meet him at the sari-sari store when Mama hid inside the house to have her baby. He'd be watching for me every day during the early morning hours until it was time.

And now that time has arrived. Since yesterday evening, I have listened to Mama struggle against the early pains of child-birth. All night, I laid in the corner of our shack, waiting calmly and quietly. Yet one thought kept nagging me: *Give your baby sister a name.* The thought was unyielding, like a command from God himself.

I knew what this little life was about to become, and I couldn't help her or give her anything, except a name—at least, she'd have a name. In between Mama's contractions, I pleaded and whined for her to choose one, finally deciding to name baby sister myself. After several minutes of me shouting at Mama to promise to give her the name that I chose, Mama conceded, *"OK lang."*

It was the last time I will ever speak to Mama. Now I stand on the highest point of my neighborhood—a hurried, five-minute walk from our home—and take a final glance down toward the Pasig, knowing I am gone forever. Facing forward, I make for the sari-sari store and wait for the man with the spiderweb tattoo to take me somewhere—anywhere else. As I press on, I hear in the near distance a final scream, and then—just barely—the tiny cry of my sister.

Angela is born.

I pause to appreciate the moment, but I feel nothing.

As I leave both you and baby sister, I wonder if you will feel for me—or at least for Angela, whose unexpected journey to finding family is just beginning.

CHAPTER ONE

Do-Gooders

GARRY

Winter 2008

I jammed my bulky 6'2" frame into the ride boat filled with my wife, two children, mother-in-law, and grandfather-in-law. As we rode Disney's *It's A Small World*, I couldn't help but sing the lyrics, not only because the chorus repeated incessantly, but also because it recounted our life at this moment, full of laughter, hope, and tears. However, it wasn't these universal sentiments that connected me to the rest of humanity; rather, my globetrotting had transformed the earth into a small, small world.

And of all the places to land, this was where I had settled—living in a theme-park town with my expanding family and business, with even bigger dreams in the making. Central Florida was not the place I thought I would end up, but it worked for now.

I was born in North Jersey to my construction-working

father and devout mother, schooled at Lehigh University and then Columbia University for my PhD in engineering. I wed a fellow Columbia grad, resided in the Upper East Side of New York City for a decade, and traveled often to India, China, and beyond for work as the CEO of a booming engineering firm, which I'd started a few years back.

And I always seem to be in the middle of the action. We were living in Manhattan on 9/11. Although we didn't live downtown, the blinding smoke and ash filled every New York City neighborhood that day, as if we all stood at the feet of the fallen towers.

That morning, I paced the crowded sidewalk in front of my Second Avenue apartment and watched as thousands of New Yorkers trudged north—away from the wreckage—sweaty, dirty, and weeping. This was just a few years ago when I lived in the City, and everything changed for me. For many New Yorkers, the falling towers distorted more than just the cityscape and our sense of safety. 9/11 ushered in an economic shift for those living within the city's geographical boundaries as well as thousands of other tri-state residents. In the three months after the attacks, 2.8 billion dollars of wages were lost, mostly from high-wage employment categories in the financial district. Depression rates shot up. Some people got angry, blaming anyone who looked Middle Eastern. During the tumultuous recovery period, many professionals moved out and moved on. I was one of those people.

My skills were marketable, so I sold our apartment and moved back into my parent's home in New Jersey with my wife and our baby son, Garret. In the basement office, I crafted my business plan. I would hire fellow New York friends who also wanted out. They would sell engineering services, making calculations and preparing construction documents for developers as they built structures across the globe. It did not matter that my friends weren't engineers because they were salesmen. They would sell, and I would engineer. The plan worked immediately, and contracts to build, inspect, and renovate homes, office buildings, hotels, and multi-family units rolled in.

As projects increased in number and scope, I realized I was going to need more space and additional engineers. The expansion prompted me and my team to relocate to booming South Florida, which promised lucrative building opportunities. Since my wife was born and raised there, it was an easy fit, and her dad rented us space in his office to establish our Florida presence.

Now I needed engineers. There weren't many because of the gap in the number of science, technology, engineering, and mathematics (STEM) graduates in the United States at this time. During my time at Columbia University, I was the only American doctoral candidate. The other students moved from various parts of Asia and especially China. I knew where I needed to go to find quality engineers.

I called up a former colleague who had emigrated from China to the States and asked him to put me in touch with a few top engineers in his hometown of Shanghai. He did, and they became my first foreign staff members, calculating building loads, designing optimal configurations for building layouts, selecting building materials, and making sure projects were planned in accordance with the numerous regulatory checks and requirements.

This global strategy predated the age of building information modeling (BIM), Skype, 3D printers, and high-speed internet, so running a foreign office wasn't simple or commonplace. I would take photos of drawings and building sites and send them via email, and the engineers would calculate, draft, and check the drawings. They returned them to me for review, asking questions and making comments via the one bilingual team member. Even though I couldn't understand most of the team, we got the job done.

Another of my early colleagues from New York was a native of Mumbai. He advised me to hire engineers from India and recommended a young structural engineer named Vijay, adding that most professionals in India speak English. I needed engineers, so I visited Delhi where Vijay convinced me to hire a whole team. Vijay was smart—very smart—and our newest office grew up around him and his hometown of Nagpur.

Visiting there for the first time, I experienced the startling reality of India, where most rural natives did not own a toothbrush, but everyone had five bars of connectivity on their phones. Twice motorbikes nearly ran me down on the crowded, narrow street in front of the new office. Our security guard lived in a tented hut outside of our place, cooking over an open fire among meandering cows that persistently roamed the streets. Nothing prepares you for your first time in India.

"Instead of worshipping them, why not use the cows to feed the people?" I asked Vijay, realizing I could solve generations of poverty with a single blasphemous solution. He laughed, but I was only partly kidding. We will develop this engineering team and find a way to do some good, I decided. Jodi hadn't seen Nagpur yet, but I knew she would agree.

The poverty revealed to me on that first trip to India demanded my attention. I'm not an emotional guy, but I could not dismiss the images of what I'd seen. Memories from that trip nagged at me, tugging me to find a way to offer something back. The scales of blessings were tipped so heavily in my favor that I shuddered under the guilt. And that's not me. I don't hang on to negative feelings—much to the disappointment of my wife, who likes to hash out issues much longer than I prefer. Confronted by my India experiences and the self-accusations of greed that followed, I took charge of my uncomfortable, guilty feelings and motivated myself to do good. And that was that.

China was much cleaner than India—both the people and the landscape seemed almost sterile. Where the Nagpur team members bubbled over with their passionate enthusiasm for relationships, food, and celebration—even amid the extreme poverty of their surroundings, the Chinese engineers remained aloof. The young team dutifully sent their paychecks back to their aging parents, but they didn't laugh and rarely smiled. I'm not sure they even liked me, but I tried not to be too American.

Still, I appreciated their zeal and skills, and my firm enabled many young, talented engineers to learn Western architecture and engineering while earning enough to support themselves and their families. One of my team members earned enough money to fund the education of a local orphaned girl. Another found that his salary would allow him to pay the social maintenance fee for having a second child—a rare luxury under China's one-child policy. Yes, in both India and China, there was opportunity to do good and make some money. Having been raised as both a capitalist and a Christian, it made sense to me.

Business thriving, I now lived on the intercoastal waterways of Fort Lauderdale with my young wife; our three-and-a-half-year-old son, Garret; and Jolyn, our one-year-old daughter. Named after her two grandmothers, Josephine and Carolyn, Jolyn Rose shone brightly from the day she was born. Her radiant smile, easy disposition, and the frequent squeals that erupted from her joyous heart reminded me daily of the reason I had children. Shockingly different from Garret, she was a delight in every way.

Garret was serious-minded—I had named him after my father, also a serious man. My dad never finished high school and began his construction company by laying block. Over the course of my childhood, he made millions, and by the time I was twelve, he'd started to train me to take over his business.

Going to the jobsites to work alongside the laborers while my father led the team, I learned the ways of construction: the lingo, vulgarities, tricks, and leadership principles. By fifteen, I was running the books, since I was the only one who understood the new computer system—I was also the only kid at Eastern Christian whose parents pulled him out on Fridays to run payroll at the family business. The school objected, of course, but my parents just laughed.

Often, my school would call my mom in for a chat. In first grade, my teacher advised my mom to medicate my so-called ADHD to help calm me down; by second grade, the teachers agreed that I would not amount to anything. I was too distracted, too wild, and too easily bored. My heartbroken mother refused to get me formally diagnosed, and Dad simply told her, "It's okay, Carolyn, he can work with me at the company. After all, he can dig a ditch."

So that was the plan for my life. From then on, rather than deal with the judgment of the teachers and other parents, my mother would drop me, lunch bag in hand, at the corner of the block nearest to the school and instruct me to run to the entrance as fast as I could. With this game, she avoided the teachers almost every time. Right before I opened my car door and said goodbye, she'd stare at me for a moment, smiling calmly and flashing her sparkling blue eyes. Then, she'd tell me to run.

Just like my mom—her namesake—Jolyn didn't allow much to deter her joy. Even after a scolding, Jolyn would immediately engage with her surroundings, finding reasons to laugh at the littlest things. As a growing toddler, she would gush over a small doll, a stroll with Grandma, or a bit of cotton candy. She was perfect, easy—making Garret's struggles more obvious and difficult to ignore.

Garret behaved differently than other kids—especially Jolyn. He was difficult. Like, I-can-rage-at-you-all-day-long difficult. But I was sure he would be fine. I had heard similar stories of my own ADHD-fueled antics from my childhood when I would escape the crib by climbing out the window and wander outside for a while until my mom found me.

"He'll be fine," I often said, trying to relieve my wife. The most calming, soothing, and attentive human I have ever met, my wife handled Garret well. *She's got this,* I knew.

Jodi was also different. I fell in love with Jodi on New Year's Eve at a formal ball held at the top floor of a skyscraper in Midtown Manhattan. That night, she wore a black dress and a knowing grin that stole my heart. But she wasn't my date; she was someone else's.

My date was lovely and funny—I laughed nonstop, but she wasn't Jodi. Jodi was not funny, but she was stunning and smart. I had heard about her from a friend. She also had attended Columbia and now was pursuing mission work, driven by a seriously compassionate heart and her ambition to make a mark on the world. When we met, I remember thinking *that's the girl I'm going to marry.* A few weeks later, I told her so. She didn't agree, but she smiled. I knew it was just a matter of time. That was New Year's Eve 1996. We were married the summer of 1997.

I was used to getting what I wanted—just ask my older sister, Pamela, who often reminds me of this fact. Things had come easily for me; life wasn't hard. When the gridlock came, I knew I could change directions. I'm highly adaptable and not very particular, and so is my wife. We can go anywhere and choose to do anything. I never believed I had any limitations, and I've always been fearless. I remember the Bible teaching me that "anything not done out of faith is sin." I believed that one and committed to never deciding anything based on fear. So, by 2005, Jodi and I had two children and were headed for entrepreneurial triumph.

That same year, a historic series of hurricanes pummeled the southeastern United States and forced me to make a move. In the heat of the summer, three significant storms hit our South Florida town. Fort Lauderdale was an older city, with electric wires hanging vulnerably above ground. Power outages were a mild inconvenience for most people, an excuse for a day off. For me, a CEO who ran his entire operation with foreign offices, it became impossible.

Late in the hurricane season—two months after Katrina had moved past us to ravage New Orleans—Wilma hit Florida on October 24. For nine days, we had no power, which was particularly unpleasant with my bored, screaming, I'm-going-to-wear-a-hat-and-sunglasses-to-avoid-the-world preschooler and his baby sister. When I could no longer stand it, I took Jodi, Garret, and Jolyn and headed to the Astro van, hoping we had enough fuel to get us out of the disaster zone to a working gas station. After a tense first hour in traffic, we made it to an operational pump in Lake Worth with an eighth of a tank left. From there, I drove on until we landed in central Florida, where we stayed with a friend for a few nights. Their home was inland, protected from the storm surges. During our weeklong stay, we toured central Florida and decided to stay for good.

In Orlando, we bought what my son called "the big house." The Tuscan-styled house on a cul-de-sac was the largest, finest home Garret had ever seen. To be fair, his first room was a 6x6-foot closet-turned-nursery in our 755-square-foot Manhattan apartment. Since leaving New York, we had lived only in small apartments and condos. Even as my business became successful, I remained conservative in our spending, not yet convinced that my business model would work.

This was our first house. My business had grown to 100 team members spread across the world. Building projects took me to the Bahamas, Morocco, Doha (the capital of Qatar), Dubai and the UAE, Nagpur, Shanghai, Sydney, and Vancouver. I could afford the big house, especially with the zero-down mortgages that were being offered. Our time here would mark the longest period of time we had ever stayed in the same place.

When Garret turned five, we had a pool party, hosting seventy-five children and parents from our neighborhood and church. It was an ocean-themed party, and the day we realized Garret needed help. To Garret's amazement, Jodi had created a two-tier under-the-sea cake, staying up far past me the previous night to craft it. Then, hours into the party, my wife noticed that Garret hadn't been around for a while.

Walking outside and inside, from room to room, she finally found him crouching in his closet, quietly building Legos. "The children are looking for you! It's your party!" she'd told him. But Garret said nothing.

When I went to help, he did not look up at me but continued playing, as if protecting himself from his own party. It was a look I had seen many times before when he defended himself against the elements, which never seemed to bother anyone else. I shut the closet door, leaving it slightly ajar and giving him the space to recuperate and later join the rest of us.

Garret's odd behavior won us judgment from everyone who knew us. How could it not? Sunday school freak-outs and angry outbursts toward his classmates earned us quite the reputation in our town. Jodi wept at Garret's relentlessly stressful behaviors, admitting that we must be the worst parents in the world. It just didn't make sense to us. Sometimes Garret screamed and grabbed like a hungry, newborn baby, and at others, he would use such extravagant vocabulary that I would marvel at his intelligence. He was clearly gifted but also saddled with anxieties, peculiarities, and an unwavering rigidity. Our child didn't sleep well, he ate fussily, and he craved sweets all the time. He raged when the tags in his shorts itched him and obsessively pulled on his hair whenever he had to do an uncomfortable task. He hit. He bit Jodi, drawing blood. He wouldn't bend his routine, even if an emergency demanded it.

Garret required our attention throughout the day, and Jodi's involvement in Garret's daily routine irked me. She and I were rarely alone, and I wondered if Jolyn missed Jodi's full attention, too. Only Jodi's mom, whom Garret called *Mema*, and my mother were willing to stay with him—and only for a limited amount of time. *Why can't he be like the other kids?* I often wondered. But I always convinced myself that he'd be fine.

Garret's strange and often publicly defiant behavior became an issue when I was asked to become an elder at our local

Christian church. As decreed by the church by-laws and the book of Titus, eldership required a reputation for being able to lead your own family: for raising children who were not "open to the charge of being wild and disobedient." In the two years since we began living in our new neighborhood, Jodi and I had volunteered and taught Bible classes to hundreds of people. I had led a men's group that began with five and grew to a hundred strong. Together at weekly meetings, we discussed what it meant to be real men who did right, often saying more than others thought appropriate about sexuality, pornography, and the need for men to open up and change their habits. Man Up—as I called it—resonated all over town.

My wife did the same kind of volunteer work in the ministry, and eventually the church offered her a position to lead the children's ministry, consisting of 700 children and 200 volunteers. With a PhD in clinical Christian psychology, Jodi was also particularly well-equipped to counsel women. She formally began to lead the women's ministry in addition to the children's team, often speaking publicly and to large groups of eager students.

One evening, we led a marriage seminar, expecting fifty people to attend. When we showed up to speak, 500 gatherers walked in the door looking for marriage help. From this ministry and the development of the church building, which I designed, the church grew from 500 to 3,000 people within a few years. In the end, I was voted in as an elder, despite Garret's reputation.

The business continued along a comparable trajectory: our growth was exponential. Theme park developers asked me to help design an expansive fun park in China and several water parks in Canada. I met with princes and politicians and designed the finest structures, including mansions, palaces, hotels, and resorts.

During our years in Florida, my firm brought in several million dollars of yearly revenue.

Our lives flowed along a similar pattern of wealth. The children attended local private schools, my wife meticulously decorated our home, and I drove a Lexus. We easily moved my mother-in-law, her husband, and Jodi's Italian grandfather near us so they could enjoy a life of retirement and ease. They lived in the condominiums in our gated neighborhood and flooded our lives with attention and love. At times, their doting was a bit too much, but my Italian wife relished it.

We bought annual passes to Disney World and spent every weekend in the parks. Our photo albums from this time are filled with pictures of my growing children posed with every Disney princess and character ever created. When my son got bored and frustrated with going to see Mickey Mouse, we also got passes to Sea World and Universal Studios. We traveled, skied, cruised, worked, and played hard. The not-actually-in-the-Bible verse my dad had taught me growing up was becoming prophetic: "The Lord helps those who help themselves."

For me, life was easy and fun. The American dream had come true. Freedom and hard work led me to "the big house," and I loved it. To my surprise, many of the men in my group accused their lives of becoming too predictable and mundane. I argued with many friends as they made the decision to abandon their suburban homes (and families), wondering what more life had to offer. But not me—my life felt perfect.

Sitting in the theme park ride, my knees scraping the seats in front of me and my weight causing the little boat to tilt, I thought, *I am truly, fully, wholly content.*

I glance at Garret's serious expression, his hat and sunglasses on, vigilant against the elements around him. If I have to name a challenge in my life right now, he is called Garret. My son's obvious pain and daily outbursts—along with the judgments from onlookers—don't go unnoticed. Neither do the emotional battles my wife faces as she parents this very uncommon child.

But Garret will be fine. I know it. I always win.

CHAPTER TWO

Too Much

GARRET

Spring 2008

Stay here; stay here; stay here! I think to myself. *Don't look around, keep your head down.* I'm facedown in the dirt about twenty feet from the back door of my school's gym. "Garret, are you okay? Garret?"

I say nothing. I'm too itchy; it feels like bugs are crawling all over the skin on my neck and my arms. The sun is so bright at 3:00 p.m., pick-up time. The nosy onlookers leave when I give no response. Mrs. Shirley stands close to me, but she doesn't say anything. I like her. I want to run around screaming, but I'm stuck here, flat. I wait until Mom drives up in the minivan. It's a golden beige one.

I'm only a few feet from where the cars pull through the crammed waiting area, so Mom hurries over. I never understood why this was the pick-up plan. Total chaos. I usually read my books as I wait and can skim a new page every few seconds. I like the Percy Jackson Series. I've read all of Rick Riordan's books, but today, I forgot my book when I ran to hide in the toilet stall in the first-grade hallway restroom. *Stupid school!*

I'm the fastest reader in my class. Last summer, I read the entire seven-book *Harry Potter* series. It was good. I even got an award for reading. Mom was so happy and told me how special I am and how she loves the big, important words that I've learned from all my books. The tests show that I'm a good reader, different but special. I don't know about that; I just like to read instead of being here in the dirt.

But more than reading, I like my games, especially ones I can carry in my pocket. At times like this, of heat and faces and words and itchy, I like to reach into my pocket to feel the smooth case of my Nintendo DS. I can run the tips of my fingers over the volume buttons and charging connection and instantly feel hopeful. The games are here for me, drawing me away from the chaos.

Pokémon is my favorite because it's the best. I wish I had a game with me today. Gaming makes sense. There's a winner and a loser; there's a beginning and an end. There's an off and an on. I don't have to wonder what's happening. Not like during my days at school. *Stupid school!* I think again.

I don't understand why I have to go to school. And why did God make the world like this anyway? My first-grade teacher tells us that He is full of good stuff. Really? What's good about this world? The skin on my arms feels on fire. The sounds and light come sharply at me from every direction. My brain is too aware right now—sometimes, I can't see what's right in front of me.

People ask me all the time, "What's the matter with you?"

Don't they feel itchy too? I wonder. *Aren't they bored? Don't they have the same need to rage against the endless onslaught of noises, sounds, and sights?* No, this doesn't seem like a great creation at all.

But I can't say that anymore because when I do, people's lips get tight and their eyes look oddly small. Everyone says it's good to always tell the truth, but I don't think they mean it. I don't hear a lot of truth—not when I have to wait for Mom as she helps the ladies or when Dad lingers long after leading his men's study group. It seems my parents are careful to tell people what is kind or helpful, but not *really* true.

And Dad lies. Last week, Dad told me we were going to Target to buy a new Bionicle that was coming out, but he didn't tell the truth. When we got to the store, the new figure was not there for us to buy. I scrutinized the other, older versions hoping I might find it pushed to the back or on the wrong shelf, but the new Bionicle wasn't anywhere.

Dad asked the man in the red shirt where we could find them. "Sold out!" the man explained. Dad told me we couldn't get the Bionicle today.

"Liar!" I screamed out. "You promised that if I earned a star every day at school, we would get it today, Saturday! Today is Saturday!" But he didn't see it that way.

Only the animals don't lie because they don't talk. God did good with the animals I have to admit, especially the fish. My fish tank, the oceans, and all the zoos and aquariums are the best of creation. I know everything about fish, even the ones no one has heard about. "I just know the leviathan still exists! I just know it!" I tell my parents. My dad says, "No way!" But mom believes me. Someday, I'll sink to the bottom of the sea and find him. Just me in the dark, quiet, blue sea. Someday.

But today isn't that day. Today, I was so bored my head throbbed. *How many times will teachers hand out worksheets to do the same thing over and over?* I'd wondered. Don't they know that when I try to write, my hands feel like silly putty?

Paper feels sharp on my skin. The worksheets have so many pictures and endless words with lines for filling. The other children rush to complete them with eager pencils and stupid smiles. Do they really enjoy this? For eight hours every day? What could possibly be okay about this situation?

Today started off surprisingly well. Then at lunch, my classmate Adam sat next to me and listened to my stories about the Mariana Trench. "Did you know that more people have walked on the moon than entered the Mariana Trench?" I asked him, aware that he didn't know.

When he had to go to the bathroom, I didn't mind; I came along with him, talking about the trench all the way. "Did you know the angler fish lives there at the bottom of the sea?" I asked. "The trench is the least explored area on Earth." I could hardly contain the full feelings in my chest—thoughts kept popping up, and there were too many ideas to share.

When Adam slipped through the narrow door to the cafeteria bathroom, I waited outside, still talking, but more loudly so he still could hear me. I don't know how long I talked to him through the door, but after some time, I noticed the cafeteria growing quiet as students finished their lunches and walked out the glass doors to the playground area.

At our school, once you are done eating and have cleaned up, you can go to the playground. *If I don't get out there soon, I won't get a swing,* I considered. Swinging is the only thing I like to do on the playground. Being in the swing allows me to see the world from above. The rushing air cools me down, and the rocking motion calms me. The people look small, and they aren't so noisy. From my high perch, the world makes more sense than here below.

I paused in my speech about the trench and refocused. I had begun to wonder about Adam. At least a few minutes had gone by, certainly enough for him to use the bathroom and wash his hands. I watched the cafeteria ladies put our trays into the trash with one large push that cleared the whole table at once. I saw my tray disappear. I didn't have a chance to eat my cookie.

I stood waiting outside the bathroom door until the cafeteria lady came to me. "You'd better run off to class; lunchtime and recess are all done now."

I think she had to tell me twice; the first time, I didn't hear her. *Maybe Adam forgot and went out the side door without me seeing,* I reasoned. But he wasn't done eating yet, and he hadn't cleaned up his tray. It made no sense. The rule was that you had to clean up your tray when done, and then you could go to recess. Because I was waiting, I had broken the rules, too. I hadn't finished lunch and didn't pack up my tray.

I had to wait until math stations for the chance to ask Adam where he had gone during lunch. "Oh, I forgot!" he mumbled softly and rushed to the next station without looking at me. I had a funny feeling about his forgetting. It was the same tingling sensation I got in my hands when I spoke to less friendly classmates. *Adam likes me,* I thought to myself. *I think he's my friend.*

After math came reading time and then dismissal. I wanted to finish my homework during the reading lesson because I was already a great reader. Still, my head felt dizzy and my stomach grumbled, so I failed to complete it before Mrs. Shirley ordered me to the carpet for the daily reading group.

The homework assignment: to write a sentence and draw a picture to go along with it. I pulled on my hair, thinking about it. My neck became itchy, and I stared at the unfinished worksheet sitting on my desk.

I could not have homework. "You're not supposed to do schoolwork at home," I had told my teacher, my classmates, my parents, and Mema. "It's schoolwork, and it belongs at school."

Finally, when I no longer could keep my body sitting on the floor before Mrs. Shirley, I yanked one last tug at my hair, pulled out several strands, and groaned through my gritted teeth. "This is a waste of time!" I blurted out, putting my head down. The itching became burning, my body growing hot, and the sides of my mouth forced themselves downward.

In a wave of hysterical energy, I jumped up, sprinted out of the classroom to the hallway bathroom, and sank down to the floor. I kicked at the door a few times. Luckily, Mrs. Shirley didn't come in until I was done with that. Vandalizing school property was a definite rule breaker.

The bathroom floor was usually a safe spot: the one-inch blue-and-white tiles lacked a definite pattern, and they distracted me. I was sure that there was a reason for placing the tiles in such a way, but in all my times on the bathroom floor, I had yet to figure out its rhythm. Finally, Mrs. Shirley came in looking for me. She was nice, but I wasn't coming out.

Then the dismissal bell rang. I knew I had to make a run for it. So, I escaped—out of the bathroom, down the hall, straight through the gym, and out the back door, into the bright light— so itchy, hungry, and defeated. So here I lie, facedown in the dirt with no book or backpack, arms and legs spread out like the rays of a lionfish. Not moving.

Until Mom comes and scoops me up. Saying nothing to the teachers, she just picks me up and walks with me back to the van. Mom's arms feel strong and thin, and she hugs me tightly. I hang loosely from her shoulders, burying my head in her neck and long hair.

When we get to the van, I climb into my bucket seat, diagonal to her driver's seat, waiting while she picks up my three-year-old sister from part-time preschool. Jolyn arrives at the car before I can get on my seat belt, bounding over to the van, all blond curls, pink shirt, and smiles. She makes absolutely no sense to me.

Her eyes are dancing, and I can see how she loves me and wants me to smile back at her. "Garret!" she exclaims, clutching my knees as she climbs in over me to her seat. I like Jolyn, but she's way too noisy. She pats me on my head and gets into her seat behind Mom's. I hear her chatter away as she clicks on her seat belt, but I don't say a word, my face feeling heavy as if it were falling to the floor. I focus on Mom, waiting for her to get into the car. *Let's go, let's go, let's go!*

But she doesn't come quickly. Mom is different. I watch her look at the other moms and teachers, as if she enjoys them and wants to hear what they have to say. Mom often listens without speaking in return. I'm not sure how she does it, but the other parents and teachers always stop to talk to her.

Mrs. Shirley approaches her, likely to tell on me. Mrs. Shirley has a lot of words, which I often ignore. *How does Mom stand there so long?* I can't even imagine. Mom is nodding and smiling, eventually shrugging her shoulders and turning back toward the van. Before reaching me, she loudly calls back over her shoulder to Mrs. Shirley: "It's been a hard day."

Adam is standing next to his mom, so I wave. He doesn't wave back. His mom is talking to a group of other mothers at the far end of the pick-up zone. She seems important, maybe a room mom or something. As Mom closes the van door, I notice Adam's mom staring at her with an expression I don't understand.

The grin on Mom's face tells me she doesn't care about what Adam's mom or anyone else thinks. Finally in the van, Mom turns the key and looks back over her right shoulder to check behind us before reversing the van into the lot. As she does, she glances at me and gives me a wink. Maybe we have a secret, but I'm not sure. I just know I'm okay now.

On the drive home, the large homes in our lakeside neighborhood stand up high, strong, and still. I picture myself wandering around in them, imagining them quiet and empty. It's not that I don't like my house; the big house holds my fish and Bionicles and has a pool, but it's always filled with people and noise. Mom says it's hospitality, and I think it's a waste of time.

Often, I come downstairs from my room to find the strangest individuals. Sometimes, they yell; lots of them cry. One time, I came in and Mom was listening to a woman who was larger than our couch. Her legs hung over the edges of the cushions by at least six inches, and she cried.

Some nights, after I go to bed, I hear other moms and dads talking to my parents about the Bible, marriage, or their children—but, mostly, I hear crying. I hear some laughter, too. It doesn't make much sense to me. Dad's voice is so loud that I hear him all the way upstairs in my bed. Mom mostly listens. My parents tell me that we welcome people into our home because we have been given so much.

The visitors seem the same to me. They come to the discussion groups and dinners. They get financial or marriage advice and eat lots of our food (especially the cookies), but they never seem to look better or happier. At least, not to me.

Always the same, they come in to say "hello," smile at me, and then they walk away quickly. Sometimes, I don't bother to look up; they aren't there to see me. Mom teaches me to say "hello" and look them in the eye to show them I care. But I prefer to keep my eyes on my DS and my attention far away from their many words and awkward hugs, which feel like sandpaper on my skin. When I do look up, I see them staring at me. I never know why, and I don't care.

Sometimes, these visitors bring over other children, and I'm expected to play with them. "Show Caden your Thomas Trains." That's the worst. I don't know these children, and they only play trains for a few minutes before they turn their attention to my other treasures.

I don't mind if they play with the trains. I was obsessed with them when I was a toddler and proudly kept them in the Thomas box Mom and Dad bought me on the day we rode the real Thomas Train at Lake Mary. I used to spend hours in the train store near one of the apartments where we used to live. It was so close that Mom and I could walk to it, and we'd spend hours there. Mom always wanted to leave too soon. Once, she had to carry me home, screaming all the way, because I didn't want to go. But that was then. Now, I'm willing to share my trains.

But no one can play with my Bionicles, especially the ones they no longer make. I place them high on my shelf, not completely out of reach, but high enough so that the other children usually don't climb up and try to touch them. My Legos are a different situation altogether. They sit in a bin, wide open for everyone. I can never understand why Mom dumped them all in there.

"Let's try to keep our toys together in one place," she says. My mother is obsessed with everything having its place. When my mom gets mad, it's usually about my things being out of place.

The Lego bucket remains the inevitable first stop for all visiting children. "Stop!" I bark at the kids who wreck my designs for parts, but I'm always too late. By the time they leave, my earlier creations lay pulled apart and scattered across my bedroom floor.

"People are more important than things," Mom always says when I get mad, even though we have a lot of things.

Eventually, Mom comes to rescue me, spending long periods of time organizing and reorganizing my room as I try to calm down. She cleans as I rest in the swing Dad bolted into our upstairs ceiling. It's an outdoor swing, but we keep it inside so I can swing any time. I have to keep swinging—swinging to sleep, swinging to stop screaming, swinging to quit pulling my hair.

Coming out of my thoughts and the stress of the school day, I see our home through the neighbor's trees. We pull up to the big house, and I slide out, feet hitting the stone driveway, making my way under the entranceway arch and through the heavy front door that's three times my height.

Craving candy, I kick off my shoes and run to the kitchen where a wall of windows showcases the waterfall and pool, which border the grassy path leading down to John's Lake. It's not the view that makes me happy, but my bug mazes and lizard habitat by the pool do make my face feel lighter.

Jolyn prances into the kitchen, also looking for a snack. Mom says no candy, but at the same moment, Mema walks in the door with a huge hug and large bag of cotton candy.

"Yes! Cotton candy!" I know Mom lets Mema give us whatever we want.

We call her "Grandma Treat," and she is mom's best friend. They talk about everything, but especially about me and Jolyn. Sitting with us like always, Mema pulls in close to me so she can hear everything about my day—including the homework fiasco and Mariana Trench. Like my mom, Mema gets me. She knows my secrets and always has the best ideas. We often wander her yard in search of Old Man Turtle, and when we find him, we feed him lettuce, taking the time to watch him eat. Grandmas are old, so Mema goes slow.

Jolyn sits up on the counter ledge to hover closer to me and Mema. As Jolyn eats, she gets even louder and jumpier than normal. Not me—I grab a sticky blue glob of cotton candy and shove it into my mouth, leaving a large chunk stuck on my cheek. Shoveling in another wad, I feel my head becoming clearer and my heart calming down. All the noise in my body quiets, and the world around me slows.

The truth is, Mom and Dad often give me candy because it calms me down and soothes my mood. Mom gives me some pieces to tuck into my pockets for the extra time spent at church when she has to work children's ministry or Dad has to teach a class.

People tell Mom she is wrong to give me candy, but she and Dad don't care. She carries it in her purse for those moments when I need it, the confusing and loud flashes when I feel frantic and bored, eventually pulling at my hair. The attacks happen when we stay anywhere too long, but especially at church where Mom and Dad take their time to meet all the visitors. Even after all their hard work, church still doesn't seem very awesome to me—just more people, a growing number of wall-mounted TVs, and a new lobby café where they don't sell candy.

The only prolonged activity that doesn't make me pull my hair out is when we journey to visit the poor people in remote places. Even though traveling to reach them feels endless (which I hate), the foreign location fits me once we get there. Faraway people never seem to wear shoes and always eat with their hands, two bad-mannered habits which I love. They also look bored and uncomfortable, like me.

I get an idea. Next time I travel with my parents to help people, I will bring along extra candy. The sweets will help them feel better, too. "Mema, can you get extra cotton candy for me to bring to the poor people?" I say as I finish my portion.

Mema smiles at me. She understands. "How about I get you bags of lollipops, so you can pack them easily in your suitcase?" she suggests.

I ponder this fantastic idea and agree. "Good idea, Mema. Thanks," I say, and march upstairs to my swing. It's been a hard day.

CHAPTER THREE

Doing Good Differently

JODI

Summer 2008

"There are 143 million orphans in the world, with eighteen million classifying as *double orphans* and needing forever families," our social worker lectures, "Most of them are not babies."

Garry and I were sitting in a corporate boardroom at the adoption agency with four other families, wide-eyed, hopeful, and well-off—ready to do some good. The social worker went on to explain that a vast number of children had trauma and attachment issues, fetal alcohol syndrome, and mental and physical disabilities. They might also have AIDS, Down syndrome, autism, heart conditions, hermaphroditism, blindness, missing limbs, hepatitis C, or disfigurement.

She showed us a slide show of pictures of children—not cute ones or young ones but children who had no noses or who were missing hands and feet. These children rarely had hair, and none of them had life in their eyes.

The social worker explained how we would never be able to predict or fully understand the host of issues that would accompany a child adopted from overseas. Furthermore, if you wanted to adopt a baby, the wait was seven years and cost $35,000, not including the cost of raising a high-needs, malnourished infant who would require frequent therapies and medical follow-up.

If we were looking for one of the magical adoption encounters you see in the movies, this introductory class wasn't it. But that was okay with me. Garry and I weren't looking for the Hollywood experience. We didn't need to adopt a strong, perfect, stunning baby—we already had that in Jolyn. A difficult child did not intimidate us either. We had one of those, too. "No one could be harder than Garret!" we had said, laughing, only partly in jest.

With Garret's struggles, we understood tough parenting scenarios, and we were not entering into the adoption process with starry-eyed expectations. We were pursuing adoption to do a forever good, a deed that likely wouldn't be done by someone else. The child might never "make it" the way American parents hope for their children to succeed in life—heck, it seemed like the child might not even like us! But if we chose a child, one who otherwise never would be adopted, one who was less "marketable" than the beautiful babies seen in all of the advertisements and films, maybe we really could change a life.

At this point, the volunteering we did at ministry outreach events seemed a bit frivolous to me, especially after we had visited overseas and witnessed truly desperate poverty. We had the means and the heart to do good—good that would last, good that would change lives forever.

In both New York and Florida, we had dedicated ourselves to counseling distressed people both locally and globally. We had given away a lot of money, supporting additional mission work across Asia, the Caribbean, and throughout Africa, but we weren't sure if transformation ever happened in the lives of the people. How do you know once you write the check?

Even visiting these areas in person did little to show us that our offerings had made a difference. After years of discussion, Garry and I hypothesized that adoption could be a way to give differently. Although adoption would only improve one life, that one life would become different forever.

Or at least that's what I told myself and our acquaintances who inquired about the reasons we were choosing to adopt. The truth was that adoption frequently did not yield happy endings. I'd heard too many heart-breaking stories of children rejecting their parents and reenacting their violent pasts in the presence of their shell-shocked families. These kept me from fully advocating adoption to others, but I knew they wouldn't deter me. I held a different motivation that didn't require a picture-perfect outcome.

When my closest friends and family asked why I was pursuing adoption—or the volunteering or mission work—I had no logical answer or grand thesis statement to give them: I only could tell them about the burden. *How could I not help?* That question accompanied me wherever I went, especially as I learned about the missing girls.

In my time traveling among hurting people, I'd realized that there were millions of lost women and children, permanently moved into the labyrinth of human trafficking. I lived in their presence daily, angels expecting me to answer their haunting calls for help. They lingered painfully out there in the world and in my transcendent reality, that mysterious part of me where the heart and will intersect. Their nagging voices spurred me—*I am forgotten, taken, alone*—their relentless call a stinging reminder to come and fix what's broken.

Their voices inside grew louder as I grew older. Years of local volunteering and global missions gave way to this decision to adopt, to take a step to reclaim one life that had been abandoned. Garry and I began our journey in China, a place where overpopulation and government policies had orphaned hundreds of thousands of baby girls. Even though I experienced fear and self-doubt in our decision, I sensed the angels' approval.

I left the adoption agency that night determined to complete the necessary paperwork. For the next month, I finalized and notarized scores of documents: introductory agency forms and fees; financial worksheets; three years of tax forms; psychological evaluations; assessments from our four home study visits and reports; medical exams for everyone in the family; local police clearance letters; national FBI clearances; letters of recommendation from pastors, employers, and friends; and affidavits from other potential caretakers in case we died while the children were still young. Every piece of paperwork required approvals, which often took several weeks to return.

Approvals meant we'd reached their standards: we couldn't be medically obese; our marriage had to be verified as being *strong*; we couldn't earn less than what the US government deemed middle-class wages; and we had to have at least enough square footage for the adopted child to have her own room. We referenced all of our local schools and therapists, along with insurance companies and potential cultural groups that promised to preserve our future child's heritage. We signed papers agreeing not to cause trouble, complain, or advocate for faster placement, no matter how long the process took.

Once this process was completed, we could view children, which we did. At the same time, I began applying for immigration and citizenship approvals, and later, a plethora of required travel documents. With each exam, document, assessment, and interview came endless questions:

Why do you want to adopt a child from overseas?

What happens when the child rejects you?

Do you get angry? What do you do when you get angry?

How do you and your spouse resolve conflict?

How would you deal with a child with severe medical issues?

What if the child hurts your other children?

I hustled to answer them and secure the necessary documents for four straight months. In between my women and children's ministry work, I pushed the paperwork, appointments, mailings, interviews, and payments while Garry focused on strengthening his firm.

It was while we were waiting for China's approval of our dossier that the economy began to slow, markets softened, and our budget got tighter. In January, Garry began to downsize his team in anticipation of the looming recession. By the end of the year, layoffs became commonplace. One by one, team members left, wishing us well and hoping to find jobs in the nascent economic crisis. Eventually, we closed the US office completely, and Garry and I transformed part of our garage into a home office, complete with eight-foot-long engineering plotters for printing massive construction documents.

With the heavy loss of his US team, Garry kept adjusting and navigating his way through 2008 and 2009 as the economy continued crashing. "It'll be fine," he assured me, and I trusted him completely. He believed in us and our choices, even now.

With the help of his boundless (and sometimes distracted) energy, his quick decision-making, and larger-than-life personality, my most insane ideas to do good became possibilities. No thought was too grand or unattainable with Garry by my side. So, I pushed on with the paperwork, sending in payments as I went and trusting that we'd be able to survive the financial disaster.

■ ■ ■ ■

What surprised me most during the adoption process was how vulnerable I felt as I wrote down every detail and nuance of our personal, professional, and financial lives. In the eyes of the social worker and the people who had to confirm our employment, character, faith, health, and intentions, I felt utterly exposed.

We had always been open people, trying to help others by welcoming them into our lives. The same presence calling me to adopt had called me earlier to help the hurting women and children around me. Garry also felt called to serve out of the abundance of his blessings.

Throughout the years of our missional lifestyle, Garry and I had taught marriage classes to thousands of people, and I had counseled countless women and children escaping trauma and abuse. In these pastoral counseling roles, we had shared intimate truths about our marriage—fights, doubts, and mistakes—to model honestly and provide a safe place for others' healing. But this scrutiny felt different.

Under the microscope we waited, paying lots of money for social workers to examine our home, parenting style, marital challenges, and psychological strengths and deficits. Not only that, but the full dossier required interviews with everyone close to us: friends, business partners, pastors, and grandparents. Everyone close to us knew we were pursuing this adoption, and everyone, it seemed, had an opinion about it.

"What about Garret? What will happen if this new child takes up all your time? Garret needs extra," Grandma Vermaas had questioned.

"Another girl! I could never love another girl as much as I love Jolyn," my mom blurted out. "I don't think this is a good idea."

Dismissing these comments as grandma-speak, I shared with my close friends how discouraged I was to proceed without their support. Garry worked a lot, and I relied on my mom. I needed her backing throughout an already burdensome and relentless process.

"Maybe your mom has a point; Garret isn't doing very well," one of my friends retorted honestly. As I stood at my kitchen sink, staring at the lake late one night while talking to her on the phone, her comment hit me wildly. *Not doing well*, I thought. *Garret has autism. He will never do well. He will never be "good." He will never be like other kids.*

Her assessment hit me hard that night, and I wondered if being in the constant mess with Garret meant that I couldn't do good for another child. *Am I so naïve to try to help another child when my firstborn never makes it through the day without a riot?*

I wept. But I was no stranger to crying. Whenever trials came, which was most days, I cried. Sometimes, I cried to Garry, but he didn't really understand. Garry tried to be encouraging, but how many times can you whine to your husband about the same unhappy story? It was all too much.

When your first child is different, you don't know it for a while. Early on, I just believed it was me. *I must be the worst mother in the world* was a common refrain among my ever-searching thoughts. Garret looked normal, completely adorable with big blue eyes and intent little expressions, but he grew upset if he wasn't near me, within touching distance. I either held him or wore him in a Baby Bjorn for the first two years of his life. He never slept through the night unless he was lying next to me.

It seemed impossible for Garret to separate from me. When he finally started to wander off on his own, he immediately hurried back, gaze set on me and mouth wide open as if gasping for breath in the storming sea of his surroundings. I was his life vest. Of course, that was my fault too, I was told. I was "too much."

I own that. I *am* too much. But when you find your toddler sitting on top of your van to escape social expectations, screeching when he has to wear collared shirts, or pulling on his hair due to a change in the day's routine, well, you become the mom who's "too much." I read all the books and visited all the specialists. So many well-meaning therapists tried to understand Garret, first thinking it must be our home environment.

"How's your marriage?" they asked. "Do you get a date night?"

Then they questioned our discipline style. "Have you tried toy jail? You must not be consistent in your time-outs. What about the 1-2-3 method?"

More questions came, but no answers. We followed all the directions but found no actual solutions. Finally, I went back to school myself to study counseling. But that's a different story.

After six months on the wait list, I finally got Garret in to see the best psychiatrist in central Florida. On the day of the visit, after filling out all of the many assessment forms, Garry and I sat in the neurological center of Nemours Children's Hospital with Garret crawling around the room, making odd noises and either hiding under the chairs or perching on top of them. This behavior had become normal to us.

"No, it can't be autism—he talks, and he is smart," we countered.

The doctor delivered a self-important pause and turned to Garret, who was back on the floor. He motioned to him, and said matter-of-factly, "How's this working for you?"

The doctor then proceeded to explain to us the full range of Autism Spectrum Disorder (ASD). Although we had understood the verbal, interpersonal, and communication limitations of individuals with severe autism, we hadn't learned about the more verbal and high-functioning qualities of someone with Asperger's syndrome.

The doctor described issues with social interactions, repetitive behaviors, perseveration with certain topics or items, and overall communication abnormalities, which illuminated our understanding. He also prescribed a careful set of medications to level Garret's moods to become more functional day-to-day.

The results of his IQ testing later came back at 131. Garret's intelligence compensated for some of his abnormalities, enabling him to function as an awkward, yet painfully uncomfortable child. At times, he could function almost normally, obfuscating his disability for a short time until he decompensated into a complete meltdown.

I wished at times that his disability was visible, so onlookers would have mercy on us during his public outbursts. Complete strangers often pointed out the need for us to improve our parenting styles. They weren't wrong, but they certainly lacked empathy.

Once, in an unfortunately long line at Epcot, Garret

experienced one of his panic attacks. I still can hear the man in front of us as we exited the busy line, declaring to his own children, "See, if you spare the rod, you spoil the child," quoting Scripture loud enough to ensure that we also benefitted from its wisdom. Garry and I looked at each other, speechless, as we carried Garret and Jolyn toward the exit as quickly as we could.

I thought about this incident when I hung up the phone with my trusted friend. The proud man's merciless judgment had stung, but hers delivered a clear and shocking message: you cannot adopt a child—especially one with special needs.

I didn't see it that way. Yes, Garret was hard. He is hard. But Garret is brilliant, and he analyzes the world in ways that simply escape me and most others. Tuning out the mundane and the ordinary, Garret embodies empathy in the most unexpected ways. Amid his autistic struggles, he can hyperfocus on a child who's being bullied, a sick member of the church, or an elderly neighbor living alone. He stays thoughtfully deliberate and feels the pain of others, even when he can't show it. No fish, frog, or bug has ever been harmed on his watch. He doesn't lie—ever. He only says and does exactly what he believes, and it is beautiful, except when it's not.

One evening as dusk settled, Garret was bitten by a bat while trying to save it from drowning in our pool. After I rushed him to the emergency room, the nurse promptly delivered thirteen shots to his pointer finger, causing it to swell around the two tiny teeth marks embedded into his skin. I assumed he had learned the lesson: "Now, please don't try to save bats again!"

Through agonizing grimaces, he had announced with conviction, "Mom, I would do it again if I could save the bat."

Such courage from a child who thinks the tags on his shirt

are "killing him!" Deep, inexplicable, embarrassingly naïve, deliberate, honest, and caring—that's what I see when I see Garret.

Not only would Garret welcome an adopted child, he might relate to her pain more than anyone else. Of course, it would be hard—I wasn't afraid of hard. My life already had challenged me. My single mom started out as a cleaning lady and raised me and my older sister to never quit and to commit ourselves to learning, doing, and achieving.

Nancy and I attended the most exclusive high school in the state on financial scholarships. Not naturally bright like my sister, I studied for hours on end to earn the grades that got me into Columbia University. The university and the city of New York both kicked my butt.

No, I wasn't afraid of hard work. I also wasn't afraid of looking bad—I knew I already did. While my friend's protestation over our adoption plans discouraged me, I understood it was my next step in life. Garry—in his usual, blunt terms—agreed: "Let's do it."

■ ■ ■ ■

A month later, we got the phone call and our referral papers:

Cao Shi Ya; A female abandoned baby was found in the grass opposite of the gate of the Chemical Garden Committee on Changlu Road in Yanjiang Industrial Development, District of Nanjing City.

Heart beating, as quickly as I could, I had read on:

She has a round face and thick hairs, found naked and wrapped in green Western-style clothes. Her umbilical cord remained. There was lots of bloodstain all over her body.

I stopped to digest this information. It was all I would ever know about my little girl's entrance into this world. I imagined a young mother giving birth in secret and immediately having her baby taken away and left for finding.

Did she ask for the baby to be taken from her? Did someone force her to give up her baby in some indecorous affair? Or was she young and defeated, never looking at the baby before she was taken away forever by a mother or aunt who knew what must be done. I felt an equivalent sense of loss for both the biological mother and the child, a deep wound that infused not only their story but also the story of so many other mothers and babies.

We gave the child the surname "Cao" meaning "hundreds."

It was the most appropriate name they could have given her, "hundreds," because there were so many orphaned daughters. Cao Shi Ya was just one of countless others. Reaching the end of the three-page document, I read the final notes on the "ceaselessly crying," underweight, almost four-year-old, who still was not yet able to walk:

Diagnosis: Motor and intellectual developmental delay.

We had twenty-four hours to decide. Shi Ya was on the "Special Findings" list. This list was made up of children who had been available for adoption, matched with a family, and later rejected by the family during the referral process. These children had been denied at least twice now, and the agency had only a short time to advocate for their adoption before they were absorbed back into the master list of orphans. The process was efficient, clearly dictated by China, and now the agency was asking me to make a choice.

Shi Ya. I knew so little about her and understood that any intellectual delay might mean a total inability to ever care for herself or a simple slowness that would improve with time, love, and attention. I looked up the meaning of her Chinese name, hoping it fit her personality in some way and could tell me more about her. Shi Ya in Chinese means "beautiful poem or story."

I loved the name, but it was clear that Shi Ya's referral picture didn't show a beautiful story. After we said "yes," we only reluctantly shared the photo with others, her bald head, serious eyes, and tiny body dressed in oversized boy's shorts and donated Western t-shirt. My mother, well, she tried hard to be encouraging. After seeing me spend years clearing the adoption process, Mema knew I wasn't changing my mind. My mother had known me to be stubborn from birth. She tried to be excited about Shi Ya, but I felt her hesitation.

Garry, on the other hand, wasn't worried at all. "She'll get cuter!" he assured me, knowing her appearance wasn't the real worry. In our marriage, we had lived a life of "yes." We had never discussed "yes" as an actual life plan, but with Garry's fearlessness and my dogged determination, "yes" ended up becoming our mission. Where others hesitated, we rushed ahead. So, we agreed on adopting Shi Ya, and we kept her name.

■ ■ ■ ■ ■

In the early morning hours of May 4, 2009, Garry and I arrived in Shanghai, where one of his overseas offices was located. A team member accompanied us to the train station, and we traveled from Shanghai to Nanjing, which was several hours away. Once there, we took a small bus chartered by our adoption agency and filled with other adopting families to meet our daughter.

We had left Garret and Jolyn with the two grandmas who stayed with them at our home, both more than willing to watch over their "favorites." The journey was relentlessly long, almost thirty-six hours door-to-door. When we arrived, we shuffled dutifully off the small, red-and-white tour bus with the other expectant parents and headed toward the government building in Nanjing, People's Republic of China.

We entered a concrete-floored lobby where we stood, waiting to meet our daughter. Almost immediately, a group of young women came in, holding children of various ages. The process felt rehearsed, as if they had put on this parade many times before.

I couldn't tell which child in the group of fussing toddlers and children was ours. They all looked similar with round faces and searching eyes, each uttering confused murmurs.

Then I spotted a young woman holding what looked like an infant dressed in yellow. She had short hair but wore a little white barrette where her hairline met her forehead. Her round face flushed under the light, and her eyes squinted.

The woman holding the bundle recognized us first and let out a shrill "Shreeeya." She pointed fiercely at us and said, "Mama and Baba." The caretaker kept pushing Shi Ya to us and insisting "Mama and Baba." But Shi Ya only looked at the present I held, a red Minnie Mouse backpack filled with toys, stickers, and books that Mema had sent for her.

Coming toward us carefully, Shi Ya didn't bother with the toys, but she quickly grabbed the papers and stickers from inside the bag and began placing them on her fingers and arms. She pulled them off and on until what once was a cute set of Disney stickers became hundreds of small sticky notes all over her body and new backpack. After five minutes, we signed a form and left, just a cohort of dazed and smiling parents with our odd new children.

The ride back to our hotel with the six other families quickly grew quiet. Shi Ya's brow wrinkled, and her eyes peered searchingly out of the window. Several mothers' eyes welled with tears. I took long, steady breaths, while Garry snapped a few photos.

Once alone, we aimed to bond with Shi Ya, as all the adoption books we had read advised. We attempted to play at the park, cuddle, and share dim sum, activities that ended with our daughter refusing to walk, touch, or chew.

Wherever she found herself, Shi Ya plopped down like a ragdoll, as if not realizing she had the power to move herself independently. The flat back of Shi Ya's head and her inability to walk correctly suggested she had spent years strapped into a cot, the typical method for keeping orphans safe when they outnumbered their caretakers. She never had experienced life outside the confines of the orphanage and could barely keep herself balanced enough to walk. Her head looked giant on her emaciated body and seemed too heavy for her to carry.

She could not talk or even chew with any vigor or coordination. She'd only ever eaten congee, the watery rice soup filled with scraps of meat that makes up the typical Chinese orphan's diet. Her belly was distended, and she had the worst breath I had ever smelled. Her teeth rotted from four years of not brushing them and eating fish parts... "No one ever tells you about that," I joked with Garry. It was as if her whole being was trying to push us away—even her very breath.

Shi Ya didn't make any sounds that first day, but she was coyishly willing to hang out with us if we fed her or gave her stickers. By nighttime, however, she wanted to go home, and she screamed all night long to make sure we knew it. I tried swaddling her and rocking her, just like the books instructed. I attempted hand-feeding her and combing her hair. Garry walked with her around the room, down to the lobby, and eventually outside the hotel.

We struggled to let her cry it out in her crib, and I tried having her lay next to me as Garret had. Neither worked, however, and she kicked at me relentlessly. When I held her close, her body stiffened. If I put her down, she screamed ceaselessly. Finally, out of ideas, we left her lying in the wooden hotel crib. But she continued to cry for hours.

I spent those hours on the floor next to her crib, talking and singing to her. In between my voice and her sobs, I heard the screams of our neighbor's baby next door. (The hotel was smart enough to restrict the adopting families to the same wing of the building in order to protect other guests from the crying and screaming.)

Shi Ya shrieked, stomped, kicked, and beat against the side of that wooden crib. Then I felt it, a sharp pain on the bridge of my nose. I lost my vision for a moment and took a second to catch my breath as pain radiated across my face. I focused my eyes back on Shi Ya and realized that the side of the crib had come down on my face. This twenty-pound four-year-old had just broken my nose.

The next day arrived with no further incident and only a few moments of rest. Bruised and exhausted, I went down to the breakfast buffet of the hotel with Garry and Shi Ya and visited with the other parents. Today was the day we would all finalize our adoptions. The authorities gave adopting parents twenty-four hours to back out. I'm sure we all considered it—at least for one serious moment.

Looking around the restaurant, I observed my adoption comrades sitting with their noisy little ones, who were now covered in oatmeal, bananas, and milk—some protesting more than others. It was then that I realized that my neighbor, whose baby

I heard throughout the night, was not there. I discovered later she had returned her healthy, eight-month-old baby girl because of the crying. Her mother-in-law, who had accompanied her on this journey, told me before they checked out, "This isn't what we expected."

We finalized the adoption and proceeded to fulfill the additional requirements. For thirteen days, we repeated the same routine, visiting various government offices and medical facilities in the mornings and touring the lakes, loom factories, and memorial sites of Nanjing in the afternoons. I think the touring was supposed to give us an appreciation of and connection to our child's culture, but I had never felt so cold and disengaged. Cao Shi Ya, now Shiya Rose Vermaas, whined, cried, fought, ignored, and pushed me away every chance she got. She did not like me, and I didn't like her.

Garry had no concerns about Shiya whatsoever and seemed to enjoy her enough. His persistent confidence did not restore my own, even though I knew he was right: *she would be okay.* My unrelenting self-doubt wasn't really about Shiya. It was about me. As a mother, not once had I felt disconnection from—or dislike for— my child. I did not recognize myself, the ugly feelings betraying my dutiful maternal instincts. Never before had my faulty humanity so terrified and humiliated me, even as the humbling experience prepared me for future adoptions.

I could not wait to go home. My heart ached for Garret and Jolyn. I yearned to reconnect to my maternal self, to release the numb and confused me who showed up with my new little one. Although friends emailed to check on me and share in the adoption experience, I found myself unable to articulate what I was feeling and thinking to these other moms. I certainly could not tell my mother about my doubts and confirm her greatest fears. Instead, I only emailed them cute pictures and kept my true thoughts to myself.

During these two weeks in China, Garry attempted to understand my struggles, but only I could unravel my darkly tangled emotions. Garry faced his own woes in China as he rallied against the economic downturn and demise of our family's livelihood. During the long days of post-adoption tasks, Garry would often leave, slipping out of meetings to work alongside his Shanghai engineers, who had traveled to see him and strategize the company's future. Throughout our trip to China, and long after we returned home, Garry fought to finance our growing family.

For the other fathers on the trip, adopting their children was the main event, but not for my husband. Garry had an equally urgent goal competing for his attention: to save his dissipating firm from the crushing weight of a collapsing economy. The other fathers would ask me where he was, and I had to admit he was working, which felt strange in the face of their doting attentiveness. They were paternal heroes, and their equally devoted wives seemed much more equipped to love their children than I.

I wondered if Garry and I were cut out to do this kind of good—and promptly decided that we were doing good a little differently than everyone else.

And maybe that, too, was good.

CHAPTER FOUR

Meaningless

GARRY

Summer 2009

When we bought "the big house" in 2005, we paid full price. Instead of placing a large down payment on the home, I invested in my firm, which by then had grown to 120 team members spread throughout offices in Shanghai, Nagpur, and across the United States. I had always believed that investing in myself was my best bet. Buying a house for nothing down was easy, and subprime loans were everywhere. Life was good, and the American Dream was thriving.

By 2006, banks were heavily invested in mortgage-backed securities and were relying increasingly on derivatives. Like so many others, I ignored the inverted yield curve that emerged that year—after all, there was a strong money supply and continuing low interest rates. I continued to expand the firm, opening a large, prestigious office in my hometown.

The original team added additional staff and together established a spirited workplace and branded technical products, winning new clients and projects as sales spread rapidly throughout central Florida. My cell phone rang throughout the day and into the night as architects and developers called, hoping to partner with us to build a theme park in Russia, an automobile-themed resort in China, and various hospitality-focused structures around the world. The success surprised even me.

Then, in August 2008, the phones stopped ringing. I remember sitting in frightening silence at my once-bustling office. Fannie Mae and Freddy Mac went bankrupt that month. Everyone wanted to blame them, but they weren't the only cause of the recession. A perfect storm had been brewing. By the following month, on September 29, 2008, the stock market had plummeted 777.68 points. My phone began to ring again; this time, however, the callers only wanted one of two things: to cancel their jobs or to tell me they were going bankrupt and couldn't pay the money they already owed me.

In September 2008, clients owed us one million dollars in accounts receivable, money that we would never see. I held over a million dollars in debt on investment loans from family members, office spaces, equipment, company cars, and salaries for 120 team members. That meant I had 120 families—as well as my own—relying on me.

As the housing market started to collapse and cause this financial decline, I was in the middle of expanding my family by adopting. I had a wife, two children, and another one on the way from China. I also had the big house, which had lost almost half its value in a matter of months. Like the rest of America, I had blown it. Living in Florida, the epicenter of the housing crisis, I felt my failures strong and early.

I quickly took inventory and began slashing my budget. I let go of our cars, salaries, and any unnecessary equipment and supplies. I gave up the Lexus and got my mom's old Toyota Camry. I reluctantly began to reduce our staff, starting with the most expensive positions. We lowered expenses as much as possible, but it was not enough. Eventually, I had to lay off many of my lifelong friends.

I paid off contracts to get out of our cumbersome lease and shifted our office into my garage. One team member worked with me in that converted space, and he rode a bike to my house each morning. Even though we cancelled leases on the rest of our rental equipment, we still owed months of payments. By the end of 2008, I only had one American team member, my good friend from New York. Each month, I continued to decrease the number of team members in our foreign offices.

By early 2009, a client from a large development firm came to me with an offer. He was interested in buying my firm to capitalize on the efficient processes we had created in the engineering space. By working with a global team spanning several time zones, we had perfected an efficient 24-hour workday. Someone was always on call. We worked smart, and he wanted in. A sale would mean giving up my firm to work for a huge company, adding on a long daily commute. It also would cost me my freedom. I loathed the thought of these consequences, but I had no other choice.

To make the sale happen, I bought out my only remaining US-based shareholder and leader of sales because the buyer refused to keep any non-engineers on my company's roster. I paid him off with the last cash I had, leaving too little money in the bank to cover both my house mortgage and the adoption. I chose the adoption and—for the first time in my life—stopped paying my mortgage.

China required us to bring $7,000 in cash to pay the China Center for Children's Welfare and Adoption (CCCWA). Stuffing seventy one-hundred-dollar bills in my bag, I left Garret and Jolyn with the grandmas and left for China with Jodi to meet our daughter. The Chinese nannies hoisted Shiya into our arms within minutes of arriving in China, and by day two, I had handed over the bank-issued one hundred-dollar bills. Sitting with my cranky, malnourished daughter on my lap in the cramped CCCWA office, I felt the rhythmic tapping of the money counter ensuring I had paid the full $7,000.

Never had money taken on such a strangely meaningful role in my life. Without the money, we couldn't rescue Shiya. Without Shiya, the cash seemed pointless. Maybe it was the money counter, but at that moment I knew without hesitation that I made the right choice. I realized we would lose our house, but Shiya was ours.

From that epiphany at the CCCWA, we still had twelve more full days of adoption requirements. After each of the obligatory, but largely ceremonious, appointments, I had to get back to work. I met daily with our remaining engineering team from Shanghai.

I had to prepare them for the upcoming sale to ensure that it would happen. "If we don't sell," I explained, "the firm will be bankrupt within three months." First, we decreased our staff even further to remain financially viable, reducing from eighty down to twenty engineers. Then, we focused their efforts on the timely delivery of flawless construction documents for the buyer's projects. Our team needed to show them our finest work if we wanted to maintain their interest. Via Skype calls and meetings, the Shanghai team and I shared our plans with Vijay, who implemented the same tactics in the Nagpur office.

What should have been a time of celebrating my new daughter became a bitter, uncomfortable turning point—a time to own my mistakes and admit the hopelessness of our current situation. I was stuck; we were stuck. It was a place I had never been before. Shiya's screaming and my wife's crying mirrored exactly how I felt inside, but I didn't scream or cry. Instead, I brokered the deal to sell my firm and begin again.

We left China with our daughter and returned to a home that we couldn't afford or sell. Our mortgage became twice as large as the plummeting value of the property. Plus, the Florida housing market became glutted with hundreds of thousands of houses just like mine.

By the fall of 2009, I was an employee of the new firm, and I hated it. My lack of inspiration on the job gave me opportunities to dedicate more time to my community. I spent extra time teaching with Jodi at our local church, which spoke highly relevant messages full of practical and spiritual insights. Marriages, families, and men needed more encouragement and help than ever before.

As I shared about my own financial woes, the ongoing challenges of raising my children, and how Jodi and I continued to push ahead in our marriage, I found a large audience of eager listeners. People everywhere were experiencing these same struggles and discovered a unique comradery, which resulted in an explosion of church membership. As the church grew, however, I began to recognize and question the odd transformation from a mission-minded small group of believers to the multi-million-dollar corporation it was becoming.

Amid my new job and the church's success, the pastor asked me to have lunch with a missionary named Ververt who had flown in from Damoh, India. At that time, the pastors were not focused on foreign missions but remembered that I had an office in India. Over a casual lunch at the local Chili's, Ververt and his wife, Neelam, described their training school in Damoh and the young missionaries who traveled on motorbikes to reach the small villages where they served.

"Many never return," Ververt shared with calmness and resolve. He hoped their visit to the United States would inspire Christian church members to support the building of an orphanage for the children of martyred missionaries.

I had walked among poverty and violence in my own mission experiences, but there was something different about Ververt. His total acceptance of painful setbacks in combination with a relentless striving to do good clarified my next steps. Ververt and Neelam reminded me of the story about a boy who rescued beached starfish.[1] In the modern-day parable, an old man rebukes the boy, who was throwing the suffocating sea stars back into the ocean one at a time. The old man saw futility in the little boy's efforts and asked him, "There must be thousands of starfish. How can your efforts make any difference?"

I could relate to the practical old man, but the young boy knew what really mattered. Picking up a starfish and throwing it back into the sea, he spoke truth: "It makes a difference to this one!"

As Ververt and Neelam shared about Damoh, I thought of my own orphaned daughter, her distended belly fastened tightly into an orphanage cot, waiting. *It makes a difference to this one!*

---

[1] Eiseley, Loren C. *The Star Thrower.* New York: Times Books, 1978.

Ververt only needed enough funds to complete the children's home. I knew I couldn't solve every problem in the world, but I could solve this one. Upon my next business trip to India, I hired a driver to take me from my Nagpur office to Damoh to visit the mission. An unfortunate stomach bug kept me nauseated most of the journey between the cities, so I had ample opportunities vomiting by the side of the road to survey the communities of rural Central India. On one stop, I witnessed men standing outside small huts brushing their teeth with sticks. On another, I made out several gaunt children wandering naked among the harvested leftovers of a grain field. Women washed clothes in the brown pond waters, faces too serious for their age. By the time I reached Ververt's orphanage filled with smiling, well-clothed children, I had seen enough scarcity to recognize the clear good happening at the mission.

Upon my return home a few days later, I advocated for the church leaders to support Ververt's orphanage and a related mission in Myanmar. Instead, the church leadership chose to invest in local expansion. Though I understood their goal of helping our own community, I did not agree with the allocation of funds and told them so—as I usually did.

It was at this time that I made the decision to no longer pay tithes to the church and instead began sending our donations entirely to overseas missions. By saving up our tithes, we were able to fund the completion of the children's home in Damoh, and we urged others to find similar ways to give.

When I spoke publicly, I began drawing attention to the importance of caring for orphans and hurting people instead of focusing solely on recruiting more church attendees. I confess I can be overly insistent and loud. Many have called me obnoxious. I say what I think and argue for what I believe is right. If nothing else, the last few years had taught me not to view success in numbers. Numbers had become meaningless to me. I'm sure I pushed too much, but I didn't care.

Later that year, the pastors told me to stop teaching. My wife, Dr. Jodi, still taught and worked with the women and children, partnering with two other women activists to support hundreds of struggling women in our community. With her pastoral counseling experience, she offered no-cost counseling for emotional and relational crises. In tandem, her fellow missionary cohorts, Mo and Jaimie, worked to provide physical assistance to any woman or child in need. Together, they changed lives.

However, I was no longer allowed to do the same. My teachings had become too black/white and controversial, alienating the pastoral team who had successfully made our congregation into the largest Christian church in the area. Not wanting to gossip or split the church, I obliged, trying to keep my mouth shut. I attended, silently, which wasn't easy for me. I never had been quiet, and it soon became clear that my mission no longer aligned with theirs. I wanted to fix it, but I didn't know how, and I couldn't reconcile what I had experienced overseas with our pastoral differences.

There was plenty of turmoil at home as well. Shiya kept screaming as she reluctantly adjusted to her new life. Most mornings she awoke bleeding from where she had scratched herself raw. My wife had to tape Shiya's fingers each night to keep her from seriously injuring herself.

Garret and Jolyn tried to play with her, but even they could take only so much. Garret especially struggled with her loud rants, and Mema grew increasingly worried about all of it: our financial decisions, my growing rift with the church leaders, the impending loss of our home, Shiya's strange and disengaged behaviors, and the effects these behaviors had on her other grandchildren. Through it all, the turmoil continued to shape Jodi and me, until the day of reckoning arrived for both me and Shiya.

I entered the house from my garage-office to see Shiya standing in the foyer of our home, crying as loudly as possible with my wife going calmly about her work, ignoring the obvious. I spotted two tiny feet planted on the green tiled floor, a round red face, a wide-open mouth, and twenty-two pounds of anger. *What's happening?* Shiya's nasally shrieks felt like sandpaper Q-tips in my ears. I cringed and tried to sneak back to my office before anyone saw me.

It was too late. Shiya shot me a determined look through narrow eyes, refusing to walk the twelve steps from the foyer to the kitchen. I knew from experience that she expected Jodi to carry her, but Jodi refused. "You're stubborn," I heard Jodi say to her, "but no one is as stubborn as I am. I raised Garret, and I can do this all day long."

And she had been. I tried to help for a few minutes, engaging Shiya calmly and warmly at eye level, as the therapists had instructed.

When I asked, "How can I help you?" she yelled louder in response, her stinking breath streaming into my nostrils. I quit. As I got up from my crouched position to head back to the garage, I recognized Jodi's resolute gaze. This was her game face. I knew this obstinate expression well. Her mouth was pressed shut, her eyes set, and her demeanor calm. I stared at Shiya knowingly. *You're not winning this battle, Shiya,* I laughed to myself, remembering my own previous losses.

In complete command of a seemingly doomed situation, Jodi declared, "Shiya, I love you, but God gave you legs and feet that work; you can do it. Take yourself where you want to go!" Over the next three hours, she said this sentence intermittently between cooking, working, and playing with Jolyn while Garret stayed hidden in his room. I heard it from the office, the bedroom, the bathroom—wherever I wandered.

"God gave you legs and feet that work. Take yourself where you want to go!"

Mema came in the front door for a visit with the children, but upon hearing Shiya's shouts, she turned back quickly and headed home.

"God gave you legs and feet that work. Take yourself where you want to go, Shiya!"

And finally, she did. Shiya walked, slowly and carefully, over to the dinner table and sat down on the red cushioned bench. The house was peaceful, and we all sat for dinner, quiet and exhausted. As I ate, I kept hearing the words, "God gave you legs and feet that work. Take yourself where you want to go!"

But this time it wasn't Jodi's voice that I heard. It was mine. Saying nothing, I got up from the table and went to my office to call a friend from my men's group, a realtor with a questionable reputation who had become known for his ability to short-sell homes. "Get it sold, no matter what it takes," I told him. Like Shiya, I had realized that it was time to surrender and move on.

A few months later, we had negotiated with the bank and sold our home, taking a significant loss on our initial investment. Before we moved, my wife and I advertised an estate sale through the local paper and word of mouth. Hundreds of people came, removing every item from our home. The furniture, the dishes, the artwork—including the black and white pictures of my grandparents—even sconce lights fastened to the wall all sold within a few hours. One harried mother snatched up my daughter's uncleaned potty from our bathroom floor and asked Jodi the price.

"Uh...$2?" she said. *Sold.*

Everything sold. At the end of the day, most of everything we had ever owned was gone. I thought I would sense the loss more acutely, or at least feel the sting of my failures. I didn't. It had all been meaningless: the stuff, the house, the status.

Sitting in that empty house at the end of the day, my wife cried—and then laughed. Mema worried out loud. Garret and Shiya hid upstairs. Jolyn danced in the empty living room. My house and belongings were no longer mine, my company was sold, and our bank ledger was back up to zero.

I was free and able to do anything. It was the richest day of my life.

PART II

STILL ALIVE

Eleven

ANGELA

I am alive; that much I know. My feet tell me so as my heels burn against the asphalt, my toes battling the pebbles and bits of glass, smashed down to splinters. From deep inside my chest, I feel my heart pounding so loudly that I don't even hear the motors whizzing by me or the roosters cackling, my feet slapping the narrow dirt path lined by overgrown hibiscus, palms, and piles of garbage.

I am running, running as fast as I can, ducking the makeshift cargo bikes, past the restless and skinny dogs, beyond the side streets near the sari-sari store, and on toward home. I have a bit farther to go and a handful of rice in the pockets of my small dress. A few grains spill out as I run, a trail of clues leading back to my crime.

I must run faster because the bad men are chasing me. I speed up the pace of my feet. The bad men want my food; they want my rice. They want me. I hear them coming after me, shouting. I don't know how many.

I can see the paved side street that will lead me home—it's the sign that I'm almost there. My eyes burn from the smoke of the burning refuse, and I begin to blink wildly, trying to make it. Before I reach my street, the stench of the river greets me. It's a smell that you remember—sharp, rotting, and sick. I quicken my feet, no longer caring about the pebbles or the glass splinters. The bad men seem to slow down, too fat to run this far, this fast.

The Pasig welcomes me home; this *Ilog Pasig* is my home. It holds our water: water to wash, water to drink, water for cooking rice. A small wooden shack that crowds the river is my house. There are many shacks along the north side of this river, the water that divides the rich and poor—or so people say. Mine is the one with the blue covering. Although the blue looks funny as a roof, it protects us much better than the slatted wooden or cardboard roofs of my neighbors. The blue came as a gift to my mother, Evangeline. A gift for what I never knew, but that blue roof marks my finish line. I'm almost there.

As I run from the bad men, I feel my lungs burning from the fires that line the riverbank, boiling pots of water for the white gold. I keep on, dodging around the people, hoping they don't follow me home. I know my way; I've learned well, and I never get caught.

From the time I could walk, I remember Mama pulling me out the door to market, using me as a shield against the curious looks. She was beautiful with thick, brown hair that hung from her shoulders to her rounded hips and eyes that searched wildly for her lucky chance. Although Rogie Nino is almost 7, he doesn't get to go to town with Mama. Just me, 'cause I'm special.

I know the streets, the crevices, the faces. I know the bad men in blue with their gold-colored badges. I know which gangs go with which tattoos. And I know the unlucky ones—the children without pants, the ones who are not allowed out because they're too sick with worms, and the ones who have no family. And then there are the distracted ones, the chatty ladies out selling their goods, who stop to brag about their latest *laguyo* or their sons who have made it to Kuala Lumpur. Mama taught me about these market ladies, whose rice sits open in woven bags, ready for the taking.

I'm almost home now, and I'm no longer afraid. Although my toes hurt from the splinters, I feel a sense of fun as I victoriously reach my small neighborhood with the prized white gold still in my pockets—most of it anyway. I make a game of outrunning the flies, but the flies always win. The river is their home more than mine.

The flies rule the river and canals of Binondo. Unlike my food, their food is plenty. The mounds of garbage and refuse, death and *dumi*, stack up higher than me along the river's edges, creating a buffet for the flies and other creatures. If the bugs get lucky, they might even feast on the latest cat drowned in the Pasig. Mama told me these cats were sick and crazed and that they had to be destroyed. The water silences them, and their washed-up bodies become food for the flies, roaches, and rats. I've never gotten used to seeing Mama take the cats down to the river to drown them. The cats seemed no crazier than me.

When I reach our blue roof, I notice the water boiling, ready for the rice. The hot pot sits on top of a rock circle filled with burning garbage, about four big jumps from the entranceway of our wooden hut. A thatched door with two rope hinges and no lock separates the outdoor cooking area from the inside of our house, which takes eleven of my steps to cross. When I arrive, Mama grins at me—a knowing smile—and I dump out my rice into the pot. Today, we eat, thanks to me.

I stand guard over the pot, waiting for the murky water to boil, the white gold becoming thicker, its fragrance crowding out the smell of the garbage. As I stir, I see the bad men crossing to our street. They are walking now and looking into the swarm of faces, tarps, and cardboard, spaces we call home. I see that there are only three of these police, their eyes searching for me—the lost child, the daylight thief, the tiny nuisance from the market. I go back to stirring the pot, allowing my thoughts to disappear into the rising steam. My stomach jerks tightly, reminding me that I am still here and that I am hungry.

As the rice plumps, Mama takes over. Grabbing a flat fragment of driftwood, she begins to scoop rice onto the small pieces of scrap metal we use as plates. I found these treasures near a motor shop on the other side of the district. She carves out the biggest scoop for herself, and then one for me. Before Rogie Nino and my younger siblings even get theirs, I've cleaned half my plate, using my hands to shovel down the food, so they can't try to share or take it. Rogie Nino gets some rice next, and then Mama scoops out what is left for my three younger brothers.

My little brothers are 1, 2, and 3 years old. The one-year-old brother gets only a fistful of rice, which he grabs and eats from the ground. Picking up the grains of rice with his tiny fingers, he and his carefulness won't get much to eat. The next two boys snatch the plate with the small mound of rice they share. The oldest steals the largest portion but—after hearing his brother cry—shares most of it with him, getting almost nothing for himself.

Later, I see him scraping the pot for anything that might be left, but despite his good efforts, he finds nothing, and his big brown eyes search for some way to explain to the youngers that there is no more.

Although the youngest two cannot walk well, they manage to tug on my shirt for more food. I have nothing left for them, as planned. I only feel guilty for a second since it's me who got the rice in the first place. The boys return to the doorway of our hut, where they watch me clean up.

As I crouch low to the ground near the river's edge to wash the pot, I stare at them with their big heads and tiny limbs. They look funny to me, dressed in only underpants, with big heads, swollen bellies, and arms and legs that look like noodles. Their brown eyes look large but also red and oozing, like small monkeys. My younger brothers have no names, so I imagine what to call them and think of Banoy, Ruzil, and Ulan, all names for heroes, kings, and nature. Playing the name game is my favorite thing to do.

Born here in this hut, Mama didn't name them, and Papa didn't seem to care. Mama told me I had a sister who named me, but she won't tell me anything else about her. She's all gone now. Before Mama became pregnant again, Papa used to come by every few weeks. I liked it when he was here because when he came, Mama would clean our house. She'd even sweep the dirt path leading to the waterway to create a smooth place for us to play. Sometimes, Papa would bring a mango. If I was lucky, I could smile big and get a slice. Papa was nice.

But he doesn't come around anymore. The last time he was here, he didn't say much, and there wasn't any fighting. I had stared through the thatch door opening to watch Papa talk to

Mama. I hadn't been able to hear him, but I remember Mama's face turning still and white as he spoke, her mouth turning down and deepening the lines on the sides of her mouth.

Papa looked different that night; he was thinner. I could see his bones sticking out his back when he removed his shirt to wash in the river. He coughed so wildly that blood came out of his mouth and onto the cloth he carried in his left pant pocket. Mama just sat, saying nothing, and that was the last time I ever saw Papa.

I, too, cough a bit like Papa. Mama pushes me away when I cough, and today is no different. It's been a lot of days since I last saw Papa. And Mama's belly is looking bigger and rounder, just like my little brothers'. Mama doesn't seem to notice the growth of her belly—or theirs. Some days, I wonder if she, too, will leave for good.

Mama, I am told, has ten children and one more on the way. The first three disappeared with their papa when Mama told him to leave because he drank a lot and couldn't get a job. The next oldest child, Rogie Nino's big brother, ran away—I have no memories of him. He and Rogie share a father, but I've never seen him. Then there's the rest of us: my lost sister and me, the next three boys, and the one coming. According to the neighborhood *tsismis*, our home is known as the place of many men, countless children, irresistible drugs, and endless stories.

Rogie Nino is the only one of us here who doesn't share the same papa. He knows he doesn't belong, as if he were only staying for a short while until his real life finds him. And he is smart, smarter than the rest of us. The day he went looking for scraps, he used a smile and some jokes to steal eggs and *tulingan* from the local market. Upon his return, Mama accused him of eating most of the fish for himself, which he had.

Rogie Nino gave no response that day. He hung his head in silence, and Mama became enraged. Her voice deepened as she called him names, revealing the evil spirits, and I put my head down between my knees to hide. I heard a loud thud and the sound of splashing water. Several boiling drops landed on my feet, burning my ankles. The sound of water slapping the ground gave way to crying screams that I had never heard before from Rogie.

Today, Rogie Nino bears layers and layers of thick, shiny sheets of hard skin on his upper left arm. It stands out from the smooth, golden skin on the rest of his body. He no longer jokes or smiles, and he always hides his scars. But like me, he is also still alive.

On the days Mama goes away, I wait until our hunger pushes me out the door to find food. Sometimes, a neighbor will share a bit of rice or scraps they've bought from the *mambabatchoy*. But often, their *pagpag* makes me feel funny, and the boys don't like to eat it. Mama had warned me that the *pagpag* brought the worms, which show up like small, white ribbons stuck in our *dumi*. I hate the worms, so I try to get the rice.

Since Papa left for good, Mama's absences have been longer. I never know what to expect when she comes back. Some days, she returns loud and laughing, holding candies and a few pesos. Other times, she wanders home talking to herself, eyes flashing and calling us *buwisit, puta, gago*. The words don't sting me anymore, and neither do the sticks she uses to swat our faces.

Mama is not always angry. I don't think she likes the boys very much, but she praises me when I bring back the rice. I like it when she tells the neighbors how I am the best rice thief around. Sometimes, I even show off to Rogie about being the best, but he doesn't seem to care. On Mama's good days, I can sit close to her by the river and touch her long, shiny hair. I don't hate her anger as much as I fear her leaving—especially when she disappears for a long time. Sometimes, she goes away for many days. *But at least she'll come back*, I remind myself, which means we are better off than the street children who often vanish with the bad men.

"Grrrahhh!" Suddenly, I hear it. I look up to see Mama crawling from the small stool where she had been sitting close to the hot pot. She had been particularly quiet today, which was unusual, and I startled.

"What's happening, Mama?" I ask, approaching her. She says nothing, only lifting her right hand from the dirt on which she crawls and extending it backward in a swift wave, telling me to move away. I obey. She has gotten a few more feet and enters the doorway, yelling, *"Labas! Labas!"* to the little boys. Rogie Nino already left after the meal as usual and won't be back till after dark. I pull the young boys to me as Mama scoots her round body into the house.

The groans, shrieks, and bad words continue for some time, until night comes, and it is not safe for us to be outside alone. The boys and I move closer to each other, making shapes in the dirt with sticks. My stick is the best because it had a sharp point. I had whittled it to use for writing. Rogie Nino and I are the only ones who can write. We learned words by studying the signs in the local markets so that we would be able to find our way.

Finally, the noise stops, but I hear no word from Mama. *Is she dead?* We wait for some time, sitting by the water and watching the reflections of the last of the cooking fires as they dance on the surface. Even the lights seem to grow tired, and we fall asleep, huddled together, not because we're cold but because touching each other helps us know we're not alone.

A mosquito bite on the back of my ankle wakes me from my

drowsiness, and I see the boys are asleep. I press my eyes shut, trying to go back to sleep and escape the shadows, but there are too many noises. Screeching flying bugs, moaning neighbors, far off laughter, and breaking glass, all of which I can hear but not see.

When I'm too nervous to stay waiting, I get up and approach our hut. Peering through the narrow spaces in the door, I don't see anything—no movement, nothing at all. Pushing the door partly open, I look in and see Mama asleep on the floor, her dress bloody with legs hanging out uncovered. I look long; she is so still. Just barely, I can make out her chest moving in slow deep breaths. Maybe we can come in now.

I shake my brothers awake, and their big eyes stare back into mine. I grab their hands and pull them to the hut, shoving them forward on their rumps. We wind around the door opening like rats around a rock, sliding behind the backside of the door, not wanting to get caught. We sneak to the opposite corner of the house, staying as far away from Mama as possible. Reaching our corner, we crouch down in the dark and lean against the back wall. My hand brushes by something soft, much softer than the woven blankets we use as bedding. I straighten up and take a sharp breath before I see what's there.

It's the baby, the tiniest baby I've ever seen, lying naked on the blanket—a girl. She is only as tall as the space between my knee and my foot, but her limbs make her seem longer. Her arms and legs stick out like loose wires hanging from the old telephone poles. *Is she alive?* Since she's so quiet, I'm not sure.

Careful not to show the boys what I've found, I make out her eyes in the darkness; they aren't open, but the lashes form two perfect half-circles that take up most of her face. Up close, I can now see her chest moving up and down—just a little bit. Mama has birthed her eleventh child, and she's alive.

I barely remember my brothers being born, except for the crying that lasted until they could no longer scream. Unlike them, this child is completely silent. I stare at her for a long time, my vision becoming clearer in the darkness. She seems almost peaceful—and she is beautiful. I hear no sound other than her faint breath, quiet, as if she already knows not to cry for a mama who will not come.

CHAPTER FIVE

Duffle Bags

GARRET

Summer 2010

"I'm not going to that school," I say for the fiftieth time. I'm on my swing. It's one of the few items left in the house. Mom sits behind me on the floor with her laptop, typing away. She ignores my argument and keeps on working. Mom is preparing a big speech she's going to give to a bunch of women. It'll be her last one before we move. I think she's sad. Her eyes dip down on the sides more than usual. She hasn't said much since the people came in and took all the stuff from our house.

Mema pulls up outside. Letting herself in, she immediately comes upstairs. "Guess what I found at work today? Someone had the Hidden Mickey Collection pin of the monorail you were looking for, so I traded it for one of my princess pins." After handing it to me, she and Mom move downstairs, and I get off my swing to get my pin collector's album.

Mema works at Disney World and watches out for rare pins. Collecting pins was my favorite activity at the theme parks. I went from one staff member to another, whether they were sweeping popcorn off the busy sidewalk or setting up ropes for the afternoon parade. They had to trade with guests, and I was the best collector. There were so many workers and so many pins, and I had to check out each one.

Sometimes, Mom got mad because I ran from her on my quest to find pins. I did lose her once, or so she says. But I wasn't lost—I was waiting right where I had seen them last. I'm not sure why it took them thirty minutes to find me there. "We've never lost a child in thirty years," the security leader proudly told my parents when they found me sitting on the rock wall across from the sweet shop.

"I wasn't lost," I insisted, correcting the self-satisfied man with the fancy walkie talkie. I was exactly where I had left them when I had spotted a blue lanyard stuffed full of pins.

The new pin Mema just gave me is magical, and I run to hook it into the correct page of my album. Shuffling through my book to find the collection of multicolored monorail pins, I pick up the many lanyards full of pins shoved into the back pocket of the book.

The pins show scenes, and each one tells a story. There are villains and heroes, princesses and Power Rangers, pirates and sorcerers. Good and evil meet each other on the face of each pin, where everyone's role is obvious and ordered.

I'm only slightly interrupted by the noisy voices I hear downstairs. Mom and Mema seem angry, which is rare. "It's so dangerous over there, and what about your children and what they need?" Mema sounds like she's giving a speech. Their voices are loud but not because of the volume. They might be fighting, and maybe Mom is crying. My arms begin to itch. Mom never talks like this, especially when she talks to Mema. She seems kind of annoyed, excited, and sad all at once.

"It's not that the poor people there don't have shoes, Mom. They don't even have pants!" she pleads. Mema grows silent for a few moments and then resumes talking, slowly and inaudibly. I think Mom won the argument.

Obviously, Mema isn't happy we are moving away, even if it's to help poor people. Six days before our sale when people came in and bought all the stuff in our house, Dad came home with an announcement: "Go buy ten duffle bags. Each of you gets two bags to put anything in you want to keep." He looked at me especially. "Make sure to pack clothes as well as toys." Then, he added, "We leave in one month."

I had never even heard of the place we were moving to: Doha, Qatar. "Qatar is in the Middle East," Dad later explained to me, "and the Emir asked me to build his palace." The palace part sounded cool to me. He must be a neat guy to have a palace.

Even though Dad assured everyone we would be safe, Grandma and Mema didn't think so. Qatar is a desert nation jutting out into the Persian Gulf, sitting next to Saudi Arabia and across from Iran. Dad had shown me the tiny country on a map. Qatar looked puny, and I knew it must be hot, but at least the Persian Gulf would have lots of fish.

The grandmas both agreed it was a place filled with terrorists. I didn't care about the terrorists, but I was worried about the new school. Elite International School required uniforms and dress shoes. I felt itchy hot just thinking about it.

Mom cried when she had to say goodbye to her friends like

Miss Jaimie and Mrs. Mo, but I knew she really was happy. She had always told me about her trips to far-off places in China, Africa, Australia, and parts of Europe. We read books together, and before we sold everything we owned, our rooms had been full of token souvenirs from all the places she had been before I was born. She had brought home carved statues from South Africa, embroidered table mats and jade dragons from China, extra-large boomerangs from Australia, and brightly colored rocks and shells gathered from faraway shores.

Most every day, Mom talked to me about these distant places and the children and widows whom she hoped we could help. Sitting with her, looking through the books about other magical places, I dreamed of traveling, too. I'd visit every zoo and aquarium in the world, I decided.

Mom had the most to say about Asia. "Many places don't have clean water or enough food," she explained, "and many of the children aren't able to go to school." The food part sounded sad to me, but I liked the idea of living in a place where children aren't allowed to go to school.

During our first year with Shiya, Mom kept pursuing other adoptions. I really didn't understand why she wanted another sister like Shiya, but she did. She *really* did. It seemed she was seeking her lost child the way she had searched for me when I wandered away at Disney.

The year after Shiya's arrival, Mom found an adoption agency that facilitated Vietnamese adoptions and began the process. Mom and Dad paid the large fees and completed the dossier, just as the nation decided to stop adoptions, citing child trafficking as the main reason. My mom had pushed back hard, as she always did, and the social worker rebuked her. "You don't want to adopt a child who was stolen, do you?"

With that, Mom got feisty, "No, I don't want a stolen child; I want to adopt one of the thirty million *other children* who don't have parents."

And that was it. Later that same year, after searching records, agencies, blogs, and groups, Mom found Saimay. Saimay is now four years old. A landmine blew up and killed her dad as he was walking home one day, and her mother had "lost her mind." I wasn't sure what that meant, but I understood that Saimay no longer had parents.

Mom showed me the only photo we had of Saimay. In the small picture taken at her dorm in Laos, a small girl sits on a thatched chair next to an old woman. She has a small smile, and her hair is long and pulled back in a ponytail.

"This girl is way cuter than Shiya," I told Mom. "She looks sad but pretty." I couldn't wait to show her my Bionicles.

Closing my collector's book, satisfied with the placement of the blue monorail pin, I head downstairs to find Mom and Mema sitting on the decorative rocks surrounding the pool, chatting about what we could fit into the ten duffle bags. The patio door is open to the humid breeze. Since there aren't couches left inside the house, I go outside to sit by the pool.

Mema seems happy again, and Mom's voice no longer sounds strange. They watch Jolyn as she plays in the pool, throwing princess rings to Shiya who does not want to participate. Jolyn's laughter and constant jumping contrast with Shiya's refusal to lift her arms and catch the rings.

Retrieving the rings herself, Jolyn tries again. She's pushy and tosses the biggest ring to Shiya, almost hitting her in the face. Shiya doesn't care. She stays stationary at the edge of the pool, chewing on her whole hand and groaning her complaints.

Shiya hates having to sit by the pool, but Mom makes her, so she can "overcome her fear," or something like that. Shiya isn't much fun, and she's still scared of everything. Even though I don't know exactly what they are, I don't think Shiya will like the terrorists.

CHAPTER SIX

A Divided Life

Jodi

Fall 2010

"You're at the wrong house," Garry tells me.

Blood drains from my face, and my hands start to tingle.

"I'll come get you and the kids."

I end the call on my clunky mobile phone, the only kind available from the local Qtel shop, and stare at it, trying to calculate how long it will be until Garry comes to pick us up. I have at least thirty minutes. Since I didn't have a car, the phone was my only refuge in this situation, and I chuckle, thinking about how frustrating it was to try to get it.

We had filled out the papers, gathered passports and sponsorship papers, and arrived at the store, only to wait in the lengthy line, which became endless as Qataris cut to the front of it. By cultural mandate, Qataris are entitled to skip the line. They're not being rude when they cut off traffic at the malls and crowded roundabouts, or when they throw their tea bags onto the street to be picked up by a Sri Lankan street cleaner. No offense is meant when Qatari mothers scold the Filipino babysitters who love on their chubby children—children who also bark back orders to the young nannies with the same stern solemnity as their robed mothers. It's simply the Qatari way.

We have lived in Doha, Qatar, for four weeks now, and tonight, Garry's Qatari sponsor, Abdullah, invited us to a party to celebrate Eid al-Fitr. The party began right after sundown following the ringing of the fourth *adhan*, the provocative, moaning call to prayer that's blasted throughout the city on loudspeakers. As the men hurried to the mosques and the women and children joined them in prayer from wherever they were—whether at home, with friends, or in a store—servants prepared for lavish parties that would break the day's religious fast.

Parties for breaking the fast delayed until after sundown. Even though it would begin long past the children's bedtimes and Garret was sure to behave poorly, politely declining the invitation wasn't an option for me. I hoped to avoid the party, because I knew it would be my job to watch the children and navigate the party without Garry's assistance. Since Qatari women only socialized with men from their own families, the men and women held separate gatherings. Each of Abdullah's wives had their own house and party, and everyone here seemed thrilled I had chosen this one. Their elation made more sense after the call.

For the next thirty minutes, I sit among a house full of treasures and onlookers, both glitteringly adorned. Bowls of brightly wrapped candies and chocolates shaped like seashells adorn the tops of marble ledges and small, round tabletops. Golden plates hold *qatayef* and other pastries, filled with pistachios and dripping with honey. Across the room on a long buffet lie hundreds of cookies, called *kahk*, stacked on a wide silver platter that Garret keeps returning to, grabbing handfuls. Unable to break away from the ladies' curious stares, I cannot stop him or find my girls, who had been whisked away by Abdullah's wife and her mother immediately upon our arrival.

I have no choice other than to sit in my velvet settee and attempt to answer the ladies' many questions. I am offered hot tea served from a shot-size china cup, an unfortunate beverage given the 122-degree heat outside. Not permitted to decline this offer either, I sip my tea slowly as I investigate the platters of foods that have been prepared.

Across from where I sit, three-foot-long flatbreads, steaming and topped with toasted sesame seeds, have just been set on the draped banquet table. The aromatic bread sits next to pounds of *baba ganoush*, *fatoush*, and *hummus*. The hummus here is delicate, flavored with citrus—not like the hummus in America, where overstated garlic seasoning masks its true flavor. Servers with platters of lamb-filled kabobs and *machboos* pass by as my gold-rimmed plate now brims with delicacies and unknowns. So abundant are the halal meats and spices that I don't even miss the forbidden pork and wine.

The entrance to the mansion opens into a large, rectangular parlor with expansive ceilings adorned with gold overlay and chandeliers dangling perfectly about every ten feet. Throughout the space, several dozen nosy ladies attired in satin party dresses click their high heels loudly across the marble floor as they come to meet "Abdullah's American." They speak careful English, though I find it difficult to understand much of what they say.

The question they ask most is, "Why are you here?"

I try several answers, including the properly scripted ones: "to experience a new culture" or "to get to know your beautiful country." But I am met with blank faces. These responses seem to bore the ladies, so I try more blatant replies: "to help some of the poor migrants in outlying areas" and "to develop some counseling programs for orphans and widows."

Now the ladies look confused, and their narrowing eyes disclose a slightly offended expression. "Who would need counseling?" one of the elder women asks me.

"We have our own charities," someone else points out. My throat pulls tight as I realize my cultural illiteracy has caused great insult. I'm unsure of what to say next.

I try again: "My husband is building the Emir's palace with Abdullah." At this, the ladies break into knowing smiles. My body relaxes as I watch their baffled expressions yield to lively chatter about Abdullah's generosity. Now that I've responded correctly and appropriately, I force my own smile. To the women, my family is here because my husband works for Abdullah, and that makes perfect sense to them. Abdullah owns a construction firm and is worth four billion dollars.

Outside of the family home, a woman's eyes and shoes are the only part of her that's visible; therefore, both are decorated with jewels, colors, and details. Of course, only Qatari women wear this uniform, and it's a symbol of wealth and honor. While Muslim ladies from other Arab countries wear looser *hijabs* that show their faces and colored *abayas*, Qatari women stand out in their flowing, black *niqabs*, etched with shiny stones and long enough to graze the ground underneath them as they walk. By the clicking of their concealed high heels—they seem intent on being noticed.

I continue talking with the women and grow more comfortable. My children run around with other children, eating chocolates and playing tag throughout the ground floor of this magnificent home. I hope they don't break anything. As I meet one lady after another, I cannot help but stare into their eyes, adorned with thickly painted eyeliner and false eyelashes that are seamlessly attached.

As an expat, I am permitted to wear Western clothes so long as my body remains covered. In truth, no one notices me in my long, cotton skirts and plain tops when they are surrounded by the elegance and beauty of these ornamented ladies. Thankfully, I'm not made to wear the *hijab*; however, I always wear a long scarf around my neck and shoulders, ready to place over my head just in case I meet the judgmental eyes of a male Qatari who is visibly disgusted by the sight of my whole head and hair.

But not tonight; tonight, I am at the women and children's party, where *hijabs* and *abayas* come off at the door, revealing gowns and jewels like I've never seen before up close. Since women are not permitted to attend male parties and vice versa, tonight is the ladies' opportunity to freely remove their outer coverings. It is a rare sight, especially after being in Qatar for almost a month now, and I'm struck by their thick, long hair, hanging down to their waists and bedazzled with jewels. Tonight, the women speak of journalism careers and new education initiatives, of Doha's rapid growth and its various fashion and makeup trends. Hearing them speak leisurely about popular topics is a welcome change. Outside of the party, I haven't seen Qatari women interact with others, except to direct servants to carry one of their children or shopping bags.

In this country, Qataris come first and grant permission to

other immigrants to live here. The class system, as explained to me by Garry's Muslim colleague, is organized as follows: Qataris first; then other Arab immigrants; then British, Australian, and American expats and businessmen; Indians, who make up the professional class of teachers, doctors, and dentists; Filipinos, who are hired for childcare or as hospitality workers; and then Gypsies, Nepalese, Bangladeshi, and Sri Lankans, who serve as street cleaners, construction workers, and bathroom attendants, among other dirty and dangerous jobs.

To enter Qatar, most immigrants must surrender their passports, get tested for tuberculosis, and sign papers agreeing to a specified wage, to be determined by their country of birth. It is the unwritten immigration policy. Americans are paid higher than Indians, Indians make more than Filipinos, and everyone gets more than the Sri Lankans.

For my required TB test earlier last week, I had waited at least five hours. Stern nurses roughly examined us alongside hundreds of other foreign moms and kids in the women and children's clinic, making sure that no one with a transmittable disease was issued a resident's permit.

Garry signed away many rights and agreed to numerous stipulations, including the "no beer" policy, which was most painful for him. He agreed to them all, except one: he refused to surrender our passports. Although it was illegal according to international law, the Qatari sheikhs and bosses always held the passports. They operated under the authority of the Emir, and no one questioned them. Relinquishing our passports was the easiest way to become lost forever in this foreign country. Thousands of Filipinos, Sri Lankans, Nepalese, and others without passports never returned to their homes.

"It is illegal for you to ask for my passport," Garry had said to Ahmed, Abdullah's right-hand fellow. Abdullah might have ejected us immediately for this, but he refrained. And tonight, I am at his party. Or his first wife's party, and Abdullah expects me at his fourth wife's house, imminently. After the thirty long minutes had passed, Garry called to tell me he was outside and ready to take me to the next party.

Embarrassed to be leaving so early, I try to get to the door without anyone noticing. If questioned, I am not sure what response wouldn't offend them, again. Luckily, they don't ask and only object, surrounding me as I attempt to locate my children, who are now hiding among the lavish furniture in the formal living room next to the parlor.

First wife's mother reaches out and grabs Jolyn by the hand and prevents her from escaping back into the game. She then places some folded money into her hand, four one-hundred Qatari riyal bills. As Garret spots the transaction, he quickly finds his place next to Jolyn. Before I can protest, they each receive handfuls of QR, their eyes dancing between the money and their generous benefactor. Shiya remains unaware of the exchange but receives more money than either of her siblings.

"This is better than Halloween!" exclaims Garret, laughing in disbelief. I go against my instinct to turn down this extravagant gift because I know the offense would be too great. We head toward the entryway, loudly giving thanks.

Garry sits just outside in the SUV, but first wife's mother grabs Shiya by both shoulders before we can get out the door. Kneeling to eye level more nimbly than expected for someone her age, she studies Shiya's flat expression as her gaze remains serious, offering no clues to whether she is being critical of this non-Qatari, non-white child. Upon inspecting Shiya's short stature and round face, first wife's mother quickly stands up and comes close to me, her face still expressionless, and blurts out, "Her eyes differ to you." The sentiment is both a diagnosis and question.

"Yes, we adopted her from China almost two years ago," I say, unsure of her opinion about adoption. Quranic law prevents Muslims from adopting children outside of their bloodline. So stringent are the policies to maintain a pure lineage that tradition still encourages first cousins to marry.

Stern but no longer confused, first wife's mother announces to the room of guests, "You did good for Jesus!" She strongly pats my hand and lifts it up, repeating the news and sharing in its victory. I only smile back and nod, speechless.

"I thought talking about Jesus was illegal," I say to Garry as we climb into our oversized SUV. Everyone drives large SUVs in Doha to handle the sand.

He grins. "I think white equals Jesus here."

Before he has time to continue, Jolyn tells him about the treasures she collected at the party. Apparently giving money to children is the commonplace during Eid festivities. "How many toys can I buy?" Garret asks.

Children have become the center point of Qatari society, and toy shops flourish in Doha. In comparison to the waning malls in the United States, the shopping malls here thrive with sweet shops, toy stores, and the finest of wares. Our new friend Omar manages the Luis Vuitton, which competes with Gucci and Dolce & Gabbana in the same section of the mall. Thousand-dollar shoes and purses sell here, and Omar regularly earns tens of thousands of dollars in sales to a singular Qatari customer.

"Can we go to the mall tomorrow to buy toys?" Garret insists.

His goal is a trip to the Villaggio Mall, replete with a Venetian waterway and a gondola that runs through the middle of the building.

"If you come to one more party tonight, we can go to the mall tomorrow," I tell him. After all, we still need to make it to fourth wife's party.

The second round of festivities transpires nearly the same as the first, brimming with doting fanfare, clacking heels, and scalding beverages, except—this time—the kids understand the high stakes. Exchanging secret looks and satisfied smiles with one another, they end the night with several hundred more dollars in their pockets.

Tomorrow is Saturday, the last day of the week, so we can go to the mall. Saturdays are the best days in Doha because everything reopens after Friday's day of fasting. Garret typically hates the mall—he becomes bored and easily overwhelmed—however, the malls here are different. In the center of the Villaggio sits an eight-story atrium where rollercoasters and Ferris wheels create an indoor carnival offering hours of play. An ice-skating rink, a game room, and a fast food court sit just around the corner from the amusement park. In between the marble pillars separating the shopping and play areas are the Islamic prayer rooms, divided between male and female supplicants. Once, I blundered by entering the men's prayer room hallway rather than the ladies' room lounge. Horrified men ran at me, yelling loudly to shoo me away from their sacred space. It's a mistake I made only once.

On Saturday, armed with $200 each, Garret, Jolyn, and Shiya shopped the Villaggio like Qataris. In and out of the toy stores and game shops, moving aggressively through all the aisles, they finished their spree with an overpriced Lego set, two art kits, and four pastel-colored stuffed animals with abnormally large eyes. Shopping bags in hand, we head to the parking lot, hoping to make our way to our favorite restaurant, Al-Khaima, for hummus, flatbread, and kebabs. We never can be sure if we will make it from one end of the city to the other—the traffic had become unbearable over the past few years.

With their new wealth, Qatari oil heirs attempted to build a city that rivaled the best in the world. The skyline rose up majestically, but the city's infrastructure was lacking, as if designed by a kid with a new Lego set: unrivaled skyscrapers, expansive waterparks, and ornate palaces were built with little attention to logistics, such as roads, sidewalks, and traffic flow. Engineers like Garry were being brought to Qatar to see if they could retrofit the landscape and improve the overall grid.

But Doha isn't fixed yet, and the traffic almost thwarts our attempts at dinner. Rows of trucks carrying migrant workers back to their camps compete with roaring SUVs to beat the lights. No one stays within the traffic lanes, and people sometimes drive over the medians and sidewalks to gain the advantage. Garry hangs his head as we get caught at the next light. The lines of vehicles extend so far from the intersection that it takes several revolutions to finally cross.

Even though Garry hates the traffic, it represents something more than a nuisance to me. I grin as I view the bustling cars, the half-built skyscrapers, and the swarms of peoples from every nation, coming together to build and *become*. To me, the traffic is a harbinger of opportunity, of the investments pouring into the local engineering and construction industry. We live at the crossroads of overwhelming resources and urgent need, of burgeoning wealth and a critical infrastructure crisis.

As we slowly make our way, I can't help but recognize and appreciate the difference between the deteriorating economic environment of America and this region's growing abundance of investments, capital, and development. Even though he knew we'd be strangers and outcasts, Garry had recognized this unique opportunity when he decided to relocate here. The truth is, we didn't have many options: as the economy back home remained stuck, we were lucky we'd escaped the crash and our debt to find real opportunity.

Of course, the prudent decision would have been to stay put in Florida and wait for the economy to improve, as we knew it would. But Garry and I aren't very patient, and we have big plans, which makes us impulsive. Many have called us "reckless" or—in Garret's words— "terrible parents."

I used to think I was special because I dreamed of accomplishing great things. Hundreds of counseling clients later, I know better. Everyone dreams big, even though life's realities defy our ambitions and aspirations. Garry and I decided to *live here now* and not wait for opportunities to find us. But grand plans cost money and take heart, and no one was going to give us either. It was up to us to make it happen.

Eventually, we got unstuck from enveloping traffic and did make it to dinner. Pulling our SUV into a narrow parking spot, Garry finally exhaled. "We made it," he said.

I knew we would.

CHAPTER SEVEN

Taliban

GARRY

Fall 2010

The remote, single-lane highway stretched out, a straight line northwest through the desert toward Al Ghuwayriyah. We had already exited the Doha expressway after passing the familiar Pearl and Redco WLL Labour Camp several miles back. Now, thirty minutes outside of Qatar's capital city, I recognized the foolishness of driving so far outside of city limits with a stranger.

Wahid had picked me up earlier that day at my office, the private engineering office of the Emir (PEO). Wahid seemed normal enough—stout, stern, and reticent. When scouting new ventures, I typically travelled with my project partner, Hassam. But for the sake of expediency, Hassam had convinced me to do this project meet and greet without him. I didn't fully understand the scope or particulars of the new job, but unknowns were commonplace for me by now. Much of my work with the Emir remained strictly confidential.

Today's project meeting did not involve the Emir—it was one among an endless line of opportunities in the burgeoning Doha pipeline, and Hassam had suggested that it might be something we ought to pursue. Without hesitation, I set out to meet the new team with Wahid as my guide. Now I wished my clever Arabic-speaking friend Hassam had come with me.

I met Hassam four years ago when he showed up at my office in South Florida in 2006 looking for a job. Hassam had studied engineering but never practiced it, and no firm would hire a Muslim immigrant with zero experience—especially at that time. Having lived all over the world, Hassam had been educated in the United States and passed the engineering licensure exam without studying. He's the smartest person I know and the shrewdest, although others have used less kind descriptors. Hassam made lucrative transactions happen, deals like this one.

When Hassam approached me about moving my family to Qatar to engineer the palace job, I jumped at the opportunity, even though I had only completed one of my two contracted years to the firm that had bought me out. Although they saved me from bankruptcy, I hated the office politics, the long commute, the timecards, and the many company rules.

Hassam had left my dwindling firm the year before the buyout and now worked for the Mideast Construction and Trading Firm (MCT), where he was the project manager for the palace. As PM, he had struggled to find a competent engineering firm to handle the enormous complexity of the building designs. Knowing my situation, Hassam suggested I proposition my US firm to bid for the job and send me to lead the project once we won it. His scheme worked, as his plans usually did, and it offered me the perfect escape from my corporate misery.

Sitting next to Wahid, though, I doubted anyone would describe this situation as perfect. Wahid dressed in the white *thobe*, as did all the Qatari leaders, along with sandals and a *ghutra*. The colors of the *ghutra* men wore on their heads had meanings: white for purity, red and white for patriotism, and black and white for freedom. Wahid wore white for purity.

He was driving eighty miles per hour down a desert highway where sand dunes and oil refineries appeared more frequently than other drivers. I looked out the window, enjoying the sight of the billowing smoke and the flares from the petrochemical plants in the distance, surrounded by white dunes.

I had taken my family to race the SUV through the mounds of sand that sloped down to the quiet shores of the Arabian Gulf many times. We would swirl the car around the dunes, the large tires making spin-art in the sands. The SUV only got stuck occasionally. No matter your ethnicity or station, someone always showed up to help pull you out. There was an unspoken culture of equality etched into the edges of the dunes. Out in the sand, the flames of the refineries never ceased to burn brightly and offer an optimistic sign of life among the dusty, barren desert landscape.

"What's the project?" I asked Wahid.

"You'll see," was his only response. That was at the start of our journey, almost forty-five minutes ago. We hadn't spoken any other words since. Only the melodious hum of Arabic newscasters and the specks of sand tapping the underside of the SUV broke the silence.

As we traveled further, we hit towns along the way, springing up like one small oasis after another. But Wahid didn't stop at these towns, and I hadn't seen another driver for at least ten minutes.

When we did slow, it wasn't at the jobsite. Wahid pulled the car off to the side of the road, its right wheels sinking into the sandy shoulder. I said nothing. Neither did Wahid. As he exited the vehicle, I spotted the rug tucked under his arm, coiled up as tightly as the illegal snakes I saw at the Souk marketplace.

Unrolled, the rug resembled the one we had laid at the foot of our kitchen sink, and I wondered if we had unknowingly transgressed the law by using the prayer mat as a kitchen rug. After setting it next to his car door, Wahid knelt on his rug facing west and began his prayers. I couldn't see his body from where I sat, observing only his hands rising up and down as he prayed toward Mecca, only a thirteen-hour drive west from here.

Growing up in America as a Christian, I owned certain prejudices that I had assumed to be true about Muslims, including a basic idea that the Quran promoted violence, inequality, and the subjugation of women. Since being here, I'd had opportunities to discuss the Quran and its teachings, as well as the stories of Abraham, Moses, and Jesus, all of whom are revered as great teachers in the Islamic tradition.

While the translated text could be used to promote poor behavior, most of my Muslim colleagues stayed far away from those philosophies and instead paid strict allegiance to the five pillars or duties of Islam: *shahadah*, or professing the Muslim faith; *salat*, the ritual reciting of prayers five times each day; *zakat*, which called for charitable giving; *sawm*, the month-long fast during Ramadan; and *hajj*, the pilgrimage to Mecca. The men I knew remained married, supported and doted on their children, prayed throughout the day, gave generously to local causes, and diligently saved money for *hajj*. In all my time here, I had never met a divorced man or a child from a broken family. Islam is a religion of great sacrifice, and I found myself respecting these men for their conscientiousness.

Still, I felt a chasm between their faith and my own, even though on the outside they looked somewhat similar. To me, the differences were subtle but pervasive. Witnessing Wahid's reverence, I found myself both puzzled and amazed, intimidated and curious. Observing his commitment to prayer and the worn-out version of the Quran resting on his dashboard, I recognized and appreciated his sacrifice and efforts.

Wahid rolled up his rug and climbed back into the SUV. We had been driving for several more minutes when he announced, "I am Taliban."

It was both a confession and a call to attention. I waited, stilled by his words as I imagined that his sacrifices to Allah might not translate into kindness or mercy toward me. Wahid said nothing else. Not knowing if he were driving me to a jobsite or my gravesite, I thought through what he knew about me. I am white and American, ergo a Christian, and, by Quranic definition, an "infidel." Hoping to become culturally competent before we came, Jodi purchased a translated copy of the Quran, which had informed me that I met the criteria for that label.

How did I get here? I thought back to Hassam's invitation to come to Doha and how quickly I had jumped at the opportunity to move. The story's many pieces began to make sense. My company had sent me here to work with the PEO and build a palace, which was being constructed by Hassam's firm, the MCT, a Syrian construction company.

A displaced band of brothers—three of the richest expats in Doha—directed the MCT and maintained a close association with my sponsor, Sheikh Abdullah, who only spoke to me via his representative, the intimidating and forceful Ahmed. Ahmed often visited with the MCT brothers and came to the PEO to pass on any instructions I needed to understand about the palace job.

Because the depth of his pride could not be completely contained, Ahmed had vaguely hinted that the MCT supported the Syrian rebels by funding their campaign to smuggle medicine, food, and ammunition to the besieged insurgents. Qataris, who are Sunni Muslims, quietly cheer for the predominantly Sunni rebels who would soon attempt to overthrow Syria's Alawite Al-Assad regime, which aligns itself with Shia governments in the Gulf region.

Looking to uphold Sunni practices, Wahid, Ahmed, and the MCT—along with the sponsor I had barely met—were potentially dangerous men with strategic ambitions to accomplish regional change under the guise of big business. Powerful leaders with access to unimaginable wealth had the motives and means to create a new balance of power in the Gulf. Although I couldn't understand the underlying motivations of everyone involved, I recognized a perilous chess game, each player stealthily advancing and willing to sacrifice pawns to gain a tactical advantage. In this scenario, I was the pawn.

Wahid said nothing else after his declaration. He leaned back in the wide leather seat with one hand loosely holding the wheel, as if relieved and encouraged by our "talk." It wasn't clear if he wanted to threaten me or if he felt obligated to inform me of his allegiances. Either way, his severe expression and set jaw relaxed into a softer, rounder shape. After several more minutes, what looked like a legitimate construction site surfaced in the distance. Dozers and rollers had already flattened and packed the sand to prepare for the construction. Earlier construction teams had paved roads around the site, and the rough ends of pre-set pipes jutted clumsily out of the ground.

Once we were out of the SUV, I met several men wearing the white *ghutra* and waited for my turn to speak. I didn't understand their Arabic, and they refused to speak English. Several times, I heard "Dr. Vermaas" spoken with a slight accent, and the group pointed both to me and to various areas of the site. Ignored but reassured that the conversation involved some kind of construction project, I awaited my instructions, which never came, and left with Wahid after only ten minutes. I knew it would be several weeks before I heard a translated summary of our meeting and found out if I had "won" the top-secret job.

Compared to the fear of imminent execution, the rest of the day seemed uneventful as we returned home toward the Doha horizon. When we arrived back at my office, Wahid got out of the car to say goodbye. As he walked toward me, he leaned into me until I could smell the spiced scent of his cologne. I wondered if he was coming in for a nose bump, the traditional "handshake" of the Gulf states, but he stopped short and clasped my hand with both of his and smiled at me for the first time. It wasn't a nose bump, but I took it as a good omen—at least for business.

Jodi had come to Qatar to do good; I hoped to do good, but I mostly came to make money, and this exchange was a positive sign. The snug handshake meant Wahid considered me his teammate and equal. *I'm now peers with a Taliban apologist*, I thought.

Strangely, it felt like a compliment. I judged myself, that I might be in over my head, but not too harshly. Turning back to my office, I paced my steps to match the rhythmic sound of the fourth call to prayer that was now sounding out over the loudspeaker. It had been a long day.

CHAPTER EIGHT

Dutiful Doha

Jodi

Winter 2011

After the first six months, living in Qatar became routine. Garry worked every day downtown, winning jobs and keeping stride with the city's development. We became used to the slower pace and mundane chores of our new life as expats. Whenever Garry and I spent time outside of the United States, we always felt traumatized by the slow pace of our surroundings.

Here, things were no different, and daily life forced us to shift away from our Western expectations of "getting it done." After many frustrating outings, we decided to set a one-per-day goal for running errands. It took an entire day to do any one task, whether it was food shopping, picking up school uniforms, or getting a new tire. Back in the States, I could accomplish several tasks in the same day, plus full-time work and parenting, but not here, where shops shut down regularly for tea break and most large purchases—like a phone or car—required a signature from our sponsor. Complicated goals, like getting your television service turned on or obtaining a local driver's license, easily took a whole month—or two.

The objective for today was to take the children somewhere fun. It was Saturday, and yesterday, we already had accomplished the weekly shopping list at the expat grocery store, which was open on Fridays. The wash hung from the clothesline that crisscrossed our pink tiled kitchen, drying quickly in the heat of midday. Homework and chores complete, we craved amusement and fresh air.

We decided to head to the Souk Waqif and arrived early enough to find a place to park. The Souk sits in the middle of the skyscraper boom, a standing relic of things past. This labyrinth of an outdoor market holds dozens of spice shops, antique weapons exchanges, booths selling jewels and semi-precious stones, Shisha shops, and craftswear boutiques. It had once been a trading center for Qatari Bedouin, who were the country's original inhabitants. Today, it is a popular market and shopping area. The Bedouin still inhabit the shops, barefoot even now and covered in white robes for protection from the heat. They wait for unsuspecting parents, who overpay for their children to ride the Bedouin's camels and donkeys up and down the bazaar's narrow streets.

My children first pull us to their favorite area in the Souk, the animal market. Teeming with dealers and cages, the open-air market resonates with the sounds of bargaining and barking, mewing and bird calls. Chickens, birds, fish, dogs, cats, ferrets, and hamsters cram close together in their respective enclosures. Confused bunnies dyed pink and blue, caged specialty birds, and oddly mixed breeds of cats peek out at us each time we pass, looking for their escape.

Around the corner from these animals, down the unevenly stoned street about a quarter mile away, stand the concrete, cubicle structures topped with metal roofs where poor Bedouin live among even poorer immigrants, the hidden people who secretly run the city. The immigrant population sweeps the streets, delivers the produce, builds the structures, tends the flocks, butchers the halal beef, fixes the flat tires, dusts the prayer rooms, mops the restroom floors, and scrapes up the garbage ground into the sidewalks.

I did not see many Qataris at the Souk. Qatari citizens remained the minority, making up only 12% of the total population. At the Souk, you find tourists alongside people from the Indian and Arab professional classes mingling with white expats like me.

It was crowded tonight and hot. I paid for the iced teas of some American soldiers who were visiting Doha for the weekend on leave from the US base tucked into the desert just an hour from here. "Thank you for your service!" I said, enthusiastic to see some familiar American faces. The soldiers told me they had been in Qatar for six months and had come to enjoy the hookah and spiced treats.

As we walked the narrow streets of the Souk, covered ladies and their male partners bumped us out of the way, reminding us of our place. Garret complained about the growing crowd of people. He was not wrong—the crowds had multiplied since we arrived in Doha last year. When Qatar won the bid to host the 2022 FIFA World Cup, untold thousands of Qatari-sponsored migrant workers began arriving to recast the old city into a thriving, tourist-worthy destination.

Hoping to send money home to their families, migrant workers from Nepal, Sri Lanka, and Pakistan entered the *kafala* system of sponsorship, which required the same loyalties as Garry's agreements with his sponsor. Earning low wages and powerless to switch jobs, they ended up in migrant camps, commuting daily to one of the many building sites: eight stadiums, one hundred hotels, ninety-two training sites, and numerous railway stations and transportation hubs. The construction boom aimed to meet the needs of the approximately 1.5 million fans who will attend the games.

The night Doha won the right to host the 2022 World Cup, the Emir announced the victory over hundreds of loudspeakers that perched on roof corners throughout the city. Thousands of Doha residents took to the streets in celebration. From our window, we heard crowds of expats and immigrants cheering, applauding the now-limitless economic opportunities. More quietly, the Qataris rejoiced in their homes, affirming that they had achieved their goal of establishing their country as the new cultural, political, and economic leader of the Middle East.

We made it through the crowded Souk, grabbing a corner table at a local favorite, Zataar Zeit, where we ordered rice and Zataar's version of pizza for the children while Garry and I opted for a more native dish. While we waited, I overheard two young men with accents—Egyptian, I believed. They complained about the "stupid" workers on their jobsite, who they described as "uneducated" and "foolish."

I had heard enough to know that many men had fallen to their death or committed suicide at these construction sites—but not because they had been foolish. The non-Qatari news stations had estimated that since the beginning of the construction boom last year, over 3,000 migrant workers have already died from sickness, falling, or suicide due to oppressive and unsafe working conditions. No one knew for sure, and no one dared to ask—except the widows. But no one seemed to care about them.

Turning back to our own conversation, I listened to Jolyn talk about our upcoming trip to India while Garret grimaced at the thought of more travel. We discussed the orphanage and school that were situated in central India, where Ververt and Neelam lived and served. Shiya asked about Ververt and Neelam's orphanage and if it would be like her Chinese orphanage, smiling in hopes that it would. Garret listened for only a few moments before losing himself in his DS.

Garret was not doing well in Qatar. He had protested vehemently that Elite International School would not work for him, and after only one month of grade four, Garret got kicked out. When Principal Fatima called him to her office that day, Garret refused to come out from under the table. Sheikha Fatima had told me plainly, "Your son is not well. We cannot help him."

The culture, the uniforms, and the bullies had overwhelmed him. Garret had difficulty following directions in English, much less understanding them in a foreign dialect. Although Elite International advertised itself as an English-speaking school, the children mostly spoke Arabic while the instructors taught in basic English, heavily accented by the languages of their home countries. Furthermore, the woolen uniforms, which mimicked those of British upper-class parochial schools of the 1980s, irritated Garret's already itchy arms and legs, especially in the extreme heat. Garret complained incessantly about these various challenges, making himself an easy target for the school bullies.

The education system of Qatar was in its infancy. A

shepherding nation until the 1970s, Qatar only recently began to develop its people academically. Professionals from India, Egypt, Lebanon, Australia, and England assumed most of the professional jobs, especially healthcare and teaching. Absent of any pedagogical leadership in the school system, the teachers relied on experiences from their home countries. Many vocations lagged in their theoretic relevance and academic footing. Psychiatric care was nearly nonexistent, which made it nearly impossible to treat Garret's unbalanced brain.

Garret took two medications to function. The first drug was an anti-depressant that also reduced his anxiety and panic. Through years of trial and error, we discovered it significantly improved the rigidity, social awkwardness, obsessiveness, and cognitive repetitions associated with Garret's autism. In Qatar, anti-depressants became available as an over-the-counter medication, largely because of the growing burden of depressed women. But Qatar had banned narcotics, which meant that Garret's second medication was not as easy to find. The government prohibited widespread use of stimulant medications, which helped reduce the problems of hyperactivity, inattention, and sensory overload experienced by people on the spectrum.

The only psychiatrist willing to prescribe Garret's medications required me to go to the "mental ward" of Doha's small women's hospital. Every ten days, Garret and I would drive toward the Lusail district to reach the single-story, concrete facility, where I presented my resident permit and Garret's diagnostic papers through a hole in the glass barrier window. Once allowed in, we wound our way down several lonely corridors to our doctor's office. The ward assistant did not authorize us to make appointments—we just had to show up and hope the doctor was there. If we were lucky, he'd be sitting in his office ready to count out ten pills.

"Autism?" he had asked during our first visit. At least he had heard of it. Certainly, Principal Fatima had not.

Our Saturday night dinner at the Souk soon gave way to Sunday morning and back to school and work. The school days there felt long. Sunday through Thursday, we would drive to school down the main road heading east, past rows of billboards stuck in the dunes and covered with propaganda images and phrases. Messages like "Welcoming the World to Qatar," "Qatar 2022," and "Celebrate" popped up frequently to advertise the country's luxuries and innovations. The school sat only five miles away, but the trip took forty-five minutes, weaving us through congested streets and roundabouts dotted with statues and monuments to the Emir. Once we had arrived, we would jump over curbs to park on the sidewalks because there was not a parking lot. New schools—like restaurants and hotels—were built every day, but parking had been forgotten.

Walking into Grade 1, Jolyn would quickly find her best friend Maha and their mutual archrival Rashid, who loved to tease Jolyn for her blond, curly locks. "Good day, Maha! Good day, Rashid!" Jolyn began to incorporate both expat British and Arabic-sounding inflections in her speech.

Every morning, Rashid slyly responded with the same, "No Hi," marching off only to glance back to see if Jolyn and Maha cared that he had rebuffed her friendliness. They didn't.

Shiya was a different story. Known only as "Habibti," Shiya had been coddled by her Lebanese kindergarten teachers since day one. After three months in their class, Shiya's teachers began to realize that sweet, cute, little Habibti was an unrelenting pain in the butt. I didn't feel responsible for their troubles; they had refused to listen when I told them to set firm boundaries from the start. Now it was midyear, and they had lost all authority and credibility with Habibti.

Today, Shiya crawled down from her high perch in the SUV to give me a distracted hug, looking past me toward her classroom and hurrying off, forgetting her lunch. Her aim was to claim the art easel before her classmates. Shiya was passionate about only two things: China and drawing. She overtook the other kindergarteners, sweetly clinging to their robed mamas whose high heels clacked across the mosaic tiles as they made their way together across the courtyard.

I followed Shiya, alone, wearing sandals and carrying her lunch box. I gave the teachers a knowing grin at the door. The younger of her two teachers, the stricter one with the French Moroccan accent, held up her phone and said with a wink, "I zwill call to you."

Last week, I asked the teachers to call me when Shiya refused to listen. The plan was to help Shiya understand that her defiance at school would be dealt with later at home. This unified front empowered the teachers, who never had won Shiya's respect.

Shiya did not surrender easily. Even though she was six years old, Shiya often acted like a toddler. Developmentally, she seemed stuck in the *only-me* stage, exploring the world to satisfy her wants with little regard for the existence—much less authority— of anyone else. She experienced debilitating anxiety toward anything new, like courtyard soccer matches or non-preferred foods, and frequently screamed and scowled at anyone attempting to introduce new activities.

Shiya had not reached fundamental kindergarten proficiencies, such as beginning literacy, reciprocal social interactions with peers, and basic coordination skills. Although she now walked well, she never jumped, skipped, or ran, preferring low-effort tasks. The teachers' continual attempts to teach her failed as she stubbornly refused to participate in even mildly challenging assignments. Only when the teachers threatened to call her *Mama* and *Baba* would Shiya reluctantly join in the day's learning activities; only under our authority and the threat of potential discipline waiting for her at home would she marginally adhere to their directions.

Other than driving to and from school, most weekdays left Garret and I shut up in our apartment while Garry went to work. I never felt completely safe on my own and preferred to stay home unless necessary. When we first arrived in Doha, we had lived in an expat community behind gated walls. The accommodations resembled a European hotel—small, but efficient, safe, and luxurious.

After a month, we missed being part of Doha's vibrant culture, so we moved to an apartment in an older building in the middle of the city, within walking distance of the local shopping district and authentic eateries. This apartment did not have the typical amenities of a Western home, like a dishwasher and a clothes dryer, but it had the most interesting neighbors.

Amu, a young female medical professional from India tackling a male-dominated profession with unapologetic confidence, came over weekly to have tea with me. We'd go upstairs to visit Hamza and Noora, a Jordanian family who often invited us over to smoke hookah. They also had a son, Christopher, who was as strange as Garret. These meetings became the highlights of my lonely week, as did the unlikely elevator encounters and lobby conversations with the Syrian, Egyptian, Lebanese, Filipino, and Sri Lankan nomads who shared our building space.

While Garry worked at the PEO every day, I attempted to homeschool Garret. Not having anticipated my third-grade teaching job, I made much of it up as we went along. Schooling him meant that I also had to stay at home, so I started an online program to pursue a second master's degree in mental health counseling.

While I had already completed my doctoral studies in clinical Christian psychology several years earlier, living in the Middle East had inspired me to study a secular and multi-cultural degree in mental health. Submitting online videos, tests, and assignments daily, I pursued my studies together with Garret, who interrupted me continually for help. From our large wooden table in our fifth-floor apartment, we toiled side by side to the ongoing soundtrack of the honking traffic and chatting pedestrians beneath our window. Even five floors away, the sounds irritated and distracted both of us.

■ ■ ■ ■ ■

One spring day, after dropping Shiya and Jolyn at school, Garret and I were listening to the daily 7:00 a.m. news brief from radio Al Jazeera. Once again, several bombings had killed dozens of people in Pakistan—it was nearly the same report that had been given yesterday, and the day before that. Tensions in other Arabic nations heightened, and the newscaster named several militia groups that were rebelling in Tunisia, Egypt, Syria, and Yemen. I did not understand the specific tribal and cultural contexts, but I surmised that the reasons for the Arab Spring had been evolving long before this moment in history. Although the newscasters offered no commentary, I sensed a subtle note of satisfaction and anticipation coming through the airwaves.

The Qatari government, led by the wealthy Al Thani ruling family and Sheikh Hamad Bin Khalifa Al Thani, was navigating carefully among its troubled neighbors in order to emerge as a kind of impartial mediator amidst the disturbances. It was assumed that Qatar assisted in the ousting of Libya's Muammar al Qaddafi and slyly funded both the Syrian and Libyan rebels. In more recent days, Qatar's involvement seemed distant, although its subtle support of some Islamist groups like the Muslim Brotherhood did not sit well with the United States and other allies. Because of the limited news media and robust internet restrictions, I relied on local news to understand these profoundly important current events.

After school that day, Garry and I picked up Jolyn and Shiya and headed to church. Even though Sunday through Thursday was our school and work week, our small house church continued to meet on Sundays in accordance with our traditions. Our "church" was a small group of eight or nine other Christians who met at an expat compound. We had found this house church though a mutual friend from New York who knew its leaders, Gordon and Fiona Ayati.

The Ayatis had emigrated from Nigeria over a decade ago with their two boys and had held house church ever since. Traditional, stoic, and careful, Gordon led worship in a monotone, yet sincere voice. He worked at Doha's Ministry for Transport and Communication, where he utilized his engineering skills to improve the overall transportation system. Untrained in both singing and preaching, Gordon's services lacked spunk but not hospitality. The house church exuded a friendly vibe, which originated with Fiona, a skilled nurse in the locally developing medical field, who received us with warm hugs, loud greetings, and plates of food. Together we sang, learned, and ate together, welcoming numerous other itinerant worshipers throughout the year.

On our way to church each week, we stopped at the local McDonald's and treated the kids to an ice cream cone—or French fries in Shiya's case, since she did not eat ice cream. In each of the countries we had ever visited, we found a McDonald's. There is something about the sameness of the vanilla ice cream cones that has always helped us feel at home, even in the most foreign places.

Tonight was no different, and we pulled into the parking lot to enjoy a cone with plenty of time to spare before picking up our friend Niluka and heading to church. A Qatari woman pushed past us to cut the line, knocking Garret into me. Pressing his lips together, Garret rolled his eyes and caught his footing, but I smiled. No Qatari waited their turn and being "less than" was a good experience for us. The line-offender ordered a *McArabica* sandwich and fries for her young son, whose chubbiness reinforced the traditional belief that fat and wealthy went together.

After we finished our cones, we left to pick up Niluka, who lived forty-five minutes west of town. A Sri Lankan immigrant living in a dorm-style camp adjacent to the water park, she and I had met the week before in the water park's bathroom as she stood waiting to clean up after us. I glanced at her and waved, my best and sometimes only form of communication. Noticing Shiya's face, Niluka had asked, "Your daughter?" and beamed as I nodded. Assuming I was a Christian, Niluka then asked if I attended church. Choosing my words carefully, I shared about my faith, eventually inviting her to join us for church.

In Qatar, inviting a Muslim to church was illegal, which made me unsure about asking her, even as the words came out of my mouth. Sometimes when I connected with people, I forgot myself. I had done the same with Ayesha, the mother of Jolyn's best friend, with whom I shared everything about my faith. Garry also struggled to keep quiet. I remembered the terror on Gordon's face when Garry told him he had invited Hassam to attend our house church. Garry had assured him that Hassam had a penchant for breaking the rules, but Gordon still gave him a lecture.

We parked at the camp dormitory next to the water park where Niluka lived. She waited for me to call her to meet us in the lobby, but first we had to present our resident papers to the official in charge of the water park. He stayed motionless in his oversized office chair as he watched us approach the lobby from his office, and Garry gestured for the kids to stay quiet. Church attendance was legal for expats, but only if we did not cause trouble or invite locals. We flashed our papers to the official from the lobby and asked permission to check our friend out for the evening. His expression remained unchanged, as we entered his small lobby office.

The official wanted to know what time we would bring Niluka back. As he leaned over his clipboard to check off the sign-out sheet, Garret announced from behind me, "Our church is awesome! You should come!"

Every head popped up and we all stiffened—except Garret who looked down and started reading his *Harry Potter* book that previously had been tucked under his arm. Garry and I turned to the official, speechless. I knew we could be arrested, and thought of Niluka, who had very few rights. The room felt heavy as Garry and I held our breath, waiting. Garret didn't even like going to church, yet at just the wrong time, he had decided that this man needed to hear the message.

"Be back by 10:00," the official told us, ignoring what had been said. He gave us a small smile and patted Garret on the head.

We left quickly, passing the vacant wave pool, its very presence a reminder of the shifting values of the region. The merciful official, like the water park, traversed between old ways and new, between traditional laws and fresh opportunities. He overlooked the rules just enough to make life work.

In Doha, everyone was learning how to live with traditional rules amidst an influx of new cultural viewpoints. Just as Qatari women splashed around the wave pools in their burkinis and waterproof hijabs, the official recognized the need for both adaptation and conventional propriety. The delicate balancing act could not last forever, and the intersection of cultures overflowed disproportionately toward the idea of freedom. But on this evening, the official's decision to maintain the fragile status quo rescued us from the consequences of our infraction.

Situations like this reminded me that I was not free. Amid the mundane daily schedules of work, school, cooking, cleaning, family, and friendships, I was not free to openly share my thoughts, wear certain clothes, or consume alcohol and non-halal foods. I could address only women and had to remain mindful of topics that should not be discussed, including 9/11, Israel, the Royal Family, and any imperfections among Qatari society. If I am being completely honest and politically incorrect, I felt nervous most of the time.

At any moment, someone could take away my rights and liberties. Transgress the rules, and authorities could detain us and deny our exit visas, leaving us prisoners within these borders. It was not a specific fear of any one person or hazard; rather, it was a pervasive concern over indefinite threats.

Those around me strove for the cultural self-awareness needed for self-actualization and did not recognize my discomfort. My new friends had grown up among strict class and gender restrictions, so much so that they could not differentiate between cultural propriety and deliberate inequality. Though it wasn't debated out loud, the struggle for freedom became apparent in the physical and behavioral strivings of their lives: dear friends Omar and his wife Eisa asked us to harbor them in the United States so they could give birth to an American baby. Garry's favorite employee, Hussein, had a Malaysian girlfriend who had met me for coffee the previous week wearing a hijab for the first time, having traded in her Catholic faith to marry the Muslim love of her life.

Whether it was with the Taliban or PEO, Hassam schemed and negotiated tirelessly to secure new work that gave him the kind of economic freedom that enabled geographic mobility. Securing freedom preoccupied the hearts of everyone we had come to love here. Whether via anchor babies or business opportunities or forbidden love, their relentless search for freedom colored and molded each of their lives.

Still, the outward rules had to be followed. And we did. As dutiful residents, we returned Niluka by ten o'clock that night, without incident.

CHAPTER NINE

Tigers, Monkeys & Snakes

GARRET

Winter 2011

"You're the worst parents in the world."

I make my voice sound like the weather reporter on one of Mom's news programs. Just moments ago, I had been bitten by a wild monkey in the middle of India. Mom is looking around frantically, in hopes of finding someone who might know how to help me. We're at the Monkey Temple, what's called the Ramtek Mandir shrine in Nagpur, Maharashtra, India. We have come to Nagpur from Doha "on vacation," as Dad told us, and are staying with Vijay and his wife, Sheetal, and their son, Aarav.

Ramtek Mandir is famous because of Lord Rama, who stayed here on some epic journey, but I didn't care much about the story. The temple has narrow staircases leading to high rooms filled with statues. Worshipers leave so many candles and flowers on the stone floors that I couldn't enter without knocking something over. The small spaces and open walkways between the statues teem with wild, roaming monkeys, which I love. Mom thought the shrine felt inhabited by more than monkeys, but I'm not afraid of any spirits. I like what lives here.

Mom stares at Dad, shrugging her shoulders. Obviously, the roaming animals in India harbor disease. Mom asks Vijay about rabies, but even he doesn't have any idea about what to do about my bite. The hospitals are far away from here—and they wouldn't have the costly rabies immune globulin.

Almost certainly, I am fine; besides, I love the monkeys. I was trying to feed one when it bit me. There weren't rules against feeding them, but then again, safety regulations aren't so common here: there are no seatbelts, helmets, or warning signs.

India fits us perfectly. The people and places are messy, but no one cares. Mom doesn't remind me to shower or comb my hair because we get dirty as soon as we step outside. Jolyn and Shiya like it too—except for the mess. Despite the unkempt streets that are filled with litter and poop, there exists a colorful, glittery facet of life here, and that has charmed them.

Indian women always look fancy—even barefoot and in the most remote villages. They don multicolored scarves and jingling anklets, and slide on dozens of bangles over their painted arms. At our first stop in Delhi, Jolyn and Shiya bought several saris and long skirts from the outdoor vendors and now wear them everywhere—even to see the monkeys.

For the first time, Shiya is appreciating something other than drawing pictures or talking about the wonders of China. In India, she collects cheap bangles and harasses Mom to buy her jewelry, stones, and fabrics that we see for sale on most street corners.

Jolyn also collects, but she prefers the animal statues and carved figurines.

Neither Jolyn nor Shiya are talking right now. They both glance at my bleeding finger, then back at Mom and Dad. Mom digs through her purse. She always has emergency supplies in there: Vaseline, lotions, Band-Aids, nail clippers, hard candies, and Neosporin.

"Neosporin fixes everything," she jokes.

"Not *yesterday!*" I counter.

Mom winks back as she opens the tube. Yesterday, we rode around the jungle for six hours, so we could find a tiger. The safari jeep got a flat tire deep in the middle of the tiger park, so the guide left us in the open-air vehicle and went by foot to look for help. For at least thirty minutes, we sat alone in the jungle without protection, waiting like unsuspecting prey. Even my dad was starting to look around for the guide.

"Tigers kill about 100 people a year in India," I had told my sisters, who were crouching with me in the back seat, now even more terrified. I liked to make big statements. When they tattled on me to Mom, I tried to make them feel better. "Don't worry, tigers aren't as dangerous as snakes. Snakes killed 46,000 people in India last year. Half of all the snake bites in the world happen here."

This additional news did not encourage them, especially Shiya, who moaned intermittently and kept demanding to go home. Just when I couldn't stand her shrill protests any longer, the guide finally returned to fix the flat and rescue us. For the rest of the day, we continued the jungle trek, not seeing a single tiger or a snake, even from a distance.

"Good to go!" Mom says, placing the Neosporin back into the

small Ziploc bag in her purse. Grandma and Mema had been correct, of course; it's not safe here. Certainly not in India with the snakes, monkeys, and diseases—but also not in Qatar.

During our time in Doha, we regularly endured the stifling heat, rigid cultural expectations, and recurrent sickness that led to frequent hospital checkups. Mom withstood numerous public rebukes, silently submitting to the strict gender policies. *Wrong place; inappropriate dress; out of bounds.* Dad, too, apologized often, for things like taking the elevator with a female or eating in public during Ramadan. Most of all, church wasn't safe, and Mom and Dad warned us repeatedly not to overshare to strangers.

I didn't want to go back to Doha. I liked it here in India, where I didn't have to wear shoes or have good manners. We traveled here to take part in helping some poor children at a mission my Dad had visited the year before. Doha is only three hours from New Delhi by airplane, and I brought lots of candy for the flight. From there, we traveled to Nagpur to pick up Vijay, Sheetal, and Aarav. We spent several more hours shoved in the back seat of a small car to reach Damoh. We often had to veer off the dirt road that workers were preparing for pavement, making hundreds of semicircular detours and extending the time of our drive by three hours. After six hours of agony, we arrived at the village, passing tarp homes and cattle, and then to the mission campus just beyond.

The property contained a home and main building, which housed a school room, an auditorium, and a dormitory. Waiting in a huddle outside the building, fifty children scrambled to greet us as soon as we stepped out of the car. They gawked and crowded around us—it's like they thought I was Harry Potter. Jolyn and Shiya embraced their celebrity status, ostentatiously hugging each approaching child. The children placed flower leis around our necks, looped with colorful marigolds that stained our shirts yellow. Ververt and Neelam also greeted us, hugging me so tightly that the frustrations of the drive faded slightly.

At dinnertime that first day, we sat on the ground with the children and watched them as they shoveled large clumps of rice into their mouths with their hands. *Jackpot!* I thought. Even though they did not speak English, I had no problem being with them and never felt irritated or itchy, even when they stared at me.

The children never had seen blue eyes, so they often studied me and Jolyn, pointing at our eyes and yellow hair. Jolyn and Shiya didn't love sitting on the ground and eating with their fingers, but they relished being the center of attention. "Can we stay here instead of going back to Doha?" Jolyn prodded Mom. I knew Mom felt the same way.

After dinner, Shiya, Jolyn, and I gave away the toys and candies we had brought with us. Jolyn passed out fake "Barbie" dolls to the girls, and I carefully handed each boy a box with a toy truck. The toys did not feel nice, but Nagpur didn't have large quantities of anything better. Jolyn had showed me how the dolls hardly had any hair, revealing lots of plastic scalp. It was funny at the time, but now I felt uneasy about giving away such cheap toys. *Maybe they won't like them.* The trucks felt so light, like they would crumble when the boys attempted to roll them across the cement floor.

Handing over the trucks one by one, I helped the boys open the boxes, putting the trash aside in the corner. As they began playing, the boys' voices turned to laughter and giddy conversation. The trucks held together as we played, crashing and roaring as we rolled the vehicles back and forth.

At first Shiya only observed, but eventually she joined in the fun, letting out rare snorts of delight. Mom and Dad spoke individually to some of the children and teachers, pulling them aside and sitting on the floor to talk and listen through Neelam's translation.

Time passed quickly, and as the sun began to set, the children disappeared upstairs for their evening routine with Neelam, while we left with Ververt. It was then that I noticed the children sneaking back down to the garbage area in the kitchen, desperately looking to reclaim the boxes that earlier had held the toys. I stared, amazed that they treasured these ripped boxes, and watched them carefully place the toys back inside. *Why would anyone want to save a ripped box?*

During our four days there, Mom spoke with many of the children, and Dad taught classes. Mom explained that the children wanted to meet with her because some of them had witnessed their parents being killed by some bad people. Many of the local couples cared for them along with the mission staff on site.

As we spent our days with the children, we got to know many of the caretaking couples, listening to their stories as best we could through their accents. Ververt asked Mom and Dad to conduct a marriage seminar for these volunteers, an event for which my parents had become well-known. On the fourth and final night, they did.

Our most momentous event in Damoh happened on that last day. Dad had hired a local snake charmer, an old man with a colorful turban and dhoti and three woven baskets. His dark, wrinkled skin told me that he had been doing this a long time. A younger boy, maybe his grandson, came with him; he was a bit older than I am and seemed to be the old man's helper. His unlucky job was to catch any snakes that tried to escape.

The old man put down the baskets and squatted low to the

ground. We created a semicircle around him to watch the show. Being shorter, Shiya and Jolyn moved in about ten feet from the baskets. Peering from behind my sisters, I watched the old man remove two lids and hit the cobras on the head with his wooden flute, tapping hard as if the cobras were a drum set. As the man began to play his flute, both cobras popped up and spread their hoods, swaying back and forth as they followed the waving instrument. After the cobras had found their rhythm, the old man opened the third basket.

Shiya grimaced when she saw the man gesture to the large python that was curled up inside. Even she could tell this snake was mad, with its tightly coiled body and peering black eyes.

"Maybe he's new to the show," Jolyn said, trying to soothe Shiya's fears. "He looks like they just got him out of the jungle."

"Doesn't matter," I chimed in. "He's clearly not excited about his new job."

With a tap to its head, the old man tried to get the python to stand up and dance, but the snake ignored his commands. When the old man moved the flute to strike again, the snake soared out of the basket and started coming toward us. The old man swiped at the python, trying to catch him before he cleared the basket, but it was too fast. He pointed to the young boy; now was his time to shine. The young boy's entire job was to grab loose snakes. He quickly reached down, but he missed the snake, too, and stumbled to his knees.

Seeing how close the python was to Shiya, the old man dropped the flute and jumped over the cobras—all the while staying in his crouched position. He reached out and clutched the snake by the tail, just in time to save Shiya from being struck. Shiya remained immovable, like she usually did when situations got scary.

Immediately, the snake looped back, striking the old man in the leg. When it bit him, the sound echoed like an unexpected thunderclap. The man's leg shot out blood in all directions, and soon Jolyn was jumping to her feet shouting "Look! He's got two holes in his leg from the snake's teeth!" Always the loudest in the room, Jolyn's voice drew everyone's attention.

The old man finally captured the snake with a blanket and threw it back into the basket. In all the commotion, however, the cobras had escaped and were now missing among us. Although Mom and Dad tried to reach us through the crowd, Shiya's usual slowness left her directly in the line of the two cobras, who had reappeared and were easily making their way to her side. Seeing the cobras, Shiya's eyes closed tightly, and her mouth opened, but she could not cry out. Seeing this unfold, the old man lunged, snatching each cobra by the jaw one by one, quickly and without a sound.

When all the snakes were back in their baskets, the exhausted man flashed an angry look at the boy—I could tell he was furious from his squinted eyes and clenched jaw. Taking off his shirt, which revealed rows of boney ribs, the old man wrapped it around his leg to stop the bleeding. Recognizing the man's fury, the boy cowered and moved away from the crowd. Shiya started screaming but remained still, stuck in her spot until Dad picked her up and carried her back inside the mission building.

The day after the snake incident, we returned to Nagpur with Vijay and his family. Then came the monkey bite, and the next day we reluctantly left for our Qatar home. After plane rides from Nagpur to New Delhi and Delhi to Doha, we arrived back at Hamad International Airport to the warm greetings of the visa-stamping machines, body searches, and awkward stares.

Mom assumes her customary task of getting all of us and herself through the "Children/Women Only" line while Dad stands off at a distance, waiting uncomfortably. His hair is curling up by his temples, out of its usual gelled-back position. His eyes look small and tired.

Smirking to myself, I holler to Dad from my place in line. "What was the best part of the trip? The tigers, monkey bite, or snake attack?"

Dad chuckles slightly, putting his head down and acknowledging the validity of my critique with a small wave. Mom squeezes my hand tightly to alert me to the annoyed onlookers. Unlike Dad, they are not smiling.

Yup, we're "home."

CHAPTER TEN

Satan Killed My Cat

Jodi

Spring 2011

Always dirty, surrounded by animals, and amazed by the beauty, I described my time in India as one long camping trip—even though we never spent time in a tent. In India, animals and people simply coexist without barriers. Numerous bats lived in the spire at the top of our friend's family home, and monkeys would frequently enter to steal fruits that had been carelessly left on the counter. Outside, cows and goats bumped into us as we averted collisions with the motorbikes and wild dogs on the bustling roads. One day after a hard rain, Ververt had told us to avoid the vipers in the grass. So, after spending ten days among India's wildlife this past winter, the children decided to push for a pet of our own.

My only request was no snakes; Garry preferred a cat. While

living overseas, our cat back home had died, so a new kitty seemed like the right fit. He wasn't a tiger or monkey, but he was something. We called him Moses, and Jolyn snuggled with him most of that first night. The next day when we woke up, however, Jolyn found him dead in the small box she had laid him in next to her bedside.

Jolyn cried—her eyes red all day long—Garret paced, and Shiya didn't notice. We went back to the Souk pet shop to ask what happened, but they did not care and wouldn't give us a refund. They did give us half price on another cat, however. The second cat was similar in color to Moses but bigger. We named him Moses II, and I prayed that we would get lucky and keep him alive.

Winter turned to spring in Doha almost imperceptibly due to the constant influx of heat and dryness. The morning's first call to prayer pours out distinctly from a loudspeaker strapped to the tower of our local mosque. *Maybe today can be a good day.*

I no longer notice the ubiquitous sound of the *adhan* and go about my usual routine, inventing breakfast out of boxed milk, rice, muesli, and bananas. I'm thrilled not to find anything crawling among the bananas—no stowaways had made the long journey to Doha from distant trees. Distant because nothing grew in Qatar. The ride to Jolyn and Shiya's school still takes too long—as usual, and we are cut off by trucks of migrant workers being carried to their jobs as I attend to mine. After dropping them off, Garret and I head back to our homeschooling routine.

The recent news has been insular and myopic, and I'm only half listening to Al Jazeera when the announcer breaks in: "Today, on the eleventh of May at 1:00 a.m., Osama bin Laden was killed in a compound in Abbottabad, Pakistan. He is thought to have been shot by United States Navy Seals."

The announcer does not offer any commentary. I look out my window to see if anyone else just heard the news, but nothing seems out of the ordinary. I drive on, hearing the beeping noises from Garret's game coming from the back seat. I change channels and hear the same emotionless report about bin Laden. Being an American in the Middle East on this day is going to be dangerous, yet I didn't sense the need to panic, even as calls begin to come in from both grandmas and concerned friends. *Will there be retaliation?* is the question posed by the newscasters. I try to care—I should care. I turn up the volume on the radio.

Since returning from our visit to India, I've noticed my steady emotional decline. Our trip had brought us to persecuted children who had witnessed horrors at the hand of Hindu extremists. The Damoh mission provided care for their physical needs, but there were no trained counselors in the village. The time I had spent there counseling these children mattered deeply to me, more than any volunteering I had ever done before. Experiencing that place alongside my husband and children had sharpened my whole sense of purpose. While there, my children were able to walk alongside peers whose lives made no sense. Garret felt at home among these lost children, going without shoes and eating with his hands just as they did; Jolyn reveled in the sweet comradery, and Shiya's face showed me that she recognized herself in their eyes.

After our visit to Damoh, Garry and I wrote a business plan to propose ongoing support for this grass-roots mission and sent it back to our US church. After our up-close experience, we believed that this time the pastoral staff would find these indigenous missionaries worthy of ongoing financial support. No mission was more deserving than the Damoh women and children's home. An impassioned researcher, writer, and counselor, I quickly produced the thirty-three-page business proposal to formally request funding.

"If any good were worth doing, this is it," I had stated in the proposal. We emailed the document, replete with pictures, the region's history of impoverishment, statistical data, and opportunities for service. Never had an occasion to serve been as evident and important, but the church's answer came back sharply, "Not now." At first, Garry and I questioned their response, which drew no reply, leaving me sleepless and rattled.

As days passed since the rejection, I began to view life through an increasingly skeptical lens. We sent personal financial support to Damoh and returned to daily life in Doha where the sting of rejection I felt from my home church exacerbated my frustrations with the difficulties of basic life tasks in Doha. Garry and I pressed on to find meaningful projects in our local area, researching orphan care, labor camps, and impoverished people groups—only to receive scolding and threats, skepticism and denial that there was any need. The constant drip of refusals and contradictions became a steady standoff in the form of blank stares, unreturned phone calls, and locked office doors that never opened no matter how long I waited.

In stark contrast to this failure to do good, the doors swung open wide for Garry's work. He not only succeeded at building the palace but also won significant side work as he tried to garner enough clients to again open his own firm. He essentially worked two jobs and traveled often, negotiating deals in the world of *ghutras* and nose bumps. As the months rolled into summer, Doha nurtured Garry's prospects for financial gain but starved our family of any opportunities to live meaningful lives.

When I didn't think any more rejection was possible, I got

the second-worst phone call I would ever receive. It was from my adoption agency, reporting that Laos had closed foreign adoptions, effective immediately. I made frantic calls to my case worker, but the adoption agency and all the funds we had spent were no more. In the wake of international adoption scandals, my agency had discontinued all adoption cases and programs.

It took a few days to comprehend that I would never meet that beautiful little one sitting on the thatched chair in her pink dress. I would never meet Saimay to tell her she was loved and chosen. Injustice had slammed shut that door forever, and I was—I am—undone. Upon hearing the news, Garry didn't have words to help me. He squeezed me in his arms, as he usually did when I became sad and he didn't know what to say.

We sat down later that day to tell the children. Garret's eyes grew teary, and he moved next to me on the couch to extend his arms for a distant yet sincere hug. Jolyn sank into the pillows, her head falling naturally onto my lap as she sighed softly. Shiya leaned in close to Jolyn sweetly, though unable to grasp the meaning of it all.

Then something strange happened: life simply went on. Saimay woke up, never to be adopted, likely to be absorbed into the dark underside of the lost girl industry. The adoption agency shut down completely. Garry returned to long work hours, and the kids kept on at school. I shopped and did laundry, studied and parented. And outside my window, the traffic in Doha continued to build. Everyone else moved on so easily—except me. I got stuck.

My enthusiasm for life, the hope I used to feel at the start of each day and the deep desire to do good, succumbed to the relentless onslaught of dismissals, denials, and rejections. Garret's future, Saimay's fate, Damoh's wish, Doha's challenges—each felt impossible and lost to me. In the last act of what felt like a mocking, real-life satire, something else went missing.

One early summer morning, Moses II simply walked out of our apartment door, accidentally left ajar to be pushed open by his little paws. He, too, instinctively yearned to escape from all this. He simply walked down the stairs and slipped through the lobby's automatic doors, never to be seen again.

I tried to convince the children and myself that Moses II might be living happily outside with other cat friends, but I knew better—in that heat and traffic, no cat was going to survive for more than a few days.

"Satan killed my cat," I told Garry, neither gloomy nor surprised. They felt like the only words appropriate to the moment. To be accurate, of course, Satan had killed three of my cats. Although hyperbolic and meant to lighten a tough moment, this expression described how viciously thwarted I felt during this season of my life.

From my earliest years, I had always believed I could make a difference in the world. Quiet forcefulness, academic prowess, and relentless energy had driven me to action. I knew I could affect change; therefore, every day I pursued it. As I counseled, traveled, and listened, the stories I heard brought to light the darkness that I did not want to see. The injustice, poverty, pain, and hopelessness experienced by others stayed with me. It incensed me, inspired me, and called me forth. Every time I wanted to quit or surrender, the voices of hurting people—the memories of those I had seen and known—reignited my passion. I heard them calling, angelic and bold.

Yet, I had no instructions, and no one ever authored a manual for doing good. So here I was—adoptive mother, counselor, missionary, nonprofit starter—stuck, arrested, and defeated. Despite all my efforts and campaigns in Qatar, I saw zero positive results and felt embarrassed by my naiveté: I was unable to change the life of even one cat.

I struggled to sleep, eat, and be present in my daily routine. The actions I took or tried to take in the service of others in Doha and Damoh—and with Garret, Shiya, and Saimay—remained doggedly unsuccessful. I began to wake early to pray, pacing around my apartment floor. Because I am unable to go outside in the dark, the living room has become my spiritual walking trail.

Each morning, before the *adhan*, I start my journey at the ten-foot long drapes, which pool on the floor beneath the window at the far side of the room. I pace the elongated living area back and forth and in big ovals, charting paths around the clumsy, wooden furniture and stopping for a moment after each revolution to study the map that hangs on the far-side wall. Even as I pace and pray for the countries on it, I feel how ridiculous are my pursuits and supplications.

The words I utter are aggressive, yet I am so broken. *Who am I to change the world?* I flush with the embarrassment of someone who keeps showing up for practice long after they've been cut from the team. I wonder if it's time to settle into normal and accept that life isn't extraordinary and that even the greatest of purposes can fall away.

CHAPTER ELEVEN

Crisis

GARRY

Summer 2011

As we reached our one-year anniversary of living in Qatar, new work projects kept emerging, even though my firm never fully supported my ambitions in the Gulf States. I had tried to convince them of the countless opportunities there and, if given the resources, the wins that we might see come to fruition. They found it too risky. After all, being a businessman in Qatar requires an odd skill set—including the ability to be forceful in the presence of competing hierarchies of power—if you want to succeed and survive.

The executives at my firm did not have these skills, and they never understood them, although to be fair, they had not needed them. Such aptitudes can only be learned in the crucible of great danger and opportunity. They're the talents developed out of necessity, not by birth or choice.

As I navigated between loyalties to my US-based employer and several uncertain business prospects, the thick cultural proprieties of the Mideast socio-political landscape forced me to adjust my economic strategies. My chief job was to engineer a palace. Licenses, contracts, and construction deals had to be negotiated among royals and rebels, businessmen and mafia. I had to secure construction firms and partnerships with interior designers, builders, security companies, and civil site authorities to complete the $20-million-dollar fortress.

Every local authority—whether they were legal or operating underground—challenged me, sometimes through fear and intimidation, and other times by making me wait for months before answering a *response-for-information*. Everyone required a certain type of cultural deference and conformity to their whims and ways. And we were rarely paid on time.

Completing deals and securing payments required relentlessness and a forceful etiquette. Once, I decided to halt the multi-million-dollar construction job because we were owed $500,000 for an increase in square footage, which hadn't been paid. Although it was unthinkable to stop working on a palace, my tolerance threshold had been met. I was thirty-eight-years old with no company or financial legacy of my own, being told what to do by the twenty-two-year-old Qatari sheikhs who ran the PEO—all the while being berated on the phone by my bosses back in the United States, my ideas being ignored, rejected, or scorned, depending on the mood of the day. I had reached my breaking point.

So, when the executives back home ordered me to obtain the long overdue payment from the local development firm, I decided to do the one thing that would force their hand: I halted the job.

Now I am being summoned to the high-rise office of one of the wealthiest and most powerful developers in Doha. Entering his office, I notice two large security details seated on either side of one angry client. *This is not good.* Usually, I don't get to meet with the actual client representative, only some less powerful agent at the firm.

"Why you stop our work?" He's yelling so loudly that I find myself scanning the window to make sure it isn't open, out of fear that one of the security details might throw me out of it.

It isn't, so I retort just as stridently, "Why do you not pay me?" My aggressiveness surprises both him and me.

"You say I owe you money?" he asks, again yelling more than asking.

"Yes, you owe me money," I say, settling into my new sense of courage. I have no idea what will happen next. He looks me in the eye, and after a few moments of staring, his expression starts to relax.

"How much money I owe you?" he asks, more thoughtfully this time.

"Five hundred thousand dollars," I report, sweat now dripping beneath my collar and down my back. I stand my ground, keeping my gaze fixed on him.

"If I give you the money, you give me your word to finish?" he asks me.

"You give me your word to pay me, and I give you my word to finish the job." Another pause. The client comes even closer now, extends his hand to shake on the deal, and nods at me to seal the agreement. Then he leaves, and that's it—and I am still alive. A week later, I reopen construction, and, eventually, he pays us every dollar.

That day, it hit me hard: *working here isn't fun.* Opportunities abounded, yes—but so did danger. With the chaotic blend of threats and chances, we were at a crisis point, balancing between multiple personalities, companies, expectations, and the needs of my family. Our financial future felt uncertain, while my wife and children struggled every day to find safety, purpose, and connection in this relational and literal desert. The balancing act could not continue. If we were to emerge from this crisis intact, I would have to quicken my pace and move forward my own way.

I took the few prospects I had collected so far and decided to start that new firm, now. I asked Hassam and Adam, a fellow Columbia alumnus, to join me. When I left for Qatar the year before, I had entrusted the remaining clients from my former company into Adam's care. These small accounts became the beginning of our new firm, Base4. With renewed hope, I flung myself into this new venture, a symbolic gesture of my newfound decision to throw away the rule book. It was time to stop playing by others' rules and to start writing my own.

Building Base4 took me to India, Bahrain, the UAE, and Morocco, where I won the engineering contract for another palace on the hilltops overlooking the Mediterranean Sea—this time for a different crown prince. Being Moroccan, Hassam had insisted on negotiating the contract to secure this job. Like me, he also spurned business etiquette. When he left for Morocco, he only told me he had connections with the officials who had been charged with building the new palace.

Unbeknownst to me, Hassam had set up a mock Base4 office in Morocco to show the officials our impressive and large firm. The day they came to inspect our operations, Hassam had rendered and fastened a Base4 placard on the door of an empty office he had borrowed from a friend. He filled the Base4 office with "engineers," who were friends he had paid to take the day off and sit in the office to "work" on their laptops. Impressed by the grand headquarters, the officials awarded us the 1.5-million-dollar contract. When I questioned Hassam's ethics, he just smiled broadly and said, "Oh Garry," gesticulating with his hand as if flapping away a pesky fly.

Although small, Base4 represented freedom. Instead of rules, I decided to build my company on four values: honesty, humility, respect, and fun. The "4" in Base4 came to represent those four values, which would guide us through all future decisions. To this day, I have no compliance officers.

As I wrapped up my time in Qatar, Base4 continued to take on a life of its own. New jobs, along with winning the Moroccan palace contract, provided me the financial security I needed to leave my current job. It was time to move back stateside. I strategized with Jodi about how I might approach the conversation with my boss, since I held substantial contractual obligations at my two-year post in the Middle East. I loathed having to make the necessary call and inform him of my plans, even as I was sure that this was the right move for me and my family.

Unfortunately, it was a call I never got to make. Before I contacted my boss to discuss my resignation, a different call came in: "They found cancer again."

Josephine's voice had trembled when she shared the news with Jodi. Jodi's mom had been in remission from breast cancer for eight years, but despite the relentless checkups and ongoing vigilance, the cancer had returned—this time in her uterus, and more aggressive than before.

Although she did not ask us to, we chose to return to the

United States to be with her. It was an easy decision to make. The urgency of some crises arrives so forcefully that it overshadows the potency of all other difficulties. Josephine's devastating news became a tidal-wave moment in our lives, flushing out all other anxieties, plans, and regrets. Within three months, we wrapped up our life in Doha, left the few items we had acquired, and flew home for good.

PART III

TURNING POINTS

Open Arms

ANGELA

I hear only screaming. We are riding in the backseat of a tiny car, and I tuck my legs up to my chest and wrap my arms around them. In between the raging protests, the combatant stops only to take quick breaths and then continues. *Where are they taking me*? I ask myself. Peeking from behind my knees, I see two of my younger brothers to my left, quietly staring out the window. They're just two and three years old, and they don't know that we'll never see our home again.

I duck my head back down, but my hiding doesn't relieve the noise. When I glance right, I see Rogie, who does not look afraid. He also keeps his head low, not making a sound. In the front seat are two bad men, talking on the phone as they drive. I can't hear them because of the screaming: so loud, so confusing. I wish it would stop so I could think—and figure my way out.

"*Tahimik!*" says the driver, looking back, but only at me. Only now do I realize that it's me who is screaming.

The bad men came to our shack to get me and the rest of us. I hate my nosy neighbor who turned us over to the bad men in blue. They showed up with their badges and told me to come with them.

"I'll take you somewhere safe," the skinny one said. But I know better. They took my littlest brother and sister, and I have not seen them since earlier this morning. That must have been when I started screaming.

The bad men keep watch on our neighborhood, taking children with no parents to some terrible place that Mama had told me about. They had never come for me because Mama hid us away, and we were good at keeping quiet. But Mama hasn't come home for a long time, so long that even my meanest neighbor came by to share some of her rice.

These past many days, I have tried to watch my little brothers and sister, but they have grown very frightened and sick. My littlest brother, just a year old, was lying on the floor in only his shirt, no diaper, soiling himself until there was nothing left in his body to come out. He wouldn't even eat the rice, and he grew thinner and thinner until he almost blended into the dirt floor beneath him. When I had the courage to come close to talk with him, I could see the worms crawling out of him. I just ignored this and tried to look away, pretending he would get better.

My two- and three-year-old brothers wandered around, useless like me. Although they had a cough and oozing eyes, at least they still walked. I tried to amuse them by drawing in the dirt, but they quickly lost interest. "She'll be back," I lied.

I knew Mama wasn't returning. The last time I saw her, three strangers from down the road were pulling her back from the river. Moments before, Rogie had seen Mama babbling to herself while pushing a naked baby into the brown water and out of sight. When Rogie cried out, others scrambled over and dragged Mama away from my drowning sister.

I had been working the *Divisoria* that morning and returned only in time to see Mama shove away the strangers and stumble down the street, opposite the way she normally took to market. I didn't call out for her.

My littlest sister was four months old when she survived being drowned. The neighbors stayed long enough to make sure she was breathing, leaving us on the damp riverbed just outside the shack. Checking over their shoulders and noticing a crowd forming up the street, they scurried back to their own homes, the meanest ones first. Rogie also left, avoiding the stares of the distant onlookers who quickly turned away once their curiosity grew to annoyance.

Baby sister wailed without stopping. The house had little food left. I thought to go to market to grab dried fish or rice, but I couldn't leave the baby. If I were to carry her, the crying would have invited unwanted attention. I rocked her. I shook her. I sang her the only songs I knew, but nothing worked to stop the crying. Eventually, the noise brought the neighbors back to our hut. They looked on, their faces neither kind nor angry. A few brought scraps of food or rice, but mostly, they asked us to keep quiet.

The crying brought the bad men back, too. In my neighborhood, no one called the bad men unless they wanted to get rid of someone who was causing problems. And now, because of baby sister, they wanted us gone. Mama had taught us to shut up so as not to cause this kind of trouble. Even at one, two, and three years old, my little brothers understood and never made a sound. Of the six of us, baby sister was the only one who made noise. Until now.

Now it's my turn. We pull alongside a big building, and the

bad men remove us from the car. My brothers go willingly, but not me. I scream at the bad men as they shove me toward the building, at times throwing myself to the ground and kicking my feet. The men lift me off the ground repeatedly, finally reaching the large front door. Placing me and my three brothers in a small room with no windows, they finally leave us alone. My yelling turns to moaning. None of us look at each other.

A uniformed woman enters the room after a few minutes and tells us we're at the Reception and Action Center. In between moans, I hear her explain that my mother is in jail. The woman says nothing else and stares at us for a moment from the entranceway. Like the busy lady at the chicken shop, this woman only speaks to give and get information.

She asks Rogie his name, but he doesn't answer, pretending not to hear her. He remains stiff and avoids eye contact, keeping his gaze straight ahead. She quickly leaves but brings back several more people. I hear them talking between my shrieks. If they talk to me, I yell louder. If left alone, I moan, but quietly so I can hear what they say.

One by one, the uniforms look at each of us, filling in papers as they observe us. "Perez Siblings," says the first line of each paper, and each of our papers sounds about the same, "Active, productive cough; bleeding infection on neck; healing wounds on arms, face, and legs; lice; worms." Because we don't allow anyone to touch us, they guess our weight and height and label us "undernourished." When they finish, they bring us a bowl of hot rice with soup and some tea. I stop screaming to shovel down the food.

The next few days, we stay in this strange place, in another small room with six small beds. Only my three brothers and I sleep here, although we are not alone. In the night, I hear the yells and cries of many other children. I stay silent and listen, hoping to hear what they say and glad that there are others like me.

In the early morning, as the officials begin their comings and goings, I scream again. Only when I'm alone or given food do I stop making noise. I should be tired of yelling, but the sounds come out naturally, as if they've been stuck inside me for a long time. The first two days, many people come to see us, including some of the bad men who ask us many questions.

They talk only to me and Rogie. "How did your mother take care of you?" "Do you have other family?" "Do you go to school?" "Who gave you this scar?" "What are the names of your brothers?"

In response, I either scream and fall to the floor, or if I am too tired, I go silent and still, staring at the white wall before me. Rogie talks, but tells only our last name, the names of our parents, and our neighborhood. When asked about my little brothers, the drowning, the cough, or the scar on his left arm, he sets his jaw and refuses to answer. I talk only when I have to go to the C.R. I point at the toilet and yell, "Ah!"

After a few more days, a new lady comes for us. She arrives early while my brothers are still asleep. I watch her enter the building from our second-floor window where I had been looking out at the cars. She is a white lady with red hair, pulled back tightly into a bun. After a few moments, she enters our room, giving a nod to the official who had walked her in to meet us. She swaddles a small brown baby. I start screaming, which wakes my brothers, who now stare at the lady and the baby slung on her hip.

The official points at us, telling her our name is Perez. Unlike the others, who examined us quickly, this lady sits down slowly on the ground near our beds, shifting the baby from her hip to her lap. She waits to look at each of us, smiling gently, her eyes blue like I had never seen before. Her calm soothes me, and my screaming quiets to a low grumble.

"My name is Sharon, and I'm here to take you to stay at my house," she says cheerily.

I have so many questions—I feel hot, my heart beats too fast, and I find it hard to breathe. *Sharon?* I never heard of that name. Unlike mine, the official's face does not change. It looks like stone, and I cannot understand what's happening between him and this new lady.

He informs her that Mama is in jail and that our father is dead. The official adds something about our dad dying from something called tuberculosis.

Is that true? The thought stings, as does his next comment: there are two other babies who are not here. He tells Sharon the doctors don't think the babies will make it, and that all of the kids—except Rogie—have active, dangerous coughing.

I hear the words, but I cannot understand them. The lady looks back at me, but she doesn't seem sad or mad or anything else I recognize. All I know is that she seems ready—ready the way I get when I walk to market to steal rice from the ladies.

"I'll take them now. Give me the papers," she says. "And I want the babies."

Only months later do I learn that the babies are my brother and sister whom I haven't seen for many days. Sharon quickly tells us to come with her. Still groaning, I get up first and grab my little brothers. *Any place is better than here.*

Rogie follows us down the stairs and into an old white van. On the sides are painted little hands and the letters "OPEN ARMS." A strange chubby man drives the van; he's young with a big smile. The van winds through traffic, people, motors, and bikes for a long time. My eyes feel heavy, but I cannot allow myself to sleep. We slow down in front of a pink, four-story building with the same letters on the top, "OPEN ARMS."

When we enter, so many children scatter around us that I stop my moaning just to look around. There are children everywhere, messy and moving about. Some play on the small playground in the courtyard. Others hang near the kitchen where I spot huge boiling pots of soup and rice. Children are laughing, crying, running, fighting, and playing. Some sit in small groups, in rooms with books and papers. Others talk with each other, laughing and occasionally pointing at us.

I follow Sharon up the stairs. The next floor has rooms filled with babies in highchairs who are being fed by chatty young women. I hear music, songs about God that are being played too loudly. Plates of half-eaten snacks and cups lay on the windowsills. Children stare at me; some grab my hands and arms. My ears start to hurt as I walk onward, and I begin to cry again. It is so loud; I can't hear my own crying.

The next floor has rooms of different colors filled with bunk beds and children. The pink room has girls who looked about my age. Sharon stops here and tells me, "This is your room." When I realize I'm not staying with my brothers, I begin to scream until she scoops me up and takes me to the next floor.

This floor looks like a big house, the kind I have seen on poster boards in the *Divisoria*. Up here, it's quieter and cleaner, like what I imagine a real house would be like.

"This is my home," Sharon says. Pointing to several other children, some with white skin and some with brown, she goes on. "These are my children, and their Papa will be home soon. He is a teacher."

I quiet down, gazing at the many chairs, pillows, tables, plates, books, papers, desks, and beds.

"You can call me Mom Sharon, and you can stay here with your brothers."

Over the next few days, I sleep in bunk beds on the fourth floor with my brothers, Mom Sharon, and her family. Mom Sharon cuts off our hair—she says it made us itch. Eventually, I only scream when someone makes me leave to visit the doctors. In our first few days here, we see many doctors who stick us with endless needles, sending us back to Mom Sharon with lots of medicines, creams, and drops. I pretend to feel better to end the trips to the doctors, but my cough always gives me away.

As we get to know this place, Mom Sharon and the other caretakers try to coax us upstairs to the fifth floor, a fenced rooftop where children go to play basketball, dance, and play outdoor games. We never go.

If I'm not eating, sleeping, or visiting doctors, I am roaming the fourth floor studying each member of this weird family: Mom Sharon and her husband, two older daughters, and one boy who looks like us. None of us talk unless we want to eat, and then we point at the food and grunt. After many days, my two younger brothers begin to play with the toys in a crate in the living room, separating from me for the first time.

Many weeks pass by; I know because the weather grows hotter. I scream less and still don't speak, although I'm beginning to learn many new words from all the talking that happens here. I practice the words in my head without saying them aloud.

Mom Sharon works in her office, talking on the phone with many people. Officials come often, and sometimes new white people visit. They talk funny, and they're from faraway places.

Sometimes these visitors bring us toys, books, and gifts.

For the first time in my life, I wear clean clothes. My two little brothers can now speak some words, and all our bodies grow bigger. I still refuse to speak when anyone asks me questions, and I often moan when I get overwhelmed by the many lights, sounds, and activities. Mom Sharon isn't afraid of my loud wailing or my stomping on the floor. Even when I try to get her to go away from me, she never does.

After the steamy weather turned less hot, something good happens. "I have a surprise for today," Mom Sharon smiles brightly, moving toward the door that leads out to the rest of the building. Noticing my hesitation, she adds, "It's a good surprise."

At the front door, she turns the handle and pushes hard against the humid hallway, unsticking the door from its frame. Two women appear, ones I've never seen before. They're holding two babies, one wrapped in pink and the other in blue. Both women smile big, even as the babies fuss. *Mom Sharon must have found more babies,* I think.

Open Arms—words which I finally came to learn—has hundreds of children. Sometimes, kids come to stay forever, or they go back to their families. Children, babies, and teenagers seem to come and go every day. At other times, moms and dads from faraway places pick up the children to take them to new families. Everyone seems happy about children leaving, but I don't really know why.

Most of the children here at Open Arms look sick and sad. I knew a lot of children who lived on the street near my old house, but none of them seemed as bad as the ones who come here. Mom Sharon chooses the worst ones. They're always unwell and usually crying, unless they're dying. Most of the time they live downstairs with other lost children, but sometimes, they live on our floor. The worst ones come to our floor. I've seen several of them die in Mom Sharon's arms, too weak to survive. I've seen her cry too, and I wonder if I'll die in her arms someday.

Mom Sharon taps my arm to get my attention and makes a loud announcement: "Here are your brother and sister!" She sees that her words don't make sense to me, so she takes the blue baby from the woman's arms and brings him close to me, so I can see his face. After a moment or two, I see something I recognize, something familiar. This baby is my brother, the one I thought died from worms, the one I hadn't seen since the Pasig. Even I smile now.

Then Mom Sharon shows me the baby in pink, and what I've wished for comes true. She's waking up from her nap on the shoulder of her caretaker and seems almost a year old. Shaking my head in disbelief, I touch her legs. She's chubby, so chubby I doubt it's her.

"This is your baby sister, much bigger and stronger now," Mom Sharon affirms.

At the sound of the crying babies, my other brothers come in to see. They also don't believe the news. Sitting down in a circle around the babies, we watch them scoot across the floor.

As I stare at them, flashes of images flood my head, but they are not from this moment. I try to concentrate on the pictures in my mind, but they come and go too quickly. I focus harder on my thoughts, trying to see these babies as they used to be, lying on the dirt floor of our hut, struggling to move and fighting for their breath. Then my mind goes black, and I lose the light.

"Angela, Angela, come back to me," I hear Mom Sharon command. I become alert to the sounds of my own moaning, and refocus my vision, looking again at the two babies. I see them now; I see eyes like mine. "Their names are Zoe and Robert," Mom Sharon informs me, pulling me back into the moment.

"Names?" I ask. It's the first word I have spoken in a long time.

"Yes, I named them Zoe and Robert," she responds. "I gave them names, as I also named your brothers, Andrew and Edward," she continues. "You're all here together now at Open Arms."

I think Mom Sharon has told me this information before, but I can't be sure. It all feels strangely distant. Behind my back, I pinch my left hand hard with my right. I want to be here.

Zoe, Robert. I practice the names in my mind and stare at their faces, looking to make a connection. Their new names are odd, but I don't care. In my head, I practice them, so I won't forget. *Zoe, Robert, Andrew, Edward, Angela, Rogie.* If I remember my siblings' names, and they remember mine, we shouldn't be lost again.

CHAPTER TWELVE

Nonprofit

GARRY

Fall 2011

"Drop him!" my friend Terry called out to the large man hoisting me above the rushing waters. I am being lifted over the waters of a flash flood in the mountainous region of western Haiti. I am on the four-hour journey from Port-au-Prince into an area of Morrisseau that's high up in the hills. To reach our destination, a small school in an obscure village at the top of a mountain, we hired several jeeps with an armed guard to accompany us. It's my first trip to Haiti, where I hope to assess the integrity of a mission that serves children at the local school. Funding for the school has dried up, and no one else wanted to make the trip to reach this place. The school and children require aid, especially after the devastating earthquake in 2010 that ruined the island, leaving 230,000 Haitians dead or missing in its aftermath.

On our way up the mountain, the flooded roads prevented our crossing at a narrow pass, so we were taking turns crossing this temporary river. After hours of waiting, I watched my friends cross over, one at a time in one of the larger vehicles. By the time it was my turn, however, the waters had risen too high for the jeep to come back for me. Stuck on the opposite side, I looked around me and saw strong, young men with machetes watching our small crew, which had now become a spectacle to the locals. I encouraged myself by remembering the kidnapping policy that my wife had taken out on me a few years earlier. *At least I will die doing the right thing!* I thought to myself, only half joking.

In the next moment, one of the men raised me high up in the air, and I figured this was it. Then something surprised me—the group of men began to cheer. My friends on the other side were pointing at me and laughing. The man lifting me up was not kidnapping me: he was carrying me across the river, so I wouldn't get wet. Seeing I had left my bag, he also sent someone else to carry my luggage, which was full of donations, across the water. How ridiculous the sight was when I later watched my friend's video footage!

But we had made it, and thus began our mission to Morrisseau, a school for 100 children who otherwise would not receive an education or nutritious meals. The school became one of several missions we supported through our growing nonprofit organization, Priority One Worldwide, or POW. While we were living in Qatar, we hadn't been able to develop POW like we had planned. Now that we were living back stateside, we had the opportunity to assess numerous potential mission partners, such as the one in Morrisseau.

Within a few months of arriving home from Doha, Jodi and I had continued working and striving for more, as we always had done, even though the landscape of our lives had been altered dramatically. To be closer to Jodi's mom, we rented a townhouse across the street from her and her husband Jim. We had owned nothing since our estate sale, so we bought mattresses, threw them on the floor, picked up some kitchenware and linens, and enrolled our children back in school. As I focused on my new firm, Jodi cared for her mom, continued to nurture our children, and completed her next degree.

I had resigned my previous post and was pouring 100% of my time into Base4 with a commitment to do work differently. Out of geographical necessity and his impending marriage, Hassam stayed with his firm in Doha. So, I—along with Adam—hired Vijay again and brought in another young engineer named Blair. Adam, Blair, Vijay, and I partnered to lead a 24-hour, global, tech-based firm ready to meet demands in the hospitality sector, meaning we could design any hotel, anywhere, anytime. Through our emerging offices in Nagpur, India; Shanghai, China; Tbilisi, Georgia; and Santiago, Dominican Republic, I was endeavoring to revolutionize the archaic architectural and engineering design processes that were stagnating the construction industry.

For the last 100 years, construction firms had relied on physical drawings and flat models, but we used 3D building information modeling to create digital drawings, portraying our renderings in virtual reality. We harnessed the efficiency of the automobile industry, creating an assembly line approach to design and engineering, which resulted in high-quality construction documents delivered faster and greener. A 40-billion-dollar-a-year industry, the architectural design and engineering field was ripe for takeover, and we would lead the way.

As Base4 found increasing success, Jodi and I lived more

frugally than ever. We didn't buy new furniture and slept on floor-mattresses for years to come. Jodi hated clutter anyway, so we remained free of chaos and "stuff." In fact, the more money I made, the less Jodi spent. We reveled in the simplicity of a rented home, hand-me-downs, and home-cooked meals. By working out of our home, I saved on office space and a wardrobe. Thanks to the internet, I had the freedom to lead a multimillion-dollar firm from my small bedroom on the second floor of my townhouse, sitting in my shorts and sneakers at my homemade plywood desk.

Never again would I be in debt. Never again would I owe anyone anything. With this new freedom, Jodi and I pushed ahead with our nonprofit missions, traveling to seek and support new pockets of people who required urgent help. When the church refused to aid the mission in Damoh, India, we had launched POW alongside four other disgruntled megachurch defectors. Together, we aimed to administer funds to well-vetted missions and ensure that 100% of every cent donated made it to the field. To accomplish this mission, Jodi and I and the other four founding members agreed to pay personally all overhead fees, such as taxes and banking fees. As a board, we collectively ensured the integrity of our donations by traveling off-site to live and work among the various groups asking for assistance.

Through honest reporting and open books, we continued to receive donations and support from many who had grown weary of tithing to local churches, preferring instead to give money that directly impacted the lives of others. Any time we found a worthy mission, one or two of us would travel to the site to make sure the funds were spent responsibly. As a result, our fellow board members Ben and Jaimie lived in India for some time, and Keith and Kristy frequently traveled to the mission in Myanmar. Jodi and I took charge of the mission in Morrisseau, Haiti, and donated the funds needed to finish the children's home in Damoh. Because none of these missions had received support from the megachurches, our nonprofit POW became the stand-in-the-gap provider.

During our first year back from Qatar, we also looked for missions right in our own backyard. Jodi signed us up for the foster/adopt program in our area and volunteered her counseling services to women and children in crisis and at a local shelter for survivors of human trafficking. We followed several local and international adoption agencies, as well as updates from the Department of State, the Florida Department of Children and Families, the China Center for Children's Welfare and Adoption, and India's Central Adoption Resource Agency.

Social workers came in and out of our small home, examining our lives as Jodi prepared for what we hoped would be more children. After losing two previous adoptions, Jodi engaged agencies with full disclosure, informing them that she had multiple applications out for various programs around the world, including programs in China, Haiti, India, and the Philippines. Often, agencies rejected our application because the square footage of our house was deemed too small or because we had three children already, at least one of whom already had significant special needs.

Being rejected while trying to do good felt particularly ugly to Jodi, who often advocated for children's welfare to parents and agencies alike. Although she struggled with despair over the polite resistance of the nonprofit world, she never stopped pushing. Many inspired women followed behind her, and the line of "how to do good" questions became her ministry. From the questioners came several other families hoping to adopt who relied on

Jodi's help and support, both professionally and personally. The shared experiences of hard work, crushing disappointments, and passion for lost children bound us tightly, and these families became like family to us.

Less disheartened than Jodi and more incredulous, I felt indignant toward the ineffectiveness of the nonprofit world. If I ran my business as did most NGOs, I would have no hope of success. Careful and content to plod along, these nonprofit professionals seem to forget the desperate millions who are waiting for someone to take bold action. That's when I met Tina.

Tina was a local teacher and fellow POW advocate. She had traveled to India and Myanmar in support of our missions, but her desire to adopt was met with several immediate rejections by agencies that would not let her apply. According to them, Tina had too many obstacles to overcome. She needed additional money, a larger home, and someone to assume a "father figure" role. As a single woman, she also must prove that she had $100,000 in cash on hand for any agency to approve her.

Tina's dilemma reminded me of the uncomfortable relationship between getting money and doing good. To adopt and change a life forever—as opposed to monthly tithing or relief donations—you had to have ready funds. The message from the foreign agencies was unmistakable: *Get the money and prove your worth!* I wrestled with these injustices toward not only Tina, but also the countless waiting children who would thrive under the care of a mother like her.

I don't like feeling unsettled, especially if I can do something about it, so Jodi and I arranged to help. We wrote letters of recommendation to India's Intercounty Adoption Board, cosigned on the lease for a larger apartment, and dumped lots of money into Tina's savings account. She qualified for the agency and submitted her dossier. After another year of paperwork, Jodi and Jolyn traveled with Tina to Pune, India, to adopt baby Anavi, a twelve-pound one-year-old with big eyes and a hole in her heart. Watching Anavi heal, laugh, and thrive under Tina's care convinced me more than ever of the importance of servant capitalism. In her case, my corporate success had become a fulcrum for turning the wheels of justice. So, I continued to work hard—not only to support my family but also to help start another.

Some people accused me of being greedy—the business tycoon who made lots of money and refused to tithe to the megachurch. The accusations stung, but I recognized the obvious tension between for-profit and non-profit philosophies. People interrogated me, trying to reconcile my growing industry presence with my unusual philanthropic activities.

Informally, people gathered around me and Jodi, observing how we lived and questioning our choices. We tried to answer them, opening our small home to both old friends and new to brainstorm new ideas for mission work and orphan care.

It was common for me to walk into our living room and find it filled with women sitting on the floor and listening to Jodi teach about mission work and orphan care. Sometimes, I walked into *pro bono* counseling sessions. Eavesdropping as I went downstairs to fill my coffee cup, I would notice Jodi listening to and sometimes crying with the women who perched around her. She rarely gave answers; instead, she shared her own struggles and defeats with alarming candor. With my typical frankness, I discussed both my nonprofit and business ventures with anyone who asked, fully disclosing each setback, achievement, and absurdity. Maybe we shared too much.

"This child is available for adoption immediately," Jodi announced one early morning, her eyes gleaming. She presented me with a photo of a one-year-old Chinese boy. Not finding success with the traditional adoption routes, Jodi had gone out on her own, searching through databases filled with pictures and descriptions of children who had been referred for adoption but later rejected by the adopting parents.

"He's been refused by his adopting family, and soon he goes back into the system, likely to never be adopted," she explained. Just like Shiya, the little boy in the photo had an intimidating medical condition—his was called *encephalomalacia*, which meant brain cell death. Understandably, his diagnosis terrified would-be adoptive parents. I also felt nervous, wondering how we would adjust to caring for a severely delayed child.

I did not have much time to gather my thoughts, however; Jodi quickly explained how the disorder ranged on a spectrum and might cause little interference with his development. She went on to describe his history, which revealed that he was hitting most of his early-life milestones. The photo backed her up: the one-year-old little guy stood strong and alert, his expression indicating vitality. Even dressed in his mismatched pink and red outfit, this baby with huge, brown eyes and spiked, black hair atop his round face was the most precious image I had ever seen.

Within twenty-four hours, we were locked in to adopt Wu Qiubao. I am not sure exactly how it happened so quickly, but Jodi knew he belonged to us and wasted no time. We renamed him William, after both of our paternal grandfathers. William Qiubao had been born in October; his Chinese name Qiubao means "Autumn treasure." Jodi made copies of the prized photo to share with everyone around us. Judgment came in the form of subtle questions and polite commentaries from everyone who knew about our current parenting struggles, small residence, and propensity to move.

To be fair, the timing was not perfect; some even called it "messy." Since returning from the Middle East, we had lived in a small rented condo with three young children—two of whom still displayed problematic behaviors. Jodi's penchant for organization and empathy kept us afloat at home while I built Base4. Our first year back stateside felt challenging and disorienting, with both opportunities and accusations, successes and noticeable losses.

Amid the chaos, Mema's cancer fight remained our daily reminder of what mattered most. Josephine was one of very few people willing to babysit my crazy crew of children, and Jodi needed her mom in her corner. Jodi wanted someone else to believe our kids were wonderful, as only a grandmother can do. We desperately desired our children to have their Mema—their sweetest confidante and biggest fan.

Like me, Josephine had fallen in love with William Qiubao immediately. She stole the picture for herself, fastening it on her refrigerator as a daily sign to stay strong and keep on. But unlike the adoption process, her aggressive cancer cells advanced quickly, outpacing the long wait for her next grandson. To the devastation of Jodi, her sister, and our entire family, she was fading quickly and likely never would meet William Qiubao.

On the night before her mom died, Jodi lingered long by Mema's bedside, which had been relocated to the downstairs living room. Her husband Jim was there, along with the hospice nurse, when I came to bring Jodi home. When I saw Mom, I had no words, my throat tight from the sadness I felt at the imminent loss. I never will understand why the good ones leave us too soon.

As Jodi reluctantly stood to leave with me, she eyed the photo of William Qiubao on Josephine's refrigerator door. Carefully removing the tape, she peeled it free and brought it home. Once there, she got to work immediately, placing William's image into an old frame, covering over the original photo and placing it back on the shelf in her office. Every day little William's big eyes and clear gaze stare back at me—a reminder of the pain and preciousness of every day and a kick in my gut driving me forward, no matter what anyone else thinks.

CHAPTER THIRTEEN

For Profit

JODI

Spring 2012

"Nancy," I said, "I think Mom stopped breathing."

These are not words you say confidently or at full volume. My sister hurried to my side, crouching next to Mom where she lay in a hospital bed in her downstairs living room. During the past week, she had not eaten, her face becoming thinned and gray. She hadn't spoken or opened her eyes in the past two days, although from time to time, she attempted to communicate with me through slight groans and eye movements. Tonight, Jim had left her side for only a moment to eat something with his children. Mom had been quiet all day, and we simply waited, glad to still be in her presence.

Nancy and I huddled near her silently. Another thirty seconds passed; then, I heard Mom inhale a quick breath and exhale with a lingering, hissing release. It was her last. The hospice nurse, who had been in the other room, rushed over because she didn't believe me when I told her that my mom had gone so quickly. The nurse had told Jim to go to dinner, given the strength of my mom's heartbeat just an hour prior.

The flustered nurse began making calls, but I understood Mom chose this moment to leave us. She had waited until both the nurse and Jim had left, so it was just the three of us—her, my sister, and me, there for one final gathering. We were alone, together for the last time, before she let go. Growing up, it always had been the three of us, so this final moment became one of the most beautiful experiences of my life as she crossed from this world to the next while in our presence.

In her last few weeks on Earth, Mom wanted to be at her home with her family. After struggling through breast cancer eight years ago and uterine cancer this past year, Mom now lay dying of a cancer that had spread throughout her body since the hysterectomy the year before. After she had been diagnosed with uterine cancer, I had come home from Qatar to be with her. The doctors had removed the cancer and all her female organs, yet one year later, the malignancy spread viciously throughout her otherwise fit and healthy body. Nancy and her husband, Brian, along with her boys, Brian Jr. and Jackson, flew in immediately. We spent a few precious weeks together before Mom grew too weak to hang on any longer.

In accepting her coming death, she only regretted not being able to be here for Nancy and me and our children. Mom cried with me and told me plainly, "You will miss me so much, just as I missed my mother." Of course, she was right.

As her days came toward their close, I thought of Mom's

gleaming face as we planned her funeral together, sitting on her bed sharing memories and keepsakes. "Jodi, I can't explain it, but I actually feel joy," she said to me.

They were words I will never forget. For the first time in her life, she felt free of anxiety, which had been her life's constant companion. Now she could let go of the plans and worries, the doctors and diagnoses, and the pressures and possibilities. She could just be.

Fittingly, Mom's last meal was on Mother's Day, and she had eaten eggplant parmigiana, her favorite. She kissed her grandchildren and bought them each one present of their choice. Although still young and saddled with autism's many relational restrictions, during these final moments, Garret's heart clearly shone through. He adored the Wii she gave him, but more than that, he seemed content to sit on Mema's bed all day, talking with her and laughing, understanding that soon she had to go. Snapping a photo of her on his iPad, he would forever miss his Mema, the person who honestly believed that he was special, in the best way. On April 24, she had gone to the hospital with some unusual stomach pains. On May 19, she died. I lost my best friend, and my children lost their Mema.

I also lost my home. Since adulthood, I had moved over twenty-two times, traveling the world for missions, work, adoptions, adventures, nonprofit leadership, and education. Over the past ten years, "home" for me had come to mean "wherever Mom lived." No matter how far we traveled, Mom remained my true north, providing the stability and direction I needed to go forth and push on. Only Nancy and I understood it, having been raised in this strength by a woman who believed we could do anything. Like other Italian mothers, she had both kept us in place and inspired us to go, cheering for us even when she doubted our decisions. I would miss her every day, my tears never completely satisfied.

The intense pain of losing my mother did not surprise me, but I was stunned by the devastating loneliness of losing my sense of home. Rather than get better, this secondary loss became more acute as the days marched forward from her death.

Gone was the physical representation of support and encouragement. No longer did the warmth of her kitchen welcome me in and invite me to share my parenting troubles. Removed were the photographs of grandchildren that used to clutter her shelves, images meant to display how my children were loved, adored, and perfect—even amid their excessive struggles and boundless challenges. The unconditional acceptance of everything about me, both great and terrible, went missing. In the absence of my biggest fan and home-team backing, the cruel scales of judgment no longer tilted in my favor.

In these moments of loss and loneliness, I had a choice: to wait to feel better, eventually, or to plow ahead even as I suffered. I chose the latter. As a counselor, I knew grieving was important work, and I traveled through the five stages of grief slowly and mightily. Still, I made the choice to push on as I healed. "I have no home," I later shared with Garry. "And I have nothing to lose."

Never did I experience such a peculiar sense of freedom, as if Mom herself were daring me to go forth with purpose. Through my daily tears amid the insurmountable realities of loss, I experienced an even greater will to move forward and do what matters. Yes, we had started a nonprofit of our own and hoped to make a difference in the lives of others. However, the 501(c)(3) world never really fit my calling. Nonprofit philosophy relied on the "wait and see" model; that is, volunteers asked for donations and waited for enough funding to accomplish the specified goal. I was all done waiting for other people.

Although I continued to support POW's work, I no longer yielded to nonprofit timetables. My polite demeanor waned—as did my willingness to wait for opportunities to take my place as an agent of change. If told to wait or slow down, I decided to move on.

I stayed kind but not docile. I paid respect but no longer avoided conflict. I vowed never again to remain silent about the mountains of useless regulations that created school systems that didn't work for special kids or orphanages that masqueraded "waiting" as a virtue. I would wait on God but not allow others to use waiting as an excuse to stand down. The world is tough and stubborn. And I would match its ferocity.

Garry always had been this way, offending others regularly with his bold vision and honest assessments. Such reckless fearlessness often got him into trouble, but it also made him free. With that freedom, he was building a firm that had taken the world by surprise. In two years, Base4 converted from an idea to the firm that everyone was talking about. What they said wasn't always positive, but Garry didn't care. *Not caring* had allowed him to blaze a path to success that few would ever experience.

The freedom that he owned naturally, I had to learn through the clarifying pain of loss. I turned my back on caring about what others thought and doing the expected. Instead, I chose to do good in a world where *doing good* might look bad. Though the world told me to "slow down," "calm down," and "settle down," I no longer considered these options. I had always worked hard, but now, in my grief, my purposes became simplified and illuminated, and I was ready for the fight.

"If your goal was to make as much money as possible," I asked Garry one afternoon, as we splashed around the local waterpark with our kids, "what would you do?"

He was surprised and amused by my question, but he responded in a moment. "I would move to North Dakota," he said. "A modern-day gold rush is moving in thousands of people who require immediate housing, hotels, and infrastructure."

The controversial fracking industry had been drawing people to this remote area of the country for a few months now. It was not the answer I expected, but I continued. "What if we decided to move wherever we needed—even to North Dakota—to make as much money as possible?" I cringed when I suggested that we relocate somewhere so far away—but not too much. "We can make money, and rather than donating it, we can use the funds to help as many children as possible without relying on anyone else."

He was listening, and—like he did with all my ideas—he had the wisdom and the guts to transform them into actionable plans.

Within one month of that conversation, we were packing up our few belongings and preparing for our move to Dickinson, North Dakota. Luckily, we hadn't acquired many belongings since our return from Qatar. It had been one year since we moved back, eight months since we decided to adopt William, and four months since Mom died. Both the impulsiveness of our move to North Dakota and our motivation for doing it brought quite a few questions from friends and family alike. The plan remained clear to us, however—and for the first time in my life, I didn't feel the need to defend it. If we failed, which we might, others could claim they knew better. If we succeeded, the outcomes would stand on their own.

In the spirit of this newfound clarity, we decided to adopt again. As we prepared to move to Dickinson, we accepted the referral for another child: thirteen-year-old Qian Jia Cheng, whom we would name James. China now advertised a "two for one dossier" option, which meant that families with an approved file could adopt two children on the same dossier. Given that children aged out of the adoption system at fourteen, the CCCWA made it easy for families to consider an older child. Since we were still waiting for William's final travel approvals, we decided to adopt both William and James simultaneously.

Without hesitation, we had said "yes" when we saw the need, pending Garret's approval. Adopting James would mean that he would become our oldest child, and we asked for Garret's feedback. Garret needed to understand the potential challenges of adopting the elder James and give voice to any concerns. If he had shown any hesitation or doubt, we would have changed our minds. As we sought Garret's reaction, we explained the situation and the dysfunction that inevitably accompanies a thirteen-year-old orphan. Unequivocally certain with all his opinions, Garret would tell us straight.

"Of course, we should do it," Garret responded without even letting us finish. "He needs a family."

And that was that. Even though the many agencies, specialists, and educational videos reminded us of the emotional hazards of adopting an older child, we had an opportunity to do true good, and we did not refuse it.

If I ever looked insane, this is the moment, I smiled and reflected to myself as we drove away from our Florida townhouse in our packed minivan. I was heading to the "Western Edge," as they call Dickinson, North Dakota, with my entrepreneurial husband, selling Base4's innovations and products to the leaders of the controversial fracking community. With that goal in mind, we drove north on the turnpike to drop our packed van at the moving company and taxi to the airport with our cast of characters: Garret, Jolyn, Shiya, and—before long—William Qiubao and James Jia Cheng. With my mom's ashes in a Tupperware for safekeeping, we turned toward our new reality, stubbornly unafraid, for-profit, and ready to do good—our way.

CHAPTER FOURTEEN

The Great Wall

Garret

Winter 2013

"Mom! Dad!" I turn my gaze up from the crowded subway floor to see the doors of our car closing. I push toward the electronic door, but I'm not fast enough, and the doors slam, forcing a rush of air in my face. From inside the sealed window of the subway door, I look onto the platform to see my dad screaming my name, trying to get the conductor's attention. It's too late, and the subway car begins to roll on to the next stop along the busy Guangzhou line.

As I watch out the window, I see my mother look me in the eye. She's not saying anything, just looking at me, not blinking once. She catches my gaze and holds up her hand, signifying with her pointer finger the number one. I think she says, "One!" before pulling her hand back and using her thumb to demonstrate a signal I knew well. It was the *get out of here* sign, which she frequently used to rescue me from social disaster. I understand; I'll go one stop and get out. I hope they can find me. There are a lot of people in China.

I crane my neck to see my family before the train enters the dark tunnel ahead. On the platform stands my dad, tightly grasping Shiya's and Jolyn's hands; my mom, who's holding little William; and James Jia Cheng, the thirteen-year-old boy who just became my big brother. I scrunch down in the corner of the car, leaning on the door as the train rumbles on. Faces stare at me, and a few speak to me in Chinese, which I cannot understand. I have never been so alone.

As the train rumbles onward, I distract myself with thoughts of our month in China. *After it started off so fun, how did it go so wrong?* Seeing the Great Wall, collecting a jade serpent, and visiting the Beijing Zoo—I had seen treasures I thought were only in books. I saw panda bears, and not just a few. Whole groups of panda bears crowded together in ornate enclosures at various corners of the panda zone. The zoo's aquarium held exotic species of fish I never knew existed. The man-eating fish and Chinese sturgeon most fascinated me—almost as much as the people were intrigued by me. All over Beijing, people pointed at me and Jolyn. Mothers had me hold their babies in my arms while they snapped photos of us together. Mom said it was because we had blond curls and blue eyes. Even though we froze in the December rain during our tour of Beijing, I hardly cared.

From Beijing, we flew to Hohhot, Inner Mongolia, where we met James. How strange to wait in our hotel lobby as officials delivered the boy who would become my brother! My parents signed one paper, and the officials left, leaving only James. It was as if they were dropping off a FedEx package, in and out within minutes.

Although I was excited to meet James, he did not feel the same way. He was still, silent, and unwilling to hug me, or my mom and dad. James was two years older than me, but he looked short and very thin. His face reminded me of one of the blade runners from my video games, sharp yet good-looking. When we got back to the hotel room, I tried to ask him if he wanted to play my games, but he did not understand what I said. Mostly, we sat quietly in the corner of the room in a large hotel lounger while I played, and he looked on.

We spent the first of four weeks in China in Hohhot, where my parents met with important adoption people while the four of us tagged along. In between appointments, we took small trips to learn about James's life in China, trudging through snow in the frigid northern province. Hohhot was barren and blanketed white, which made December in Dickinson, North Dakota, seem pleasantly mild.

We first visited an icy bridge in the center of town, reportedly the spot where then seven-year-old James was found abandoned almost six years earlier. The location was so ordinary that onlookers stared as we stopped to take a picture. James didn't understand why we were there either, and it was too cold to stay for long.

The first seven years of James' life remained largely unknown and undocumented. There was a lady he called "mom" who lived in the army barracks where she stayed in bed most of the time. Apparently, his dad was an important military man who visited her every now and then, but no one told us anything else about them. We didn't have a chance to travel to the farm where James had been "adopted" to work as a laborer, but Mom was determined to find the other two places James had lived, two orphanages on opposite sides of the city. When we asked to visit James' most recent orphanage home, the officials refused, but Dad found out the address and hired a private car.

Our driver took us to a gate at the entrance of what looked like a hospital. The building guard gestured to stay out, but when James gave a knowing wave to him, he ushered us in through the automatic doors. The director was not there, so we got to wander around anywhere we wanted. I saw some children, but not as many as I expected. The children looked older, and some appeared blind and moved in funny ways. A few could not get up from their chairs; others could not hear us.

James moved about quickly from room to room, leaning on his friends and sitting on their beds as we awkwardly said *hello* to each one. A teen girl signed to James who responded by immediately helping her find her stuffed toy. It was the first time I saw James express warmth of any kind. The orphans surrounded him, and he appeared to run the place. We met his teacher Mr. Lee, whose affectionate handshake contrasted with the coldness of the other adoption officials. With Mr. Lee, I saw James smile for the first time.

It was Mr. Lee who told us the only stories we came to know about James and gave us the address of the first orphanage where he had lived between the ages of seven to eleven. The government had closed that facility two years earlier, and James had transferred to the new compound. Mom wanted to see the first orphanage, so off we went again with the hired driver. Entering an older, dirtier part of the city, we arrived at James's first orphanage home: an abandoned, disintegrating three-story building at the end of a congested street.

If the new orphanage resembled a sterile hospital, the older orphanage, where James had resided for most of his life, looked like a prison. Walls made of concrete blocks created small bedrooms that only held broken windows and cracked tile floors. In the bathroom, the toilet was a hole in the ground, and there was no shower, only a small basin area for washing. The hallways between the rooms were freezing and dirty and led to an old kitchen with only a stove and a few wooden tables. James proudly walked us through the deserted building, pointing out the two-story boiler in the back where he used to roast sweet potatoes over the coals. According to Mr. Lee, James had often escaped from his window on the second floor to steal and roast potatoes or buy cigarettes from the tiny markets down the street. I would try to escape too if I lived here; I could not wait to leave.

After seven obligatory days in Hohhot, we were free to fly to Guangzhou to complete the second week of the adoption process. Also in Guangzhou, we were set to meet our next brother, William Qiubao. We would then finalize the required embassy documents for both boys.

At this point, I began to struggle with boredom and crave normal food. My skin felt extra itchy from wearing clothes that had been overused and roughly washed too many times in hotel sinks. By the end of the first week, our socks and thick shirts became moldy and damp, and by week two, we verged on looking homeless. Luckily, in Guangzhou, we found our McDonald's! I'm sure I saw choirs of angels descending from those golden arches. It wasn't the same, of course, but it did have chicken nuggets and ice cream.

In contrast to Hohhot, Guangzhou lay within the tropical weather zone, meaning I could ditch my winter coat and walk without the weight of my stinking outer layer. Guangzhou was where we adopted William, and he was way more fun than James.

We picked him up one day in a crowded office building in the middle of the city. Other families had been waiting to meet their children, and we had to stay a long time, watching as young Chinese ladies carried little wrapped babies to their waiting families. All the groups looked like us: big, white, friendly, and out of place. How different we seemed from the sad, stoic ladies handing off children they would never see again!

William came to us dressed in a bright yellow jacket with huge brown eyes, sucking his lower lip. He didn't cry and walked dutifully over to us as the young lady who had placed him on the ground yelled out, "Go to Mama! See Mama!" He came to Mom, and she picked him up, teary-eyed and smiling. The girl who let him go walked away waving, also crying but not smiling even a little.

William joined our family on Christmas Eve morning, and we spent the week of Christmas and New Year's waiting for our visa appointment at the Embassy. During this third week in China, Jolyn and I tried to play with William at the hotel, but he didn't seem to know how. Jolyn poked fun at me, saying William reminded her of me with his odd habits and anxious behaviors.

William examined his surroundings; he smelled everything and often paced around the room studying its many new objects, such as TV remotes, door latches, and toilet flushers. He napped standing up, with his head leaning sideways on the foot of the bed while clutching a small blanket and sucking on that bottom lip. He seemed ready to go at any moment, and so was I.

By the third week, even Jolyn began to complain. I yearned to be home so I could eat normal food, hear English words, and find some order in my very disordered daily life. Still, we had to wait until the end of the week for James' and William's meetings at the US Embassy. Once we received their visas there, we traveled to Shanghai for one last stop: Dad's office.

During our fourth and final week in China, Dad held numerous business meetings at his Shanghai office while Mom stayed with us at the hotel, where we wandered around looking for something to do. Boredom crept in again, and Shiya and Jolyn grew restless. They asked Mom to take us to the local stores to buy some toys or coloring books, but I preferred the safety and predictability of the hotel room. I threw a few fits in the stores, but Mom did not let that deter her from gathering a bag full of activities for William and the girls. James carefully chose a model airplane, which he never opened but kept tucked in his jacket for the rest of the day. I chose a train and ripped open the box as soon as I got to the hotel lobby.

Later that week, we rode the two-hour train ride to visit the Nanjing orphanage where Shiya had lived for three years. The atmosphere of this place captured the spirit of the two other residences we had explored with James, capturing both the sterility of the his most recent orphanage and the shabbiness of the old one. Shiya rarely showed excitement, yet for years she had begged to see her Chinese home. Knowing how much it meant to her, Mom and Dad made the additional effort to get there.

The Nanjing Social Welfare Institute had been expecting us, so we arrived with some fanfare. As we rode the elevator from floor to floor, Shiya hardly spoke. When we reached the sixth-floor preschool group, Shiya cautiously approached her former playroom, as if walking on the ledge of a tall building. She pressed her nose against the window that separated her from the children barricaded on the other side of the glass. She stood there a long time, staring at little girls who wandered aimlessly around the empty playroom. Even though the children were only a few feet away, they seemed miles apart from us.

The preschool teacher waved at Shiya from inside, using the arm of one of the girls to wave *hello*. The girl who mimed the greeting did not smile or seem to notice us at all. Backing away, Shiya moved on to tour her former bedroom, just a few feet from the playroom. In there, she inspected the rows of small cots equipped with girdled fasteners meant to keep little kids in their beds.

A once inquisitive Shiya turned increasingly solemn when she saw the sleeping areas. Studying the fasteners, she seemed to stare off into another dimension, like one from my video games. She assumed the same flat demeanor as the orphans in the playroom and began to look as lost as the roaming girls behind the glass. After a few minutes in her former bedroom, she stopped talking altogether.

Upon leaving the orphanage that day, Shiya's attitude toward all things China changed. No longer did she ask to visit or imagine a magical life in Nanjing. In fact, she told us plainly on the train ride home that she had decided never to return to China again. I understood.

The subway car jerks abruptly, and my thoughts return to my own unfortunate circumstance. The train gradually slows, and I ready myself to fight the crowd of commuters already pushing toward the doors of the still-moving train. Struggling to stand from my crouching position, I feel someone tug my arm and lift me off the busy floor. As the doors open, I exit the subway with the rushing current of irritated passengers, heading left whether I want to or not. Once on the platform, I feel the cold air pushing through the vents from the street above me. I spot the big red numbers on the clock suspended above the stairs on my left. It's 9:03. Other than the clock, I see only people—hundreds of people—pushing, turning, and driving me toward the exit. The crowd reminds me of Lookdown fish, which travel in hoards, going nowhere quickly. But I'm too scared to think—even about fish. Everyone has somewhere to go, except me.

By 9:06, I've successfully shoved my body over to a metal column where I hold on and wait. I imagine I am back at Disney World and think about how my family found me because I remained in the same spot. I deliberate hard, like when I strategize my chess game victories, and then decide it is my best move. I will wait here. The clock ticks onward, one slow minute at a time.

At 9:08, after most of the crowd has disappeared up the stairs and out of the station, I notice a police officer. He approaches me, but I don't understand his words. At 9:10, the man in blue stops talking and stands by me quietly as I remain planted in place, pulling on my hair and beginning to cry. It's 9:11. I keep my eyes fastened on the clock as the officer waits with me, the isolation of the emptied station now aggravating my lonely feelings.

At 9:13, I hear the next train rumbling toward the station. Before the doors open, the passengers huddle against the glass, ready to exit and come at me. I grip the metal column hard with my hands, which are tucked behind me as I stand with my back to the column's edge. I take a breath as the doors open. Then I see him.

First off the train, about five cars down, is a large white man, yelling, "Garret!" He looks funny among the smaller Chinese men and women who follow him out. "Dad!" I yell back, removing my hands from the column and moving toward him. But I am unable to make my way through the pushy crowd, so I plant my feet, put my head down, and wait. In a moment, he grabs my arm and pulls me close as the people push beyond us. I see Mom holding William in his yellow jacket, with Jolyn, Shiya, and James close by. They all smile and hug me, everyone except James who seems unsure of what to do.

My dad thanks the officer, but I am not sure what for. Turning to me, he says, "You're smart, Garret. I'm so sorry!"

Mom still has William in her arms and gives me a crowded hug that lasts too long. Once she pulls back, she looks at me eye-to-eye and says, "I'll never not find you. You did right. I'm so proud of you."

We don't talk much the rest of that day. After thirty days in China, we cannot wait to go home. The night before we leave, several of us begin to feel sick and vomit throughout the night. Shiya, Jolyn, and William went first. By the next day, every one of us, except James, was exhausted, nauseated, and feverish. We had no choice but to go to the airport, pulling the car over when we needed to throw up or find a toilet. Mom discarded soiled underwear and vomit-filled t-shirts in garbage cans along the way, still making sure the essential items, like my jade serpent and the adoption certificates, made it all the way home.

PART IV

UNFLINCHING

Together Apart

Angela

"The question is whether or not you want to stay together," Mom Sharon says, "because staying together means it will be harder to get adopted."

I understood the question. I had seen many children leave with new families over the past three years, and most of them left alone or with one other sibling. No one adopts a group of six, and I knew my younger brothers and sister had a better chance of being adopted if Rogie, Edward, and I did not come along. When compared to our younger siblings, the three of us are older, tougher, and less fun.

Zoe, Robert, and Andrew are just three, four, and five years old, but they look even younger than their ages. Like me, my three younger siblings now have no tuberculosis, infections, or worms. But unlike me, they are smiling, playful, and cute, even with their scars. They also attend preschool, and even though they don't know many words, they're smart enough to get a family. According to our social worker from the Intercounty Adoption Board (ICAB), they are ready to be placed on the adoption register.

Mom Sharon did the needed paperwork to put Rogie, Edward, and me on the adoption list, but we likely will remain here, finding work as cleaners and caretakers when we grow up. I am an excellent cleaner, and the nannies tell Edward he takes good care of the babies in the nursery. *We can stay here.*

I am used to living among the swarm of other children. Many kids leave, but our number usually remains around 150. Others stay for a long time, until they grow up and must leave—or go to school. I won't make it in school because I got kicked out. Although I learned to read and do math faster than they expected, the teachers told Mom Sharon I was too difficult. It is true. I often screamed at them, although I tried hard not to.

Some people bother me, and I fall to the ground in heated protest to make them stop, or I put on my angry eyes. No one crosses me when I wear my mean face, which I do many times each day. The younger children always want something from me. They need help finding shoes, reaching the food, or understanding the day's schedule. And they never stop yelling over each other to get my attention. If they don't find me, they bother someone else. They creep around taking what's not theirs, tattling on one another, and playing pranks.

The older kids remind me of Mama or one of her boyfriends. One girl locks me in closets, and the others laugh at me about things I do not understand. Many of the teens don't speak well, and some of them have bad tempers.

I try to avoid them all by staying in Mom Sharon's fourth floor home. I would rather shop with her or run errands, and I love to clean. Housework makes sense and lets me avoid people. When I clean downstairs, I sneak into the kitchen to steal some extra food like bagged crackers or leftover fruit bread. It's not that I'm hungry—we get three meals a day. But extra food in my belly calms me down when I am scared and angry.

Today's ICAB social worker is Ms. Amelie, and she's nice enough. She explains to me and Rogie that our mother is in jail for stealing, drugs, and "other things." She won't get out for a long time. Rogie Nino grunts. "Good," is all he says.

Ms. Amelie and Mom Sharon tell me only a little about their visits to the jail where they got Mama to sign the adoption papers. Three years have gone by since I last saw Mama, and I try hard to remember her face. I wonder if I should miss her, but nothing comes to me.

Mom Sharon says it took a long time to gather the needed documents, but they did it. "You have birth certificates and adoption paperwork ready now," she says.

Mom Sharon knows I like to hear all the information, even if I can't understand it. The more I know, the better I feel. The many visitors who come to Open Arms think orphans want toys and new clothes, but they are wrong. What orphans really want is information. Information is the currency of the orphanage that keeps me alive and ready for what comes after the adults walk away. At Open Arms, I always carry the most currency.

During the rest of the ICAB visit, Rogie doesn't say much, only asking about our other family members, which I think are many. "No one else in the family has the money to care for you," Ms. Amelie explains, "so adoption is the best way to find family."

Adoption, I've been told, is God's plan for children when the big people really mess up. I think it is true, for the most part.

Almost every month, I see moms and dads come to our orphanage to take home their new children. Most of the toddlers that were here when we arrived already have left, following loud celebrations and prayerful goodbyes. I mostly feel happy for the ones who leave, but sometimes I am sad. The cook makes *halo halo*, and during the goodbye parties, I study the faces of the new parents, wondering what made them come. Once I got the courage to ask a mother, "How did you come to adopt *her*?"

The answer to this question was the information I most needed, but she only smiled and whispered back, "God brought me."

Her response did not tell me anything I didn't know already. I have met people who took home two siblings—and, once, even three siblings—at the same time. But in all my time here, God never has brought anyone to take home more than three. Six children at once! Not even God can do that. We still pray for it. Every night, with Mom Sharon, we pray— and wait.

When Ms. Amelie asks us again if we want to be adopted together, I understand. Maybe it's time to decide to separate. Little Zoe, Robert, and Andrew could find families. Mine might take a bit longer, but someone might even adopt me—if it's just me. Separation makes it possible.

A mumbled voice disrupts my thoughts. It's Rogie's: "I think we should stay together."

Rogie never willingly speaks to ICAB. He rarely tells his opinion, preferring instead to stay away from the scuffles and sounds of the orphanage. If Rogie isn't playing sports on the rooftop court, he is either at school or with older kids. He's hardly ever with me or his younger brothers and sister. Sometimes, I think he doesn't care much about us.

Rogie is the smartest of us Perez kids, so smart that an

organization paid for him to attend a fancy school in the area, one where only the best children get to go. From our orphanage, only Rogie and one girl attend. With all his brains, he rarely says what he thinks out loud. That's why his decision to keep us together makes me feel uneasy; his forcefulness in declaring it makes me wonder if he knows something I don't know.

The next day, Sharon presents us and her tight binder of papers to the serious officials at the ICAB office. I never have been here before, but I recognize Ms. Amelie right away. Welcoming us, she groups the six of us for a photograph. Zoe and Andrew begin making silly faces and dance movements at the camera. Robert stands next to Edward—still, like a careful gentleman—while making angry eyes at Zoe, who bumps into him as she sticks out her butt. "Stop!" I scream at them, too loudly. "This is important!"

Edward pulls Andrew away from Zoe and to his side, wrapping his arms around both his little brothers in a tight hug. To the left of them, Rogie and I stand off together, apart. "Rogie and Angela, pull closer to your brothers and sister!" I hear Ms. Amelie say. We shuffle over just a little as Zoe sneaks up front.

"Smile and say, 'Family!'" Mom Sharon calls out from behind Ms. Amelie.

Several bright flashes capture the moment, and our picture is later placed among hundreds of others on the "Special Findings" list. I am told this list holds pictures of "special" children. But I know that "special" really means unadoptable.

CHAPTER FIFTEEN

The Boom

GARRY

Spring 2013

"Aim slightly below the target," Justin instructed from about twenty yards away across the field. "Come on and squeeze the trigger slowly!"

I never have shot a gun before, so visiting our new friends gave me an opportunity to do something new. And I love doing new things. Still, I hesitated. "Guns scare me," I had told Justin's wife, who was standing next to me. "No one has guns in New Jersey other than the police and the gangs."

Sweet as she was in her long skirt and pretty smile, Jessica laughed at me, incredulous at my freshman status. "I always carry my .22 in my purse when I go to town to buy groceries. You never know," she explains. In North Dakota, not only does Jessica have a gun, but so does everyone else. Justin runs 150 head of

Black Angus cattle on his fifty-acre ranch. Jessica, his wife, home-schools their three children, who tend the ranch alongside their father. Life here works, and it works simply.

I left the ranch that day having shot a gun for the first time in my life and feeling grateful to be in a profession that didn't require one. On later visits with Justin, I learned that each head of cattle auctions for $1,000, making his daily work of tending them well worth the effort. Winters make it hard, especially when he has to calf a cow in the frigid North Dakota night, yet he never complains, nor do his wife and children, all of whom seem settled and content to work hard and keep it simple. Most of the people I have met here in Dickinson remain satisfied, and we fit easily into the helpful and serious-minded community of self-made, independent capitalists. My children have made friends and settled into school and play. Even Shiya has begun to engage with her classmates. Jodi homeschools Garret and watches William while she finishes her degree and works as a counselor in the evenings. Mental health care is meager in rural areas, so she works in partnership with a local counselor who commutes between Dickinson and other small towns to meet the need. They have no office, so I drop her at the local church which moonlights as a counseling center.

Dickinson has one elementary school, two grocery stores, and a single-level shopping mall. On the weekends, we travel the plains to see buffalo and prairie dogs roaming freely on our way to Teddy Roosevelt National Park, where we hike the Badlands near Medora, a town of 132. In the Badlands, the rock formations, hills, and plateaus rise toward expanses of sky that give way to eagles, sunlight, and a 3:00 p.m. dusk. The spaces and places provide unique opportunities for exploration and healing, especially for my new son James, who stays on the edges of our family life, often isolating himself in his room.

Behind the simplicity of this place, however, a boom has been rumbling. Between 2007 and 2012, North Dakota moved from being the eighth to the second largest oil-producing state in the United States. Largely due to the hydraulic drilling method dubbed "fracking," oil on this 200,000 square-mile Bakken area became viable for extraction and transport, moving the United States toward energy independence. The US Geological Survey predicted that 7.4 billion barrels of oil could be recovered from the Bakken Formation.

As mineral rights owners in the area started to receive royalties, a local official estimated that 2,000 North Dakotans would become millionaires every year. Thanks to the attention of tycoons, industrialists, and itinerants, North Dakota moved to the lowest unemployment rate in the entire country with the influx of jobs required to operate the oil rigs as well as transport, buy, and sell the oil. In some counties, populations doubled. When I arrive, there are 180 rigs, each requiring 125 active rig attendants and 10,000 job openings to lay pipe. For every new well that went up, 25,000 workers arrived and needed a man-camp to house them. Tiny towns like Williston were developing rapidly and now demanded shopping centers, accommodations, and infrastructure.

That's where my company came in—we came to build. Oil executives, migratory workers, business leaders, and engineers were arriving in large numbers every day, and they all needed somewhere to stay. A half-mile away from my rented townhouse, I found many workers living with their families at the local hotel and calling it home. Given the obvious need for temporary and extended-stay housing, my growing firm pivoted to building hotels. My youngest partner, Blair, focused on marketing, and Base4 developed from a modest engineering company into a niche design firm, specializing in engineering for the select-service hotel market.

At this point, our clients were architects. They hired us to engineer what they designed, to map the structural, HVAC, plumbing, electrical, and fire safety plans onto the construction drawings and make it all work safely and efficiently. As our client base expanded, I realized I didn't like working for architects. These career designers dallied with their projects, taking pride in their hand sketches and looking down on the engineers who just wanted to get the job done. I hadn't used pencil and paper for a decade. These architects with their antiquated methods often delivered late, and they loved to blame us.

Architecture encouraged a mentor/mentee model, which silenced the innovation and insights of the younger generations. Stuck in this conventional training model, architects questioned the effectiveness of technology and machine-learning when it came to expediting and reshaping the design progression. Their slow timelines and archaic methods both bothered and bored me.

We can do it better. The thought came to me one day as a client cursed me out on the phone to cover his mistake. I was done working for architects, and I set out to build my own architecture division, bringing the entire design process together under one firm. The only problem was that none of the partners were architects. As technology leaders and engineers, we would need to rethink how to do architecture.

When I floated the idea to my partners, they argued with me vigorously. Being three very practical engineers, they accurately assessed the persecution we would receive from our clients, who would now be our competitors. I countered them, certain that we could build an integrated architecture, engineering, and construction (AEC) firm on the robust systems already in place. Like the car industry before us, we would automate and perfect the design/build process.

We planned accordingly and began to search for a few rebellious young architects who understood the advantage of a tech-savvy approach to design efficiency. Being cloud-based, we could hire architects from anywhere in the world. And we did. Our first architect lived in Wisconsin, and over the next several months, we hired pioneering architects from Nagpur, Tbilisi, Santiago, and Florida. It didn't matter where they lived as long as they understood the vision: harness the power of technology and teamwork to create a product that was faster, greener, and better.

No longer the middleman between developers and architects, Base4's efficiency earned us a place at the table with Hilton, Marriott, Hyatt, IHG, and Choice Hotels, and we became regulars at their conferences and lecture series. Jobs began to pour in, and we expanded the team across the world, adding educational marketing campaigns, visualization teams, virtual reality experiences, and interior design to our list of products. What began as a unique opportunity to build hotels in North Dakota became the inspiration for a cutting-edge hospitality-design firm doing work all over the United States. Once we had firmly established a business presence in the Northwest, it was time to focus on our global architectural team. I had completed the mission in North Dakota, and Base4 needed me in a more central location to sell our new product.

We chose to relocate back to South Florida. We stayed inland this time to avoid the most severe hurricane damage and to be closer to Jodi's dad and his wife, Linda. The location made sense. Being in South Florida brought me closer to some of our clients in the southern United States and the Caribbean—and to my partner, Adam, who lived in Boca Raton. As a bonus, my parents wintered in Boynton Beach, allowing our five children frequent access to all their living grandparents, who showered them with pool parties, gifts, and sunny experiences. After being far away from our families these past few years, the opportunity to reunite with them and solidify intergenerational connections encouraged us as we settled into our new South Florida home. The hot weather was also a plus.

From Florida, I traveled often to win clients and build offices, ignoring the architects and developers who said we couldn't do it. We bid on jobs everywhere: Russia's largest theme park resort; China's newest amusement park; a nine-story Hyatt Place Resort and Casino in Aruba. We walked alongside government leaders and high-stakes developers, meeting influential power brokers in each region. Some jobs we won; others we lost, but I always said "yes" to trying. Whatever we did not know, we could learn. Whatever others built, I knew we could build it with better speed, efficiency, and quality—if just given the chance.

CHAPTER SIXTEEN

Learning Differently

GARRET

Spring 2014

"Your son qualifies in two out of the three required areas for gift-edness," said the counselor. "His IQ is 131, which qualifies, and his creativity score also remains in the gifted zone. However, his achievement score doesn't measure up."

Mom bristles in her chair. "Of course, his achievement was not commensurate with his abilities; he has autism. His social anxiety and communication challenges are the key reasons for his current IEP."

She is right. Now in middle school, I still find myself on the bathroom floor sometimes, and most of the other kids don't talk to me. The aides keep me in easy courses to keep me from freaking out; however, the classes are so simple that I get bored. The only thing worse than my anxiety is the boredom. *If I must come to this terrible place every day, at least the topics should be interesting.* Last week, I got in trouble for reading books during class. When the principal asked why, I explained that the teacher was boring.

He knew I was right. "Still," the principal had said, "it's important to show respect and pay attention." I did not agree about paying attention, and now we're sitting in this meeting, surrounded by lots of people who claim they want to help.

"I understand your concerns, and the team is committed to making sure Garret does well," the counselor said without commenting on the research Mom had presented.

Mom's eyes narrow, and her face seems to fall under the weight of her frown, much like mine does. "I'm not signing this form."

The room stared at her, speechless. I think having lots of people, papers, and fancy words intimidates other parents to agree to their kids' IEPs. But these people didn't know my mom—and they also did not know what to say.

The IEP, or Individual Educational Plan, is for atypical learners like me. James, Shiya, William, and I all have IEPs. Only Jolyn is normal. Mom attends meetings a lot. I see her at campus often, and the school's administrators get to know her well, no matter where we live. Last year, Mom consulted with her attorney (my shrewd Aunt Nancy) and a doctoral-level special education advocate (my clever Aunt Pam) on the school's legal responsibilities for educating James: the principal had declared James incapable of earning the regular high school diploma due to his language challenges.

Mom's jaw clinched down when she talked about it, refusing their decision and citing the importance of the diploma as well as James's right to receive the assistance needed to secure it. She researched the state and federal educational regulations and informed the school administration how the law ensured equal access to education, which meant translation services for James in every subject other than English. The school pushed back and threatened to hold him back a grade level due to his poor grades and progress.

They didn't expect my parents' response: "We don't care if he fails a grade or has to be held back. Keep him in high school the allowable six years, so he can graduate." For emphasis, Mom added that James wasn't allowed to go to school for his first thirteen years. "He's smart," she said, "and now he gets his chance to learn."

But it will take a while. My brother James cannot read even a menu. When we eat out, he orders the same thing every time, a cheeseburger. He knows every restaurant sells them, so that's his order, every time. I like cheeseburgers too, but sometimes, you need to eat something else.

Over the past three years, James has learned to navigate America with little language, using his iPad to translate anything important—like the dialog on his Xbox game or my mom's text messages—into Mandarin. Even though James seems distant, he often comes to my room where we game together; he asks me to translate the commands and share the backstories of the characters. I like James, even though he doesn't talk much—or maybe *because* he doesn't talk much.

Mom attends a lot of appointments to help James and the rest of us. After my disastrous IEP meeting ended abruptly and without an answer, she plopped down on the kitchen stool that day, holding her scheduling calendar, and announced to Dad, "This year, I have met with teachers, IEP teams, specialists, ESL leads, counselors, physical therapists, occupational therapists, psychologists, neurologists, principals, lawyers, and policymakers ninety-four times." Then she gestured with her hands, placing them on her chest, and took a deep breath, tears welling in her eyes. I waited for her to make a point—as did Dad, but she just left it there.

Mom battles hard for me, so I try to do better. People aren't so bad. I want to be respectful when I explain to teachers why their points don't make sense. Busy work shouldn't make me so bored and crazy. I wish my heart didn't beat wildly when teachers assign me homework. I take my breaks at the water fountain and do my breathing exercises to stay calm. In these frantic moments, I don't want to be bad. I remind myself of "what's true" and the other counseling techniques that help me do better, succeeding only for a few days, and then something unexpected happens. A schedule changes, a teacher forgets, the projects begin, people tease me—and I lose it. And Mom is called in for a meeting. Another one.

I have lived in Orlando, Doha, Dickinson, and South Florida. In every place, I have gotten myself kicked out of school. Not officially, but that is what really happened. Eventually the schools run out of ideas, their many pages and plans incapable of supporting me. What looks good on paper often falls apart in the hallways and at the lunchroom table. In the end, the administration labels me a behavior problem and sticks me in classes with kids who do not want to learn. But that's not me—I want to learn. I just don't learn their way.

Our current school system is in South Florida, where we moved to live near our grandparents. Everything Papa and Nana

Linda do is big. That means loud family barbeques by the pool, twelve-foot Christmas trees at Papa's house, and gooey treats overflowing from Nana's kitchen. We also get to see Grandma and Grandfather Vermaas, who spend winters not too far from us in a retirement community. Although quieter than Papa and Nana, they make me feel loved, even celebrated, just for being me.

Every weekend, we fight over who to see first. Jolyn and William vie for the opportunity to swim at Nana's pool at the fabulous Parkland Golf and Country Club. Shiya and I nag for Grandma and Grandfather to come over to play card games and poke fun at the old people in their neighborhood. Even James comes out of his room when Grandfather comes over.

Unfortunately, we can't live at the pool or with the old people, and the schools just don't work for us. Other than our grandparents, the people here are mean. A group of high schoolers called James a "yellow" and cursed at him on the bus. He didn't have the language to explain the relentless harassment, so he endured it for six months before a neighbor kid who rode the bus felt so badly, she told Mom. Shiya also reported bullying: "Someone called me disgusting." "Jake said I have cooties." "Sue said I couldn't play." It was normal elementary-school stuff, but it happened every day.

When I got bullied, I became desperately frantic and erratic. I would flail my arms and pace around in circles, engaging in a war of words with onlookers that usually ended with me yelling. Kids blame me because I am always the loudest. After one rant with a neighborhood boy in my grade, his parents came out to the cul-de-sac to swear at my parents. Their point was clear: "You need to keep *kids like him* in the house." Mom no longer let me play outside alone after that.

But it wasn't just *kids like me* who struggled here. Jolyn came home from school crying one day, wanting to be homeschooled. Jolyn never came home in tears. I overheard Mom tell Dad later that some girls had interacted with her in "graphically inappropriate ways." I didn't know what the words implied, but I knew it was serious. For the next few years, every night, Jolyn experienced anxiety attacks before going to bed.

"We can live anywhere," Dad said one day after returning from a business trip and hearing the news about Jolyn. "It's time to go." And we did.

Since Dad and Mom could work from anywhere, they began the search to move us to the right schools and better people. "Right" didn't necessarily mean rated highly or "best" by regular standards. After all, James's high school, Marjorie Stoneman Douglas, was rated a perfect 10 on the school ratings chart. The "10" means it is a perfect school for perfectly normal kids, but that's not us. We needed a place to fit.

After a few weeks of research, we moved from the Sunshine State to the Bible Belt, near Nashville, Tennessee, to live in a small community known for its traditional values, good schools, and kind people. Also, Mom's sister, Aunt Nancy, and her family live there, too. We moved into a rented home, sight unseen, just down the block from them.

The Eckert's are the cool side of the family. Uncle Brian is a musician, producer, and studio owner, while Aunt Nancy excels as an entertainment attorney. They know all the famous and important people, and they own a second home in the trendy part of the city. My cousins, Brian Jr. and Jackson, are karate champions. We are their awkward, funny, and brash relatives, but they like us anyway.

After living in Tennessee for some time, we heard the shocking news about the shooter who killed seventeen people at James's former high school in Parkland. "It could have been James," I spilled out to Mom, who agreed. Even though he is tough, I am certain the move to Tennessee saved James's life—in more ways than one.

CHAPTER SEVENTEEN

The Push

Jodi

Winter 2015

I typed the choice into my computer: "Tell us if you want us to be your parents or your legal guardians." Underneath that sentence, I wrote, "Parents," *space, space, space,* "or Legal Guardians," and the phrase, "Circle one." Above the choices was a simple explanation of our legal responsibility to care for James until he was eighteen and that he did not have to accept us as parents. Either way, we loved him fiercely.

If he circled "Legal Guardians," we would tend to his needs, make sure he received an education, and help him move back to China once he became an adult. We would not expect love or even relational engagement. If he chose "Parents," however, he needed to make some changes. Being part of the family means he would have to come out of his room for school, dinner, and church, and that he had to be kind—or at least not mean to anyone. Those were the stipulations. I used Google Translate to translate the note into Mandarin and printed it. With the sinking feeling of impending loss, Garry and I knocked on James's door and entered to lay it on the edge of his bed. He had one day to decide.

No adoptive parents wish for this story. We adopted James because agencies told us he longed for a family. China advocated for him before he aged out of the system. At the time, we knew to ask if he wanted to be adopted, given that he was thirteen years old. The CCCWA assured us he wanted a family. A year after his adoption, however, he spiraled into a deep depression. After months of asking him questions in every way we knew how, I finally asked the right one: "Did you know we were coming for you?"

In limited English, he told us, "No, the lady tells me the day before. I choose not to come. That lady always lies." His words cut my heart deeply, but we were not surprised. It fit.

James was angry and resentful, and—over time—we became the safe depository for all his anger and pain. Even though we attended the seminars, read the books, and understood the diverse sequelae of trauma, nothing seemed to help him heal. And no matter the love, patience, listening, or counseling, James did not respond. He refused to leave his room, going days without eating, showering, or moving his body. I am not even sure he went to the bathroom. He did not attend family events and often groaned about going to school.

We were still living in Florida when he stopped going to school. This was a red line for me and Garry. Hurting children hide, but they require discipline and expectations just the same. Feeling sorry for his past would not help him; love with strict boundaries was required.

When he began to skip school, I called the local police and reported his truancy. Part of loving my children has always been allowing the natural consequences of their bad choices to become manifest in their realities. Although maternal instincts told me to call my own bluff on the tough love, I stuck with the plan. James did not tell me much about his conversation with the officer, who was eager to partner with me in this effort. Still, the conversation inspired—or at least terrified—James enough that he never cut class again.

James was not belligerent, just stubbornly committed to not wanting anything. If I gave him a new coat or shoes, he replied, "I didn't ask for that." After spending two days crafting a Chinese dragon birthday cake for his first birthday with us, he did not acknowledge or look at it, saying, "I don't have birthdays." When addressed or hugged, he physically recoiled in disgust and ran away.

Kind words did not register, and typical teenage discipline didn't work because there was nothing to take away from him. He made no friends, played few games, and wished for nothing, except to die. Yet even death required too much desire and energy, so mostly he remained in his bed, unless he was reporting for school.

In our home, James expressed such quiet hostility toward his new life that we made the hardest choice we ever had to make. With much doubt and few options, we offered him the freedom to reject us, the choice of living with us like a foreign exchange student with no relational expectations. We made the hard choice to let go, leaving the translated note on his bed that night to let him make his decision. For the first time in James's life, he received total control of his destiny.

Although we believed giving him freedom was important for

him to take the next developmental step, we honestly did not know what else to do. We were certain he would choose "Guardian" or nothing at all, refusing to answer us altogether.

Early the next morning, Garry went to James' room to retrieve the note from his bed, where he lay, awake. In pencil, he had circled "Parents." Garry and I, amazed and tearful, took the note and acted like nothing had happened, realizing that our excitement might reveal too much expectation. It was a turning point.

From that decision onward, James was not pleasant, but he became dutiful, going through the motions of attending school, church, and nightly dinners, as contracted. In these routines, he joined the rhythm of Vermaas family life. He came to expect our moves, the holidays with relatives and grandparents, and the passing school years packed with IEPs, tutors, and ESL. James spent the most time with Garret, whose autistic world remained undisturbed by his quiet Chinese companion. In a way, the brothers bonded in their preference for isolation. Garret accepted James with no hesitation, excusing the weird moods, eschewing his callous remarks, and favoring the strategic physical distance James kept between them. Often, I found James sitting on Garret's bed watching him play games on his iPad. Sometimes, I even heard them laughing.

Still, I often felt self-conscious in my own home. For me and Garry, parenting James required a new level of self-denial and sacrifice. I chose my few words deliberately, showing empathy without physical affection, asking questions—but not too many—and challenging behaviors without pushing him away into his dim pit of uncertainty.

When I touched him, I deliberately put a strong hand on his shoulder so as not to startle him. He hated it, but I practiced it anyway. And I fed him Chinese cuisine. Food became the love language through which I communicated. Hot pot, fried noodles, pot stickers, dumplings, and noodle soup with egg and scallions became staples. Together James and William bonded over soup, eating it for breakfast each morning, to the rousing complaints of my other children who hated the stench of fish sauce, vinegar, and sriracha.

When James did venture out of his room, he often found himself overcome with insecurity and terror. Keeping his head down and his expression firm, he intimidated most people into staying away. On our quiet drives to school, I would open conversations with gentle questions, seeing if he would give me any clues to his thoughts and experiences. I longed to know him as a mother understands her child, but I remained cut off. I kept pushing. Sometimes, he ignored me; other times, he responded with short, but powerful words and questions. "If you could find me," he asked one day, "how come my parents never did?"

The orphanage told James he had gotten lost, and that his parents could not find him. It was his fault he was left behind, and that lie intensified his shame. It took three years, one bit at a time, for James to explain the military barracks, the mental state of his "mother," the "sister" who also called herself his girlfriend, and the time he was sold to Chinese farmers and later returned.

Language came slowly for James, reading even more gradually. I commiserated with the challenges of learning a new language, having spent significant time in foreign lands, linguistically baffled for most of it. I encouraged him to keep speaking his native Mandarin as he studied English, a dual process that made the assimilation progression slower but preserved his cultural heritage and identity.

The truth is that many people have criticized us for taking children out of their native lands into a new culture where they must learn the language and acclimate to a whole new world. It is hard. In one of those rare, willing moments, I asked James if he would have preferred to stay in China. Immediately, he replied, "I think it better here; here is love. Over there, is no love."

Still, we often stumbled upon crisis moments that were completely unexpected. After a haircut to trim the long hair he used to hide his eyes, James became enraged in the backseat, grinding his teeth and setting his expression as we rode home from the hair salon. When Garry asked him to share what was happening, he began punching himself in the head. We had to pull over so Garry could move to the backseat and shield him from his own blows, while he cried, saying "I'm so ugly! I hate myself!"

Uprisings like this revealed my son's inner life, his grappling with loss, shame, and self-identity, living among virtual strangers who called him family. They were terrible moments—and important. As we journeyed through the pain together, we did not hide the challenges from our other children, speaking openly about every complicated situation and emotional breakdown. As our children watched one another struggle and learn, their hearts grew increasingly empathic, shaped in ways that even they did not yet understand.

With vulnerable, wrenching moments happening routinely, the family learned to measure progress differently. For us, just showing up was a victory. When James appeared at a holiday dinner, it was a triumph, even though others thought it rude when he did not banter with the guests. Garry and I appreciated the courage it took for him to sit at dinner in front of the watchful eyes of people he didn't know—or understand.

Don't get me wrong; it's not easy to let go of the world's definition of achievement and accomplishment. I had attended prep schools and an Ivy League university, using my education and mainstream success as my mantra. My children taught me to measure success differently.

Still, onlookers made their critiques known. The neighbors reprimanded William for his bus stop antics, annoyed by his incessant leaping off the curb. Where they saw mischief, I recognized a boy who was beating the odds, overcoming brain damage through his boundless energy for life.

I admit we were not good parents in the traditional sense. My kids never won awards or had lines in the school play. They did not make special lists or win over any hearts. Teachers tolerated them, but most did not understand them, finding their quirkiness irritating and misinterpreting their social efforts as rudeness.

Neither teachers nor students understood Shiya, whose communication delays made her difficult to understand. Labeled as weird, Shiya would draw for hours, elaborately sketching the faces of the people she so desperately wished to know.

Garret struggled the most. He had grown old enough to appear nearly normal sometimes, so classmates expected typical prosocial behaviors from him. When he melted down, big as he was in his early teens, he startled students and teachers alike.

Even Jolyn didn't secure any trophies or honors. She did not join the sports teams or walk among the talented dancers and cheerleaders. She preferred skateboarding and baking, raising farm animals and dialoging with adults. She was a foodie and a travel buff. With her natural proclivity for people and deep connection to all things human, Jolyn's natural leadership talents developed exponentially among her challenging siblings. She knew what was happening, and she always jumped right in. Still, at school and among peers, her unique set of skills didn't win her popularity.

"Are we terrible parents?" I often asked Garry, a notion he quickly dismissed. It was hard not to doubt myself. Should we join the sports teams and push the dance lessons? Do I persuade them to dress trendier and take them shopping more often? Should I scold them for being antsy or making lots of noise, even when their exploits are innocent?

I wondered about therapies, medications, and activities, and whether online school, private school, public school, or IEPs worked best for each child. I was willing to try anything (and I did), but my choices needed to match each individual child on their unique developmental trajectory. Some of my children, like Garret and Jolyn, benefitted from an online environment for schooling, while others, like Shiya and William, craved the social interactions at school.

In the end, Garry and I chose to accept our children wildly, leaning heavily on kindness with less emphasis on social graces. The sign I made for the boy's bathroom read: *Be Kind and Pee in the Toilet.* That pretty much summed up our beliefs about outward appearances. Garret often wore his shirt backwards, and most mornings James's bed head showed off hair sticking straight up. We went with it, choosing to correct heart matters instead of the hundred other issues that could have been the target of our improvements. We granted our kids freedom to spend their time drawing, bouncing, cooking, and gaming. A's were not mandatory, even though total effort was assumed. Although we expected our children to be kind, we did not ask them to fit in.

Unlike me, Garry always felt like we were winning. In all

things family, we moved forward and backward, making progress and experiencing losses, sometimes failing wildly and publicly. Never did I consider stopping or slowing down, a resolve inspired by my love and stubbornness. I knew the good was happening amid the setbacks, and I continued to push on every door that presented itself. Sometimes, the doors opened wide.

PART V

RELENTLESS

Waiting

ANGELA

Slowly and quietly, I creep out of my bed to avoid waking up Zoe, who always wants to follow me around. She is very annoying and noisy. Once my toes hit the concrete floor, I begin to tiptoe across the room. If I can get through the door without waking anyone else, I am free.

I sneak out of Mom Sharon's apartment to the stairs without making a sound. I quickly step down each stair, one foot then the other in the dark, down one flight to the guestroom. No one will hear me now because of the nightly worship music blaring out from the speakers on the children's floor to mask the crying. I see that the large wooden door is ajar, so when I reach it, I peek inside.

In the bed are two white people, here to adopt Lucas. I overheard Mom Sharon talking about them. They came from Australia, and although I don't know where that is, I know it's far away. After Lucas, another family will come to adopt Frederick. In December, I heard Missy and Mia will be leaving, too.

I am not sure about the schedules, but Mom Sharon seems to be making plans, so it all must be happening soon. The families who adopt the children come to live here at Open Arms for one week to see the place and meet their children. When they come, we must be on our best behavior—and smile.

After seeing many families come and go, I have learned that they are all similar. The moms and dads smile big, though they seem unusual to me—and out of place. They don't know where to sit or how to understand us. The new parents often stand around waiting for us to tell them what to do or where to go. One thing I do know: families always bring bags full of small toys and candies for all of us. And they never find out when two or three treats from their stuffed bags go missing, especially in the noise and excitement of the house.

Lucas's parents are no different. I peer into the room, spotting several oversized blue and gray duffle bags. One overflows with clothing, socks, and shoes. The other one, only partly open, reveals the prize: brightly colored bags of candies, the good ones, not like the ones I took from the sari-sari store next door. Without taking my eyes off the candies, I slink into the room toward the bags, crouch down before the one with the candies, and reach in to feel the plastic bag filled with round chocolates. Pulling it out so very quietly, I grab three balls and turn around to leave the room.

Then I see faces, three small boys in the doorway. I squint my eyes tightly, as if my scowl will push them away, then I point for them to move out of my way. They giggle and begin whispering loudly—my little brothers. Recognizing the problem, Edward noisily warns them, "Shhhhhh!" But it's too late. *Flip* goes the light switch, and the white people sit up in bed, unsure of what to say. I grin awkwardly, shoving the chocolates into the pocket of my pants, and move toward the door. Before I can get away, I see Mom Sharon's shadow on the stairwell, and Zoe following close behind. We are caught.

"Angela is stealing!" yells Andrew with an accent that only Mom Sharon and I can understand.

"NO," I yell back and point dramatically, "It was Zoe!" It wasn't my best lie, since Zoe had just arrived, so I had to explain more. "Zoe has been in here all night, and I came to find her when I woke up and found she wasn't in the bed."

Robert, confused yet full of resentment toward his annoying younger sister who always takes his things, agrees with me, "Zoe did it. I saw her."

Mom Sharon looks at Edward, the one who doesn't know any better than to tell the truth. "Edward, did Zoe come in here first?" Edward's big eyes look to me, and I look back, coolly.

"Yes, it was Zoe." He did not lie, of course; he had seen her in here earlier and assumed the worst.

Zoe whines, "It wasn't me!" By this time, the family in bed has excused themselves to go to the bathroom. Mom Sharon takes Zoe back upstairs, and I sit outside on the stairs with my brothers.

Soon Mom Sharon returns and orders my brothers to bed in the boys' room one flight below, and I quickly hurry back to my room, where Zoe and I live apart from my brothers and most of the other children. When the older children go to school in the morning, I stay to help with the babies who are sick. Sometimes I get to help Mom Sharon during important meetings. She asks me to bring coffee and get papers from her desk.

When I go to her office, I try hard to read the documents, so I can know what's going on. I have taught myself to read many of the English words by practicing with the books from the schoolroom. I must learn to read more quickly, so I can understand the important papers before I give them to Mom Sharon. The papers might tell me if anyone is coming for me.

I have seen my name on the medical reports, but I can't understand them. I know that the "DR" letters mean "doctor," and I think the papers tell others I am sick. I used to have TB, which are letters that mean some other big word that I cannot read. All of us, except Rogie, had the TB. Even though we got better from the worms, bruises, belly aches, and big cough, we still have the lice. Mom Sharon takes us on the same day every week to the clinic for check-ups. The doctors take pictures of our chests and tell me I am OK. Still, if they can get rid of the big cough, I wonder why they can't get rid of the tiny lice.

The only other papers with my name on it have the picture of me with my sister and brothers under a fake tree. Below the picture are our names and birthdays. It's the same photo all the children get when they're ready to be adopted. The photos show up in the suitcases of the parents who stay in the adoption suite. I hope my picture looks good enough, so someone comes for us.

Lots of friends leave with families, one by one. Edward cried hard when his friends left, especially David and Rinnel. He cried all during their goodbye party, but I didn't. My face mostly looked like the mad face on the "How Are You Feeling Today?" therapy map that hangs on Mom Sharon's office wall. She told me to be happy our friends got adopted. Getting adopted means being chosen, feeling special, and getting extra treats.

But I'm not chosen or special yet, I think to myself, as I sit on my bunk bed where Zoe has already fallen back to sleep. My thoughts stay with me for a long time. Feeling my eyes water, I remember the chocolates. I reach around my waist to retrieve the stolen treats hidden in my pants, finding them only a bit softened from being in my back pocket. I shove all three into my mouth so that no one takes them from me or gets me in trouble later. The sweet taste dissolves my tears, and I feel my heartbeat slowing down. Tucking the chocolate-smudged wrappers under Zoe's pillow, I lie down next to her. It takes several more minutes to finish chewing through the thick chocolate, its gooey taste cheering me up just enough to drift off to sleep.

CHAPTER EIGHTEEN

Again

JODI

Fall 2015

"Hello, Jodi, this is Melissa," said the social worker on the other end of the phone. I had just shoved several bags of groceries into my trunk and gotten into my car in time to pick up my phone. I recognized Melissa's phone number and knew she called only when there was a referral opportunity. My heart skipped as I eagerly pushed the button to accept the call.

"I have a referral for you," Melissa told me. "She's from South India, and she's seven years old. Would you like to review the file?"

Adoption social workers get straight to the point when it comes to referrals. They have limited time with each file, especially the types of files for my family. As was the case with many of my children, this little girl's file had already been rejected by other families in the adoption process. Now the agency had only a short time to find another family before returning the file to the child's home country. Returned files damaged the agency's reputation.

"Of course," I replied.

Within a minute, the file appeared in the inbox on my phone. Still in the car, I viewed the electronic files on the small screen. The file listed the child's name as "Lekshmi *FNU*," which stood for *First Name Unknown*. Lekshmi came from Karinjapally, Kerala, Southern India, where she lived in an orphanage after being found in the baggage compartment of a train, nearly dead. The handwritten medical report said she had been beaten so badly that she lost sight in her left eye and movement on the right side of her body. For six months, she had lived at the hospital, partially paralyzed and healing from seizures, bruising, and states of unconsciousness caused by traumatic brain injury.

Now, four years later, she resided at an obscure facility in the hilltops of Kerala. Her most recent medical exam showed her to be moving almost normally with sustained damage to her right hand and left eye. The local police ran advertisements in the paper for this "lost girl." Ads like this were common formalities, stuck in the back pages of many of the local newspapers. Someone had beaten her and left her for dead underneath the long-distance train headed to Mumbai. No one claimed her. No one wanted her. No one came for her. Until now.

Garry and I accepted the referral immediately, certain that the smiling girl with the wild eyes belonged with us. After having satisfied the post-placement requirements for our previous three adoptions, we were eager to adopt from India, the country that had earned our affection from the first moment we stepped onto her dusty, bustling roads. We had petitioned to adopt an older female child because of the millions of girls who ultimately vanished into the unseen—yet thriving—industry of child trafficking. With this adoption, there would be one less victim.

The adoption process in India did not follow the same organized timeline as Chinese adoptions, taking eight months for the initial paperwork to secure the stamps of approval needed to receive an initial referral. On the application, we had checked off dozens of special needs and diagnoses that we were willing to accept. Now, Lekshmi *FNU* would be our sixth child.

After locking the referral through the payment of a large fee, the paperwork cleared every foreign and domestic agency with surprising ease. To avoid future mispronunciations, we decided to spell her name Luxmi and anticipated meeting her within a few months. We filled out the travel forms and needed only one final approval from the hometown judge in Karinjapally, so she could receive her passport and visa to travel to the United States with us.

Just one signature away from bringing her home, we hit a stubborn impasse at Luxmi's local court appearance. The judge simply refused to let her go. For ten months, we waited and heard no update from the Central Adoption Agency Resource (CARA). Although we called weekly for news, our agency reported no information and would not advocate for us to CARA out of fear of looking rude to the local authorities.

By the time we hit one year from the receipt of the referral, Garry had had enough and called the CEO of our adoption agency to drive the process. Only then did we learn about the judge's reputation and that he had seen Luxmi twenty-two times in his courtroom and denied her paperwork every time.

The CEO told us that our Christian faith made it unlikely that this strict Hindu judge would ever sign off. The only option would be to appeal to a higher court to petition her case away from the local authorities. He warned against this move, which did not suit the "don't rock the boat" motto of most adoption agencies and other NGOs. Having spent lots of time in India, we were convinced that the provincial judge would not change his mind. We decided to rock the boat, knowing full well that we might jeopardize the entire adoption by offending the local jurisdiction.

This challenge to the higher court forced me to hold on to Luxmi's adoption with a measured grasp, not too tightly or loosely. We had learned to approach all our adoptions this way, fighting fiercely for the desired result yet surrendering to the possibility of no outcome at all. And just like that, the high court judge did approve our petition to grant the passport to our new daughter.

■ ■ ■ ■ ■

"Why would you adopt this ruined child?" barked the doctor, his face distorted in disgust. It was our final appointment in Delhi before we received permission to bring Luxmi home. Shaking his head, he checked off the remaining boxes on the medical form, releasing my grinning, fragile child into our permanent care.

Over the past eight days, we had traveled from Southern India to various adoption appointments throughout Delhi and to the Taj Mahal with Garry, Garry's mom, and my three daughters. We had endured numerous vomit-filled car rides, fought with the orphanage director, and fended off rabid dogs in the heat of the Indian summer. I couldn't wait to leave.

Officials, judges, and doctors criticized, ignored, or reprimanded us for taking this child. Some—like the doctor—found Luxmi worthless and cursed, while others yelled after us for carrying a Hindu child away from her homeland. Many expected soft bribes, and our agency back home was powerless to help us navigate the untamed process. Garry's mom frequently looked uncomfortable and nauseous while Jolyn and I continually checked our heads for lice, which we both found by the end of the trip.

Since we met her, Luxmi has done only three things other than smile. She has made "beep" noises, chewed on bottle tops, and sucked in the sides of her cheek to make fish lips. Affectionately, Garry and I called her Mowgli, as she had spent the last four years wandering the grounds of a secluded jungle orphanage, barefoot and aimless. She did not get to go to school, and it seemed like no one had ever spoken to her.

As we readied ourselves to leave India, I tried to prepare Luxmi, sticking both my arms straight out from my sides to mime the upcoming flight. She responded by turning her back and flinging her hand in the air like a diva exiting her concert stage. Then and there, I knew: *This girl will be alright.* She expressed no hesitation about her new life, and from that moment on, we have been her favorite people.

I left Tennessee with two daughters and came home with three. Luxmi Rose joined Shiya Rose and Jolyn Rose in the tradition of The Rose Sisters. "Rose, because all roses are different, and all are beautiful," I tell my daughters, as often as possible.

Adoption—whether of children, people, or causes—had woven itself into the thematic pattern of my life. I didn't wake up every day looking for children to adopt; rather, I woke up to my messy life of working, parenting, and chores, just like everyone else. I recognized that we had much to give, and I was determined to give it.

Garry and I do not have hobbies or follow sports. We don't enjoy shopping for cars or planning sophisticated vacations. We buy clothes from Target for convenience, picking out shirts and swimsuits alongside our milk and dish soap. Time, our most valued commodity, is spent extravagantly on people.

After Luxmi's adoption, I pursued new ways to push the orphan agenda. I published my doctoral research on interprofessional collaboration between clergy and mental health professionals, hoping its findings would empower both groups to work together for the children of their communities. Through POW, I helped raise money to educate special needs children living in impossibly destitute places. My friends and fellow board members, Jaimie and Ben and Kristy and Keith, chose to adopt some of these children. Together, we also began a *pro bono* adoption service, offering no-cost adoption counseling to potential parents and kids. In these efforts, I again found opportunities to counsel survivors of sex trafficking. As I did, I attended to teenage girls whose reports of human slavery could have been the stories of my own daughters, if not for their adoptions.

Not all our plans bore remarkable results; sadly, many initiatives ended in little actual change. Few people paid attention to my research or advocated for improvements. Even with our help, many potential parents decided adoption was too expensive and uncertain. Even the young women rescued from trafficking often made their way back to the streets, preferring the terribly familiar over the frighteningly new. Change is hard.

The months pushed forward as did our efforts, with little progress made either inside or outside our family. William entered kindergarten with his IEP and medications in hand. He struggled to keep up with his peers, especially in speech and self-control, and was often found somersaulting down the school's hallways, walking along the high walls outside, or sticking his fingers in someone's ear, "just 'cause."

Being new to the school system, both he and Luxmi kept the special ed teachers fully occupied. Lunchtime and toileting often turned disastrous, with me receiving alarming phone calls from frantic teachers nearly every day. I was the mom-on-call, although I usually did not have the answers.

It was at this time that Shiya began to laugh out loud. Always the extreme introvert and wildly distracted by her own thoughts, Shiya caught up to her peers in reading and math, although socially she lagged years behind them. By the end of the school year, she still hadn't made one friend. Neither had James, or Garret.

But I wasn't looking for results anymore. I took the perpetual bad news in stride, learning to take my licks and own the setbacks. After all, the angels still cried out, their watchful presence beckoning me forward to do good.

CHAPTER NINETEEN

More

GARRY

Spring 2016

Luxmi grew into a functional human, learning to use toilet paper, speak basic English, and attend school. When the school principal first met Luxmi, he asked us to wait to enroll her and give her time to "settle in." That was code for *we can't handle this untamed child!* We sent her to school anyway, and she loved everything about it.

Outside of school, Jodi enrolled Luxmi in occupational therapy, physical therapy, and visual therapy in between her many visits to tutors, neurologists, and ophthalmologists. As Luxmi's first school year progressed, I often went with Jodi to the school meetings as the "muscle," to insist that Luxmi receive equal academic opportunity instead of being labeled as "special" too quickly. As we had done with Garret, James, Shiya, and William before her, Jodi and I became the parents that the schools loved to hate. We expected more from them. While Jodi researched the latest educational tactics, I bluntly challenged the red tape and endless forms.

I began every meeting the same way: "Thank you for seeing us today. I don't have a lot of time, so I want to get right to it. I understand we're in an adversarial relationship: I want what's best for my daughter, and you want what's best for the school."

At that point, the room inevitably insisted that they were on our team, to which I countered: "Jodi has two PhDs, and I have one, and we will fight for what we know is best for Luxmi." We are a bit much.

With additional attention and focus, Luxmi thrived at school, immediately becoming the ESL and IEP leaders' favorite student. What Luxmi lacked in IQ, she more than made up for with infectious joy, kindness, and social ability. She learned to speak and read quickly, proving that her brain held phenomenal potential despite her history. During her six-month hospital stay after her attack and abandonment, numerous brain scans revealed sporadic pockets of dead tissue. The irreversible damage limited her short-term memory, keeping her stuck in the moment, unable to predict what was coming or remember what just happened. The vicious abuse had limited her capacity to learn, yet she became a social phenomenon.

In between working and parenting, I partnered with Jodi in her relentless pursuit of doing good. While she counseled, advocated, and researched, I knew I had to make the money to support her efforts.

Rather than focusing on selling Base4 to more developers, I chose to focus on the team and our four values of humility, honesty, respect, and fun. By providing educational resources, opportunities to learn new skills, and willingness to hear their ideas, team members would stay engaged and our product would become unparalleled.

My focus on training manifested so obviously that one day the janitor at our Nagpur office asked to join the drafting classes. He did, moving from the position of janitor to junior drafter within six months. Everyone wanted to learn and do more, and many team members' skills surpassed my own as they became experts in their respective disciplines.

I personally wrestled to live out the honesty and humility I expected of my team. If I made a mistake, I chose to own it, publicly. I apologized to people every day, which made me into a humbler human as clients reprimanded, lectured, and at times, cheated me. Although I loved to win an argument, I knew it was better to shut up and take it.

I balanced my humility with blunt honesty, saying what I thought to clients and team members alike. If I was going to own my mistakes, others would also admit theirs and we would all learn together. Whether I was talking to a billionaire or a construction foreman, I always called out when something could be built faster or better. Most people appreciated my candor, but others refused to listen, and I was not afraid to let go of clients unwilling to salute our values.

Within a short amount of time, my reputation as CEO had become well-known in my industry; some people loved me, and others hated me. In any one day, I might receive a "Best Design Firm" award, an invitation to speak at a national conference, and a retaliatory lawsuit from a disgruntled architect or developer chastising me for challenging the status quo. Yet I woke energized every day and ready to inspire the team, persuade the doubters, and fight the critics.

I intended to disrupt the AEC world. In the past fifty years, the only things that had changed on the construction jobsite were that workers now wore hard hats and carried cell phones. Other than those advancements, the field had remained the same for a half century. To onlookers and professionals alike, construction persisted as the only business where innovation seemed unfeasible. I believed innovation was not only possible, but essential.

Our modernization efforts caught the eye of the industry. We won a contract to design a resort homestead for one of the top-ten wealthiest families in America. Although it was not our typical hospitality project, the 20,000 square-foot structure resembled a hotel more than a residence. Big wins like this catapulted Base4 to astronomical success and proved to everyone that our design processes worked—even for the most luxurious and highly scrutinized projects.

By 2016, I asked Jodi to join me at Base4 as Chief Leadership Officer and Executive Coach. With her PhD in Counselor Education and Supervision, she had just accepted a professorship at the online counseling program of a prestigious university. At the same time, my partners and I knew it was time to invest in leadership and human capital because Base4 had exploded—both in the number of projects and team members. At a partners' meeting in the summer of 2016, we decided to hire someone to train leaders and invest in our teams. Being engineers, we certainly were not equipped to nurture team members and listen to their needs. The day Jodi accepted her coveted teaching position, I presented her with a counter proposition: "Come work for Base4 instead!"

At first, she declined, nicely but firmly. It reminded me of her dismissal of my dating proposal two decades back. I pressed again, this time reminding her of our decision four years earlier to focus on making as much money as possible in order to do good. Even though becoming Base4's Chief Leadership Officer was not her dream job or even her chosen field, her leadership training could provide the professional development needed to advance the firm to the next level of financial success.

With our goals clarified and aligned, Jodi walked away from her university position, knowing the opportunity likely would never come again. In the "publish or perish" hierarchical culture of university-level professorship, timing and experience were vital, and she was leaving the race.

She chose to sacrifice her individual opportunity to build the firm with me and make as much money as possible to support our drive to accomplish good in the world. To her university colleagues, she looked foolish for rejecting the allure of higher education to join the evils and corruption of the corporate world. Yet like me, she also knew our professional lives did not really matter unless we could leverage what we had—and as much as we were able to get—to change lives.

At Base4, Jodi led the Leadership and Human Resources Department. Because traditional HR inevitably involved time-cards, rules, and compliance, I had never had an official HR division. I eschewed conventional models of compliance and team training, preferring to lead a flat organization marked by more aggressive training methods, global collaboration, and professional freedom.

Instead of timecards, we taught respect for one another. In place of gender equality and cultural awareness seminars, Jodi created individual training programs, coaching sessions, and data-driven assessments derived from the servant-leadership model. Where others used recruiting agencies and tactics that emphasized job security, we unleashed a unique talent management campaign that called applicants to professional development, values-based teamwork, and industry takeover.

Team members in the United States worked out of the comfort of their homes, connecting to one another via Skype, Bluebeam Live, and cloud-based file-sharing. In our foreign offices, the firm's values made Base4 one of the most coveted places to work. We had more applicants than we needed and higher levels of talent than we had ever imagined. Jodi's targeted training in human behavior and her servant leadership expertise empowered her to grow our team from sixty to three hundred incredibly caring, innovative, and passionate team members with offices in four countries and across the United States.

As the team grew, so did Base4. By 2017, we had several hundred team members in five countries and ranked as the twenty-fifth largest hospitality architectural firm in the world. This ranking was significant because we had started off as an engineering-only firm. Within thirty-six months of adding architecture to our practice, we had become one of the largest architectural firms in the industry.

■ ■ ■ ■

The explosive growth meant I had to visit my offices more often. Since Vijay's Nagpur office had the most people, it made sense— at least to me—to move my family to Nagpur for the summer of 2017. Living in the fourth-floor apartment above the office without a washer and dryer, oven, or elevator proved challenging for my family of eight. Jodi and I both worked at the office in the mornings, then Jodi took the kids to find food and essentials with a driver named Siddarth in the afternoons.

Too prideful to follow the map on Jodi's phone, Siddarth lost my family twice—once while traveling to the milk-and-eggs store and another time looking for the butcher. The roadside stand for fruits and vegetables luckily wasn't too far from our apartment, and Jodi could walk there with the children. Of course, washing and sanitizing these items in the kitchenette required extra hours of prep work, and I was often called in to fix the line of endless mishaps: "The sink is flooding!" "The power is out!" "The water is brown!" Focusing on work tasks became nearly impossible, and I was exhausted the entire summer.

During the weeknights, we would dodge the roaming live-stock and herds of motorbikes to take the kids to find adventure. Most of the time, we came up short. One evening, we tried the local playground because the number of people there suggested it might be fun. When we got to the edge, piles of fly-infested gar-bage caught our gaze first. Reviewing our options, Jodi gestured for Luxmi to avoid the torn scrap metal dumped dangerously close to the swings. I encouraged the children to try the plastic slide, which seemed much safer than the rusty jungle gym. Always ready to climb, William ran to the slide. Reaching the top in an instant, he discovered one dead rat and two rotting birds inside the domed landing, big eyes sprinting back to tell me. No one played that day.

Another late afternoon, we tried again—this time, the zoo. Warning signs to stay off the grass welcomed us and soon gave way to the barbed wire fencing that would be our guide. The sharp barrier framed the dirt pathways, designed to keep guests on the proper route to view the parade of grimy cages. We walked single file. The concerning conditions of the grounds reflected in the furrowed brows of my children, who expressed intense pity for the animals who had to live there. We left quickly, after seeing only a few tired farm animals, some lonely fish, and a collection of lizards.

Jodi and I attempted to make up for the experience with ice cream. On this humid summer night, the corner sweet shop drew in crowds of patrons as well as swarms of nipping flies, so many that the children threw down their cones to lure the stinging insects away from them. By the weekend, our exhaustion and frustration required a reprieve.

Every Friday night, we exited Nagpur to visit different parts of India for some much-needed R & R. We traveled to several tiger safaris and the beaches of Goa; we toured the historic treasures of New Delhi and royal city of Udaipur. Our days filled with spice-laden gourmet foods, animal expeditions (free of cages), and shell-filled beaches. We encountered the usual snakes and monkeys that typically complemented our South Asian exploits, but these were refreshing distractions from the quirky challenges of Nagpur living.

The days in India passed slowly for me. I did not sleep much, and the stress of my family's boredom and discomfort weighed on me. Nonetheless, we accomplished great work with the Base4 team. Jodi and I led workshops for the developing leadership group, and I sat next to Vijay every day to strategize next steps for the office. Numerous team members sought out Jodi. One young architect relayed the story of how she had been attacked on a train and had to throw her attacker off the moving car to survive. Filled with anxiety, she came to Jodi for coaching—more accurately described as much-needed counseling.

As we spent more time with our team, we learned that stories like hers were not uncommon. Our leadership coaching and presence among the group was important work. Still, I worried about Jodi, who tried to make life fun for the kids amid the chaos, commotion, and restrictions of daily life. Our twentieth anniversary was only a few days away, and I could not help but feel a bit guilty for the odd set of challenges we were facing.

One day, as we sat next to the full clothes lines adorning our living room and ate grilled cheese sandwiches, I apologized to my family for bringing us to India. Although the sights had been notable, so had the hardships. In response, my children laughed and proceeded to roast me. James and Garret mocked me for the time we dined with a team member whose family had fed me something so spicy-hot, I'd believed I was having a heart attack. Jolyn also joined in the teasing, retelling our six-hour journey to a tiger safari resort that had closed for monsoon season the week before we arrived. William, Shiya, and Luxmi reminisced about our joint disgust at the local masala-flavored pizza and spicy mac and cheese.

I sat looking at their smiles and hearing their jeers, fully impressed and relieved. My children—despite their own limitations and needs—understood how to embrace the messiness of our life. They discovered humor and comradery in our shared struggles. As their Dad, I beamed with unexpected pride.

Jodi and I celebrated our twentieth anniversary in my office building, surrounded by my six resilient children and one hundred of our fellow team members. Ambition, momentum, and the aromas of coriander and cumin filled the space. This would be the year my firm topped ten million dollars in sales. It would also be the year I realized I could give more.

∎ ∎ ∎ ∎ ∎

When we returned to Tennessee at the end of the summer, I didn't feel right. While I was glad to get some rest, I recognized the abundance of extra time in my schedule. No longer fixing broken appliances and rescuing my lost family from the streets of Nagpur, I worked and enjoyed my family with few interruptions. Jodi easily completed laundry and shopping in a fraction of the time it had taken back in India. I did not need to walk the groceries up four floors, retrieve the clothesline extending from our balcony, or shoo the cows from in front of the car. The extra time—and our wealth of resources—made me restless.

I thought through my options. I loved spending time with my family and winning in business, both of which I did every day. For hobbies, I used to enjoy skiing, motorcycle riding, flying, metal music, and jumping out of airplanes. Flying and parachuting were too risky for me now. As a father to six, I could not justify either flying a plane or jumping out of one.

I planned a ski trip with Adam, just the two of us for one week, staying at an extravagant slope-side resort in Vail. We skied in the morning on the back bowls, reveling in the frosty sunshine, and returned for lunch at the lodge overlooking the ridge. After late afternoon runs, I soaked in the tub, had a beer, and enjoyed steak dinners. It was a flawless trip—for the first three days.

By day four, I missed home—but worse than that, I grew bored. I had skied perfect trails in ideal weather in an idyllic location—and I was done. I told Jodi over the phone that I had an amazing time and never needed to ski again. This conclusion not only surprised me, it terrified me. Life no longer impressed or filled me. I wasn't unhappy, or even discontent, but I knew I had more to do.

Upon coming home, I considered buying a motorcycle and got my fill of metal music. I took in some concerts and joined a gym again. Jodi and I traveled to our school in Haiti and investigated additional needs in both our local and international circles. We volunteered to foster with the Tennessee Department of Children and Families, but they didn't allow fostering in any families that already had five or more children.

Other private agencies said the same. We could donate funds, but not be directly involved because we had too many children. *Directly involved* is how I operate, so I kept looking for the right fit. I didn't donate money; donating was easy. I wanted to be in the middle of the good work, using my time and money to motivate both myself and others to give our best.

A neighbor contacted Jodi about a Chinese orphan exchange program, whereby orphans came to live in the United States for two weeks to have the opportunity to meet their potential families in person. Prospective parents came to know them, and it inspired the adoption of hundreds of older children. We agreed to meet with a nine-year-old boy named Evan. He'd been staying an hour away in a small town west of Nashville.

On the night we drove to meet him, even James asked to come along. All eight of us ventured out to meet Evan at his small rural residence. His host family greeted us warmly while Evan hovered close, but distant enough to escape my high five. The exuberance of my children soon won him over. Within minutes, they were playing together on handheld games, communicating through gestures, and laughing amid the awkward newness of a first meeting. Jodi and I talked with the parents, who later recommended us to adopt him.

As we drove home that night along dark country roads, the

children chatted excitedly about their new brother. Even James wanted to adopt him. To them, it was that simple: Evan needed a home, and we liked him. The meeting changed their life—and Evan's. But not for the reason we thought.

Jodi and I began the arduous process of adoption, securing a contract with his placing agency. Within one week, however, the agency reported that he was not available for adoption. Unsure of what had transpired and unable to get any clear explanations, we now faced six children who eagerly anticipated Evan's arrival. I did not know what to say, just as I hadn't been able to rationalize the loss of Saimay. Both times my explanations fell short and felt deficient.

The children's faces dropped when I told them the news. James spoke up first: "What about another boy?" Because of how rarely James asked for anything, his request had the authority of prophecy. The other children quickly joined him in the appeal, and I realized our next move.

We started in China, placing inquiries about a little boy with a serious heart condition and researching his medical needs to understand the prognosis. We viewed dossiers of sibling groups in Hungary and inquired about the adoption processes in Russia, Haiti, Guatemala, and Uganda. We encountered the typical challenges: the heart condition was too serious for the child to move; Russia closed adoptions to Americans; Uganda demanded families relocate to Uganda for twelve months; Haiti didn't return phone calls. The shifting stipulations and lack of transparency exasperated Jodi's sense of injustice, making her more determined.

It didn't rattle me much, as I had learned to expect the ongoing procedural and regulatory excuses habitually made by countless nonprofits and government workers. After my firm found success, I increasingly recognized the pitfalls of the nonprofit world, where rules prevented many people from doing good.

Accomplishing change required more than submitting a dossier and a donation; it demanded full engagement in a frustrating and intimidating process. I needed to dive into the mess, walk with the hurting, question the stagnant policies, and rouse the right people. And I needed a ruthless business acumen to get it done. The more I tried to do good, in fact, the more I became a capitalist. I needed to be my best capitalist self to disrupt the impotent world of government agencies and well-meaning NGOs.

We chose Haiti. In my experience, nothing had transformed me or the lives of others more than adoption. I had been to Haiti enough to understand both the need and the barriers.

We delivered our translated dossier to the Institut du Bien-Être Social et de Recherches (IBESR), petitioning for any child or children aged four to fourteen, healthy or with specific special needs.

In a formal written response to our agency, IBESR told us to expect a delay of two to five years, and they placed us on their list. Considering the number of orphaned children there, the timetable didn't make sense, so I began to call and check, asking both the IBESR and my contacts in country. I also planned my visit.

At the same time, Jodi continued to show me pictures of other children. From our many failed attempts, she knew that successful adoptions were the exception. Every day she searched agencies, websites, and governmental blogs and news sources, in case Haiti rejected or postponed our appeals. A few months into the push, Jodi emailed me a forty-two–page monthly e-newsletter filled with photos of children from the Philippines. I knew nothing about Philippine adoptions, but it wasn't uncommon for Jodi to send me pictures, lists, and articles of various children in need.

I viewed the newsletter, deemed the "Special Findings" list, and marveled at the sheer number of children who were approved and waiting for families. Special needs toddlers, older children, and sibling groups filled the pages. Two boys on page thirty-two caught my eye. Their grinning faces reminded me of William's mischievous ways. We had hoped our next adoption could be a boy near his age, since Garret and James were nine and eleven years older than he. Jodi inquired about the boys via a phone call to the placing agency, only to receive a quick denial one week later. The social workers assigned to the boys' case refused our inquiry because of our family's size. Since orphans lived in group homes among hundreds of other children, I wondered how a family of six children could seem "too large."

One month later, we were on a flight to Haiti—not to complete our adoption, but to drive the process. On the plane, Jodi passed the time by scrolling through the same forty-two–page list, which she had saved in her inbox. I knew the pictures and stories of the children inspired her to hope.

"Look at these children!" she said casually, showing me a picture of six Filipino children standing under a fake tree. "These children are on the 'Special Findings' list, even though they have no special needs," Jodi explained. "Their 'special need' is that there are six of them."

I pulled her hand close to me to bring the phone nearer to my face. Six beautiful faces stared back at me. The younger three smiled playfully while the older ones smirked out of obligation. Under the picture, a caption read "Perez Siblings."

No one wants six. *Six is crazy,* I thought to myself, but I didn't say so out loud. People didn't want six because of the excessive

cost of time, money, and effort. I knew because I was already doing it. Six was hard.

But six was also wonderful. I recalled my boredom and
restlessness, then assessed my wealth and time. I had more to
give—a lot more. I thought about the past decade of striving for
success while struggling mightily to do good. I considered the
many doors that had closed in our faces—even the resistance we
now confronted in Haiti. By the time the plane landed in Port-
Au-Prince, my reflections had become a call to action: *Go get the
six-pack.*

CHAPTER TWENTY

Stonepile

GARRET

Winter 2017

"This house makes me sad," Mom says from the middle of an empty living room. Her face doesn't look sad to me. I am fifteen now, and I know what lines between the eyebrows mean: *stressed out*. I glance around the room, and I like the size. It has four floors, eight bedrooms, a pool, and twenty-two acres. Dad doesn't say anything, but he likes the house too—he's always wanted to own a home in the woods. Living unnoticed with no visible neighbors or people excites me. *No more bullies*—a definite advantage.

I start my tour in the basement and begin to understand Mom's remark. The back stairs leading from the basement to the main-floor kitchen creak, and the tiles are missing, revealing the black grime on the concrete floor underneath. The brass and white kitchen lights clash with the silver metals on the knobs and faucets. One of the kitchen walls is poop-colored brown, the same dark shade of the heavy velvet drapes that adorn most of the windows. All these colors and fabrics undermine the intent of the orange Spanish tile. In the center of the room hangs a crooked tan ceiling fan, spinning, as visible flecks of dust soar across the space in the wake of its wind. The kitchen stove is disconnected from the wall, its vent permanently stuck open, and the sink, which used to be white, is now cracked and stained several shades of grayish black. The smell drives me into the next room.

The bannister of the back stairwell lies on the steps, which used to have carpet but are now only covered with plywood and staples. The second and third floor bedrooms are large, which is their best quality. Their stained carpets smell like cats and crunch when you walk on them because dried bugs had gotten stuck in the fibers. Numerous loose wires collect in heaps where the floor and walls meet. Most rooms have at least one unhinged closet door, and the cool spring breeze whistles through several broken windows. In some places, it's hard to see due to broken or missing ceiling lights.

Back on the main floor are an unusually large number of mirrors, especially in the master bedroom and the formal living room. Both of those rooms also have ornate fireplaces that now appear grotesque with their mantels and frames covered by the same unfortunate poop-colored brown. Like other items in this house, they are a regrettable legacy of what used to be a magnificent home.

Overwhelmed by the odors and the dust, I open the double doors to the front porch and step into the fresh air. The view of Middle Tennessee's rolling hills from this high perch renews my optimism about the house—until I look down to see the crumbling front stairs. I counted twenty-eight brick steps, stacked and separated from the side of the structure. Seeing me examine the gap, Dad quickly explains: the original builders did not extend the concrete footing to the stairs, and the weight of the bricks pulled on the house.

The whole front section of the house dropped two inches and sloped the main floor down toward the stairs. Fascinated by the design flaw, I go back inside and walk from the back of the house to the front, using the slanted floor to propel me forward, in jest and for the benefit of my now amused parents.

The walkaround leads me outside where I find Jolyn critiquing the leaking pool. It has an exposed concrete floor, dead leaves, muddy water, and a large toad. When Jolyn screams about the toad, William and Luxmi run to capture it. The entire lawn seems to have been unkept for years. Trees, grasses, underbrush, thorns, and bushes overgrow every corner of the lot. Shiya does not even venture outside, preferring to sit on the only beautiful space in the house—the steps of the grand double-spiral staircase.

Although the home sits high on the property, it is impossible to see from the house to the entryway gate. Too many tall trees—rotting, dead, and leaning—block the view. Whether it's the driveway, the back patio, or the brick façade, most of the exterior has sections of missing stones and bricks, either cracked or crumbling. And that's what we can see. What we can't see, my dad reads from the realtor's listing sheet: termite damage and mold.

I'm not so sure about this house after all, I decide and head to the car where James reclines playing with his iPad. I join him, waiting for my parents to come to the same conclusion. They did, and we spent the next three months looking for just the right house.

More than any other parameter, our home must have lots of sleeping spaces. We look at every house in the county big enough for a family of fourteen and far enough away from neighbors to avoid judgment. We tour horse farms, homes on pastureland, large properties wedged in country-club neighborhoods—all of them costing at least a million dollars. "When did we get rich?" I wonder out loud. "And why don't we have nicer stuff?" I joke in Dad's direction.

Obviously, we need a sizable house for our large crew, but we also need to be near schools, therapists, and food stores. And Mom asked to avoid HOAs, if possible. It's not that my mom doesn't like people, but—to be honest—our neighbors don't enjoy us very much.

Except Al's family. We moved next door to Al when we relocated to Tennessee. Al is just like me; except he does way better in school. Al and I speak the same language, assume similar nerdy identities, and stand fully capable of solving the world's problems together. He gets me like no one else: we game online, discuss politics, debate religion, play D&D, read manga, eat pizza, and pace around the house while talking incessantly. Our parents make fun of us, but we don't care.

Al and his family are our favorite neighbors of all time, and Al is my first Tennessee friend. In fact, we told Al's family about the new siblings before anyone else, even before we told the grandparents. My parents delayed telling our extended family until the adoption was approved. No sense freaking everyone out should it fail. At first, Al and his family did not believe us, until Dad showed them the picture.

I have seen too many incomplete adoptions, and I hoped this one would happen. The idea of doubling our kid count would be a great story I could tell. Also, if any children ever needed help, these were surely the ones. Dad held a family vote a few months ago, explaining how the kids almost died from TB, dysentery, and neglect, and describing our opportunity to adopt them. He also explained that adopting six meant more chaos, additional challenges, and extra love.

I also anticipated more noise, lots of extra words, and many intrusions into my stubbornly autistic world. But I didn't feel itchy or nervous about it. I was sure. It was a unanimous "yes" vote among the original six of us. My only comment at dinner that night: "How could we say 'no'? This is a no-brainer." Everyone else agreed, especially Jolyn with her big smile and endless commentary.

In expectation of doubling our kid count, Mom sought lots of advice from big-family blogs. The most radical idea she adopted is the notion of the "Family Laundry Room." This special room houses our clothing in cubbies or shelves, one for each family member's stuff. Nothing leaves the room unless it is being worn, which eliminates the need to put clothes away. I like this idea because I hate putting my things away.

Along with these new ideas about raising a big family came the endless paperwork: home study reports, immigration applications, and psychological and physical health screenings. The social worker interviewed James, Jolyn, and me, and we had to take pictures of our eventual house to prove we had enough room. To me, this adoption process resembled all the other ones, but not to Mom. She seemed to research and prepare more than ever before, still looking for the perfect house to nurture a family of fourteen.

Then one day, it happened. "I bought it!" Dad informed Mom one weekday afternoon. Doing online school at home meant Jolyn and I heard all the news in real time.

"Bought what?" she asked.

"I bought the first house," he responded.

"The one that's falling down?" asked mom, more calmly than I would have thought.

"Yup, I got a good price, and I went for it."

Dad often made life decisions without fully consulting Mom. We all came to expect it, and in the end, it usually worked out. My parents both moved fast, but they moved differently. Where Dad was hyper and, at times, offensive, Mom was calm and wise. When Mom became sad or afraid, Dad showed courage and confidence. They talked about everything, and they both chose to spend time with each other and us over anyone else. That was good, because with 11,000 square feet to renovate, we would be seeing a lot of each other. And we did.

Over the course of six months, we often drove to the house to work alongside flooring specialists, plumbers, HVAC technicians, sewage consultants, foresters, pool renovators, window installers, painters, electricians, and contractors. My parents named our house "Stonepile Manor" after the Old Testament story of the courageous men and women who crossed the Jordan River into the Promised Land, picking up twelve stones as they went, to keep as a reminder of the power of God.

My parents even made a sign that they fastened to a flat boulder that was pulled out of the ground by a local forester: *Stonepile Manor. Est. 2017* to commemorate the lives of twelve children and remind generations to come of what happens here. The name seemed a bit too assertive and hopeful to me.

We moved the week of Thanksgiving into a mostly functional household, except for not having internet. We had to purchase several cell phones and use mobile hot spots to access it. I freaked out a bit at the thought of my internet access being interrupted. After all, my games and schooling required it. Dad seemed to have it under control, but still, you never know. On moving day, Dad declared with fatigue and excitement, "I'll never move again!" Of course, none of us believed him.

Now in, the house remains a full-time chore. It takes six more months before we get the internet lines extended from the town, to our road, and into our property. For the excessive cost of $30,000, we laid down the infrastructure for highspeed internet, which Dad required to run his business. Expenses like these made me nervous, and I hoped we wouldn't run out of money. Twelve is a lot of children, and how would we afford food, toys, and school for everyone, not to mention the cost of the fifteen-seat passenger van?

Dad assured me he had it covered, but I still worried because we didn't seem like people who had a lot of money. Mom wouldn't even buy Dad's favorite cereal unless it was a BOGO; "I'm not spending $4.50 on a box of cereal" is all she would say. None of us had fancy clothes, nor did we need them. We each had three pairs of shoes: sneakers, church shoes, and water shoes. We drove a Kia or a Ford and stayed home for almost every meal. When we did buy something special, like my Nintendo Switch, we saved for it, and Mom usually found a sale.

After fifteen years in this family, I still don't fully understand our fiscal habits, but I've begun to appreciate the results. My parents are not afraid to spend money if it means doing something big and important in the world, and they work hard to earn it. At the same time, they never budget significant resources to any cause or item they don't believe will make our world better. They remain generous but intentional, rich but frugal, and fearless but deliberate. They love capitalism and compassion, and no one tells them what to do, even though they willingly place themselves in terrible places and risky situations.

By the New Year, I expected them to travel to another terrible place to pick up my brothers and sisters, but that didn't happen, of course. This time, the delay wasn't paperwork mishaps, or an unjust judge: the agency called my mom to inform us that two of the six children tested positive for TB and weren't allowed to enter the United States. Since they had been treated for TB in 2013, Mom knew the shadows shown on Zoe's and Andrew's chest X-rays were likely only scar tissue or a mistake. But the approving physician held back all six visas. Pushing hard against the agency, Mom got four of the six children approval to leave, but the doctor said Zoe and Andrew would have to stay behind.

Obviously, these people didn't know my parents. The day they heard the news, my parents sat in my dad's office and met as if they were in the war room, strategizing and researching a way to bring home all six. I didn't dare interrupt them. When they emerged, they immediately got to work.

Mom contacted the Center for Disease Control and Prevention (CDC), and Dad called his old friend from New York who worked at the US State Department. In between working, schooling, and shuffling us to our many appointments, my parents made calls throughout the day, every day for two weeks. Whether waiting for James at the tutoring center or at the doctor's office for Shiya, sitting at the back of my 4-H meeting or hiking through our property, Mom and Dad kept watchful eyes on their phones to ensure that no questions or updates were missed or postponed. By the end of two weeks, Dad had found an attentive diplomat at the US Embassy in Manila, and Mom had talked to the TB specialist at the CDC; both worked together on our case, giving us some hope.

During this waiting period, I began to get those itchy and hot sensations on my head and arms more often than usual. Since moving to Tennessee, I had done much better with keeping calm. The online school worked for me. I still got belligerent when Mom made me do the "suggested practice problems," but I controlled myself most of the time.

Now, I felt unsettled by living in this huge house meant for six more people who might not ever get here. In the family laundry room, there were sets of superhero underwear, rows of light-up sneakers, and a labeled shelf for each new sibling, reminding me they weren't where they were supposed to be. Six empty beds, made up perfectly, sat in the bedrooms waiting for little sleepers who have not come. Our custom-made 160-square-foot dinner table remained half empty, and dinnertime felt ridiculous. I could barely see my dad across the table from where I sat.

Everything is so big. The table, the house, the fifteen-passenger van, the twenty-two acres—everything points to missing people, waiting children, and empty spaces. Often, I just hide away in my room playing video games or reading, getting lost in fantasy worlds and pretending not to care. But I do care. I really do.

PART VI

ADOPTABLE

Not Yet

ANGELA

Life feels so big. The children, the noise, the loneliness; everything reminds me I'm a missing person, a waiting child, an empty space. Often, I just hide away in my room, playing card games or reading, getting lost in fantasy worlds and pretending not to care. But I do care. I really do.

It has been five years since the police brought us to Open Arms. I don't remember much before coming here. Sometimes memories come out as bad dreams or angry fits that throw me to the ground for hours, leaving me exhausted, confused, and alone. I cannot make out the memories in my mind.

Rogie tells me stories of our bad mom, terrible men, and being hurt, and I pretend to know. The feelings are stronger than the memories, and I feel like I'm locked in a dark closet at the bottom of a deep, black pit. I am lost and no one can find me. *It's not your fault* is a phrase I hear from the workers, along with *you are loved* and *you are special*. But I don't agree. I think their faith hides the truth.

I can read well now, and I have seen all the papers. Little by little, our file grows. "The Perez Siblings" have updated medical papers, doctors' notes, growth reports, and new birth records with names. Counselors, social workers, and teachers have all written down their comments, most which say something like, "Angela is learning to talk about how she feels and can calm down after breaks. She can read and likes to help around the house. Any family who adopts her should have experience with trauma." I am not positive what "trauma" means, but I don't think it's good.

With these documents, we wait on the list to be adopted. Mom Sharon asks everyone who comes here to tell others about our story and to help us find a family. Every time guests visit, I overhear the social workers who admit they don't think anyone will adopt all six of us.

I sneak around the orphanage and hear all kinds of discussions. They are not always about us, but when they are, they end with this statement: "We'll pray for a family to come forward for them!" But I don't need prayers.

I used to feel mad and sad when others left with their families, but I am used to it now. My younger brothers and sister still talk about getting a family, but not me or Rogie. I am ten years old now, and I can do a lot of things. I'm good at cooking and cleaning, and Rogie's the smartest one here. Even though he doesn't spend much time with me, I watch him talking with the older boys, learning their ways or tricking the younger ones into giving him their extra treats or toys. He's not waiting for a family either, and we are safe here. No one hurts me anymore, and I know better than to trust anyone.

Zoe and Andrew trust everyone, and they smile and laugh easily. Everyone who visits gives them special attention, and even the workers dote on them. Zoe always leaves her mess for me to clean up when there's something more fun for her to do. And Andrew runs around playing with anyone in sight, forgetting his shoes and shirt for me to find later. I do all the work. It's not fair, so when trouble comes, I usually blame one of them. They deserve it.

Edward and Robert are more serious than Zoe and Andrew, so I spend more time with them. Edward tries to be like Rogie, but Rogie doesn't want to be around him. Edward and I try to play with Robert, who stays alone a lot, wandering around aimlessly. Being only six, he doesn't have much to do except draw, which he does a lot—unless he's making fun of Zoe who loves to mess up his artwork and ruffle his neatly kept things.

In the past two weeks, we have seen each other a lot more, going to extra doctor's appointments. We even visited the passport office to get our pictures taken, which took all day. Mom Sharon promised to take us to McDonald's afterward, so we tried harder to listen. Of course, Zoe and Andrew did not obey and ran around the office, talking to the people and trying to steal pens from the desk cubbies. When I heard that Zoe and Andrew had additional trips to the doctors, I felt glad inside. They probably did not listen to the doctor and had to redo their x-rays. They deserved that, too.

"What did you do at the doctor's?" I asked Mom Sharon that night.

"Just a check-up," is all she said, but I knew there was more.

I know when Mom Sharon feels worried because her eyes squint small and she moves more quickly around the house. She also makes a lot of phone calls and stays in her office too long. Mom Sharon usually tells me what's happening, so it's strange that she didn't answer my question. That night, I lie in bed, unable to sleep. As is my custom when I feel bad, I sneak down to the kitchen to steal some noodles.

When I finish, I tiptoe back upstairs, but this time, I turn into Mom Sharon's office on the second floor rather than going back to my room. I look on her desk for new papers, or any other notes I might be able to read and understand. There are many documents from ICAB and several reports from the social worker, but I do not find anything that I have not seen before.

As I'm getting ready to leave her office, I spot the wide, brown bag that Mom Sharon carries to town. Inside at the bottom, I spy several identically sized picture books that are wrapped up together in clear plastic, which I quickly unwrap. On their covers, each book shows a picture of a large brick house sitting on a hill. It looks beautiful and far away. Opening one of the books, I view each of the pages, which are filled with pictures of white people, Chinese people, Indian people, and old people, each with inscriptions underneath that say names and roles like "sister," "brother," and "grandparents." It was a weird group of people, and the house looked way too clean.

Children who are lucky enough to get a family also get a picture book. The books come many months before the children get to have them because adoptions don't always work out. I have seen Mom Sharon throw out books when families changed their minds or got turned away. They are filled with pictures of parents who were expecting to meet their children, only to be informed that they were rejected. Many families don't pass the test. Sometimes ICAB found problems with them, and other times the kids got sick.

I am not sure how long these books have been tucked away in

the brown bag, but I do notice that there are many of them. I start counting, one, two, three…and, yes, I count six books. Six family books for six children. Six! Only the Perez Siblings are six. *Can it be?* I study the books, checking whether they each hold pictures of the same odd family members. They do.

Someone has hand painted names on the top of each book. The silver ink is hardly visible in the dark office, and I almost can't make out the letters. I stare for many moments, until I can finally make them out: "ZOE" says the first in careful handwriting. "ROGIE NINO." And then I read mine, "ANGELA," written in fancy letters with pretty loops. Someone—somewhere—has written these letters for me. My cheeks feel hot, and my heart beats faster. *Someone is coming for me.*

Days pass by, and I wait but hear no news. I might burst trying to keep the picture books a secret. Each day, I wake up early and hope it is the day for the big announcement celebrating that a family is coming for us. *What's happening?* I put on my mean face more than usual and try to get some attention and news. Mom Sharon tells me nothing, and I shoot my angry eyes at anyone who gets in my space.

Late one night, I hear her talking on her phone to a nurse about x-rays. I listen closer when I hear her say Zoe's and Andrew's names. She's arguing with the nurse about some tests, and I suddenly recall how those two had visited the doctors over and over again. My chest tightens and I cannot breathe, knowing the awful truth that I've seen too many times before: Zoe and Andrew are sick with something bad. With them too sick to travel, we've all become "unadoptable."

CHAPTER TWENTY-ONE

Too Old to Die Young

Jodi

Fall 2017

Dying before forty is dying young. I watch the lady across from me who has lost her hair as I await my own lab results, alone. She cannot be older than thirty-five, and she is lovely. It wasn't Garry's plan to be out of town during my testing, but he was due to speak at a conference, so he was gone these three days. Plus, it might be nothing.

Since trying to conceive Jolyn, I have known my hormonal system was unbalanced. For years, I experienced the well-known yet under-researched physical dilemma of being female. In addition to my body's occasional warning signs, I understood my mother's history, the trifecta of female cancers—first breast, then uterine and ovarian—and the sequelae of their effects that ended her life too soon. As my physical problems exacerbated this past year, I took note. So did my doctor, who sent me for additional scans, ultrasounds, and tests.

Sitting in the office, bored and anxious, I exchange knowing smiles with the young woman across from me. *If I die now,* I decide, *I'm way past dying young.* I'm forty-five years old, and it hits me: *I'm too old to die young, and too young to die.* These are the peculiar reflections of an uneasy woman left alone in a doctor's waiting room. Thankfully, I am called in soon after.

The gynecological oncologist is tall and probably about my age. Her words are few and her stance strong. She grabs the intake form from the dutiful nurse next to her and reviews a few questions with me. Then she evaluates the results and symptoms: large growths, plummeting hormonal levels, and a recent history of bleeding and pain. She says, simply, "You're a ticking time bomb."

Briefly reviewing the history of myself, my mother, and my grandmother, she recommends I skip any additional diagnostic procedures and undergo a complete hysterectomy, immediately. I had received other opinions and done all the research. Whether or not I have cancer now, I am certain to get it soon.

I think about my husband and children. If I do not have cancer, I can reduce the odds of my getting it by removing the potentially dangerous parts. If I have it already, I need to cut out the malignancy quickly to increase my chances of staying alive.

Unfortunately for us, the timing of a potential cancer diagnosis impacts more than my life and future; it would forever alter the lives of the six children waiting for us in the Philippines. If it is cancer, the adoption stops. Both the agencies and social workers do not recommend unwell parents to adopt. Garry and I are in the middle of an adoption battle, pressing the CDC and authorities to clear the Perez siblings. The timing couldn't be worse.

"Cancer or not," I tell the doctor, "let's take out everything."

I call Garry to tell him the seriousness of the findings and my decision. He trusts my judgment, and I have no doubt about choosing the most radical course. The timing is critical. The oncologist only has one opening for the rest of the year, and it was for Friday morning. With the adoption and my health pending, I agree.

It is Wednesday, and Friday arrives before Garry reaches home. He struggled to get the earliest morning flight to return in time; however, a last-minute cancellation moved me up to the first surgery slot of the morning.

Because Garry is not yet here, my sister picks me up at 4:00 a.m. to drive me to the hospital while Tina stays with my sleeping kids. During the car ride, thoughts of my waiting children flip through my mind. *They don't even know I'm coming for them.* I recall their little faces from their photograph and imagine them waiting for their family to come. But it's hard to stay quiet, especially when the tears begin to swell. I shouldn't share my thoughts with my sister since we are not yet approved, and the adoption remains in serious jeopardy. I say a silent prayer that I will be able to bring them home.

Thinking of the children occupies my mind during the long car ride, keeping my own fears at bay. Still, I feel out of place without Garry here with me, especially as I sign the intake forms and consents. He might not make it in time.

After registration, the nurses take me to a small presurgical room and give me my hospital gown. I shed my clothes—along with all sense of independence—and put on the striped blue robe.

It's cold in here, and my stomach growls for breakfast. Sitting on the bed, waiting for my surgery, and watching the clock, I look for text messages from Garry. Nothing. My sister tries to keep me preoccupied, distracting me with fun facts about the latest stars in country music. Numerous nurses and doctors come to check on me while I continue to check my phone.

As a first for me, the doctor is running early. She comes in fresh and fast to ask me if I have any questions, which I don't, and tells me she will see me in surgery. Glancing at my sister, the surgeon announces that she will send updates if anything goes wrong. A line of different nurses follows her in to give me pills and a few shots in my abdomen. A noticeably young anesthesiologist reconfirms my bracelet, checks for allergies, and begins the sedation process.

I check my phone one last time prior to receiving my IV; Garry still has not landed. Lying down flat on the gurney, I begin an unusually long hallway ride to the surgical room. As I wheel away from my sister, I think about my family, husband, and children, and a small tear rolls down onto the sanitized pillow. It is not sadness, but fear mixed with an awed sense of peace. *I have lived and loved at high speed and full volume, and I have no regrets.*

In my life, I have been called nice and naïve at best, but also foolish and misguided. Condescension lingers in the remarks. Although people wonder about me and ask, they often dismiss me as a do-gooder—someone to be appreciated, maybe, but not taken seriously. Many laugh off discussions about child trafficking and poverty, visibly discomforted and desperate to change topics.

Others tease me for waking up too early—4:15 a.m., even on Saturdays because I can't wait to get the day started. They tell me to "sleep in," "sit down," or "take a day off," as if life doesn't deserve that much effort.

Garry and I have dared much and—with that bold risk—earned the skepticism of many. We have pursued life to its maximum capacity, working fast, pushing hard, and talking loudly. The intensity does not go unnoticed. Christians remind me about God's grace, and everyone else tells me to slow down and enjoy life.

They are right in some ways; still, as I wheel down the hall to surgery, my life's choices make more sense than ever before. I have pressed on, pursued the impossible, and left it all on the field—decisions that never seemed righter. *No regrets here!* I affirm, beginning to count backward at the anesthesiologist's instructions.

When I wake in the recovery area, I am overcome with pain and take only shallow breaths. It takes a few moments for anyone to notice I am waking, and I can't get their attention. "I hurt," I push out in a whisper, but the nurses can't hear me. "I hurt!" I say louder. The nurse comes to me with pills and a small cup of water, but I cannot sit up. The man next to me pushes the button on his morphine pump, but when I reach for mine, I realize I didn't get one.

My belly feels on fire, my body puffed out and aching. Blood seeps out like after childbirth, and I find it difficult to get enough air. After several tries, I can lean on my left side and gulp down the pills.

After some time, but not enough, the nurses wheel me from the recovery area back to a room, informing me that both Nancy and Garry are waiting outside. The news of Garry's arrival boosts my spirits for a moment, but the unrelenting physical pain so unnerves me that I ask to stay alone, powerless to focus on anything else other than the burning sensation across my midsection. After many more minutes, deep breathing, and a heating pad across my belly, I begin to regain myself.

Before I can ask for my family, my sister explodes into the room. "You're cancer-free, Jod'! They didn't find anything!"

Tweaking her announcement, the nurse quickly adds, "Of course, we won't know until we hear from pathology, but the doctor found no visible cancer."

When I hear the news, I erupt, crying so intensely that I shock even myself, which triggers my stomach to tighten with a flow of stabbing vibrations. Garry comes to sit by me on the bed, smiling big and wondering at my tears.

"Now we can adopt the kids," I whisper as I weep uncontrollably, surrendering to the pain triggered by the cathartic blast of emotion.

It wrecks me—how close I came to losing them. James, Garret, Jolyn, Shiya, Luxmi, William, Rogie, Angela, Edward, Andrew, Robert, and Zoe are my twelve reasons for having chosen this radical surgical choice. Being and staying cancer-free was the critical component for completing my mission of rescuing and raising our kids. The sanctity of that purpose—and the dread of not accomplishing it—provoked an assault of tears. But now, the path before me lies clear, and—except for the CDC—I am going to get my kids.

CHAPTER TWENTY-TWO

The Six Pack

GARRY

Spring 2018

"If I ran my business this way, I'd be bankrupt!" I said as kindly as possible to our case worker. After several months of working with the CDC and State Department, it was our adoption agency that refused to join us in the fight. When they would not petition ICAB to move up our case, I lost it. The case worker on the other end of the phone obviously didn't like my response, as she defended both herself and her agency for several minutes afterwards.

It is true. For-profit companies expect their clients to inform and improve business strategies with their many comments and criticisms. Successful companies figure out ways to meet client demands, or they close—both of which I have done. In nonprofit land, the typical do-good corporations react to criticism with a friendly, but cowardly "I'm sorry you feel that way, but…" That is okay if you're donating to the Arbor Day Foundation and waiting on trees—which we do. It is *not* okay when it's children wondering if anyone is coming for them.

It had been more than a year since we began pursuing the Perez siblings. I had contacted the CDC and gotten confirmation that specialists would follow the children's cases in the United States, but ICAB did not care. Via our case worker, the doctor in the Philippines clarified that the agencies on both ends of the adoption would not budge on their protocols. They required six more months to re-run the TB test before they would issue exit visas.

"If my children don't get cleared in one week," I told her, "Jodi and I are flying over to meet our children and talk to the authorities ourselves."

The formal guardianship paperwork had already been signed, and nothing in the law said we could not be with our children. It was not my preferred idea to live in the Philippines and wait there for them, but we refused to wait around any longer.

Three days later, we received clearance from ICAB to pick up our children under the guidance of the CDC. Their quick turn-around shocked everyone, even our case worker who congratulated us on doing what never had been done before. The CDC, my contact in the State Department, and our threats to come uninvited had prompted their immediate change of mind. Within the month, Jodi and I began the twenty-four–hour trip to the Philippines.

Arriving on a Saturday morning, we rush to find the orphanage, using Grab, the local Uber. The short trip takes some time as we find ourselves wrapped in Manila's stand-still traffic, finally leaving the highway after thirty slow minutes and entering a smaller neighborhood overflowing with tiny shops, roaming chickens, and whizzing bicycles.

When the car slows to a stop, people surround us, bumping the sides with their elbows and bags. The odors, crowding, and garbage do not bother me—it's nothing compared to the masses in Mumbai or the stench of burning tires I had experienced in Port-au-Prince. Although I never have been to the Philippines before, I feel comfortable in this environment.

As we drive, my breathing quickens, as I think of the children I am about to meet. Jodi taps her hands on her knees, sitting forward and searching the street signs. "Our children come from District III, which should be that direction."

Craning our necks to peek down the side road, we barely make out a blackish waterway in the distance. "There's the river," Jodi says as she compares the street signs to the map on her phone, but I know we can't be sure. Much of the area looks the same, with canals and unmarked streets all strikingly similar. Faces, too, seem to blend into the afternoon commotion.

"This is the street," says our driver, pulling into a narrow way crammed with small cars and motorbikes. Checking the address, we spy in the near distance a small white sign attached to what looks like a four-story Manhattan walk-up, only the plaster's painted pink. I pay the man, and we make our way to the entrance of the building. The thought consumes me: *Life as I know it is over.*

It jolts even me: I am now the father of a dozen children. In the struggle and fight to adopt them, I almost forgot that the children are real and coming home with us. Today they become our responsibility. Everything that has led to this moment—the searches, rejections, social workers, doctors, paperwork, surgery, house, van, interrogations, pushback, and $40,000 in adoption and travel fees—are complete. Today the hard part begins.

We know what we are getting. In previous email exchanges,

the orphanage director had described the unusual and difficult behaviors of our traumatized bunch. She admitted that some of our children lived with her because no other person in the orphanage would watch them. They outsmarted all their caretakers, and every babysitter quit with tears and complaints. Several other adoptive parents had met our children when they traveled to pick up their own. They had heard that a family was coming for six Perez siblings and called to bid us a friendly, "Good luck," followed by "you're going to need it!"

The entryway of the building is crowded with people, mostly teenagers and older children hanging on the stoop, talking to one another in a dialect—Tagalog, I presume. A larger man, about twenty, stands up to greet us in English.

"Who do you want?" It is the most informal greeting to an adoption procedure I have ever received.

"We are here for the Perez Siblings," is all I say.

Jodi smiles politely, then we glance at each other as if to question whether they know we are coming. We follow the man through the heavy red door into the building where fifteen small people greet us with hugs and loudly ask our names. Nudging our way through the gathering, we walk down a long hallway toward a bright-blue, painted stairwell. Speakers play contemporary Christian music as children crawl, run, and climb everywhere.

Down the corridor is an enormous cooking area, a patio play area, and rows of rooms filled with bunk beds. Other smaller children come to their doorways to peer at us, the new visitors at Open Arms. Before we reach the kitchen or patio, we turn left and follow the man upstairs, past several old plates of food sitting on the floor, articles of clothing that have been dropped in corners, and signs that read, *You are loved, You are wanted, You are safe here.*

At the top of the stairs are several more rooms, one of which says, "Adoption Suite." He leads us there so we can put down our bags and tells us to wait. Many children sneak looks at us and run away giggling and whispering. I cannot understand much of their language, which sounds like a mixture of English slang and Tagalog. We sit on the bed and wait, listening to the sounds of scuffling feet and motorbike horns. After about five minutes, a tall girl with a video camera shines the record light at us as she enters our room. Behind her is a line of children. I study the little faces coming at me and recognize my own! Their haircuts are different from the pictures, but their eyes and smiles are the same.

Before we can match each face with a name, several small ones jump into our laps, giving hugs and touching our hair and faces. "This is Mom and Dad!" cries Sharon, in a voice that's half command and half announcement. "This is Rogie and Angela," she introduces us to the older two, who offer shy smiles in our direction. "This is Edward," she points to a boy who shakes my hand and looks me straight in the eye without saying anything. "The ones hugging you now are Andrew, Robert, and Zoe," Sharon finishes.

Andrew lets go impulsively but then begins shouting something unintelligible. His voice booms, and his wide grin takes up his whole face. Robert and Zoe refuse to let go of me as I stand to embrace the others. Rogie offers me a quick hug as he stares at the ground. Jodi crouches down to meet the children and embraces them one by one. I am less careful, picking up the little ones and tossing them into the air. Everyone eventually joins in the nervous laughter and group hug, except Angela, who leans on the wall by the door, several feet out of reach.

PART VII

THE DOZEN

I Belong

Angela

MAY 19, 2018

The common room of Open Arms fills with the normal number of kids, but tonight it's just too many. A new child named Felix sits half on my lap, half on the wooden bench where we bunch. It's the goodbye celebration for another toddler—a girl they named Joelle. Her family seems nice enough, but I have nothing to say. The sweet coconut cookies we eat fall apart in the humid air, and the warmth of the crowded room makes it hard to breathe.

"As we wish Joelle goodbye with her family, we have something else to celebrate," Mom Sharon announces. She has a twinkle in her eyes I haven't seen for some time. From behind her back I see her holding a pile of small books. Bringing them forward, she declares it's true: "A family is on its way for Rogie, Angela, Edward, Andrew, Robert, and Zoe."

The children erupt into clapping and loud chatter as Mom Sharon passes each one of us our special family book, the ones I had seen months ago in her office. Until this moment, I never had believed we would become adoptable.

I want to shout out something happy, but my throat tightens as the other kids turn to look at me. I sit still, hands sweating as they cling to the photo book. Felix nudges me to open it, but I have already seen all the pictures.

"They're coming?" My words are soft, and Mom Sharon walks over to hug me. Zoe and Robert also doubt: "Are they real?"

Andrew and Edward have begun to dance around, sharing the photo books with their bunkmates. Off in the corner, Rogie thumbs through his book, studying the pages as if they are homework. He is quiet but smiling. Then a small voice in my head speaks, *It's my turn.*

For the next few days, I questioned Mom Sharon so often that she tries to avoid me. "Why are there so many of them? Where do they live? Why do they look so different from each other? When are they coming?"

She dodged most of my questions in the hustle of her day, only answering the last one: "They come this week!"

My family was coming for us fast. Usually parents don't travel for some time after the books. Our family arrives this weekend—and already it's Friday.

Zoe, Robert, and Edward start asking me too many questions, and I don't know the answers this time. Andrew and Rogie joke with their friends, doing as they have always done, playing basketball on the fifth-floor roof and running to find other children to bother. Their steps and words take on a quicker pace than usual, and I can feel their excitement. At Mom Sharon's request, we search Open Arms for the items we want to pack and a few small gifts from her: a charm, a Bible, and toy *turumpos*. I know she will miss us.

Saturday morning, we wake early, dress in our cleanest shirts and pants, and wait. We wander and play, until it's past lunch. "Where are they?" we ask Mom Sharon—pestering her until she sends us to her apartment.

Hours pass, and I begin to doubt again: *Are they late? Or not coming at all? Did they die on the plane?* Too many thoughts, I push them all away.

"They are coming," I persuade Zoe and Robert, but mostly I try to convince myself. "I'm sure they will be here soon."

And they are. From the fourth-floor window, I watch a strange car stop near our building. Two tall people—a man a woman—quickly shut the door and cross the street. *Mom and Dad!* I yell to my brothers and sister in the next room, pushing them to line up on the stairs heading to the adoption suite, as we had planned. Rogie and I slip into our places at the back, just as images begin to flash in my mind. My steps become slower as we make our way down, and the familiar stairwell feels strangely different. I see scenes from the *estero* and twisted mean faces. I hear screaming and coughing and the cries of drowning cats. I feel my little brothers tugging on my dress and crying for food.

I grab the railing to keep myself steady. Then, the sudden moan of painted doors being unstuck—I startle as Mom Sharon throws open the adoption suite to see Mom and Dad. Even from the far side of the room, I can see their joy: it's real.

Mom Sharon's daughter films the moment of our first meeting, catching Zoe, Robert, and Andrew jumping on Dad as Edward and Rogie approach Mom. I watch this new lady as she opens her arms for a full embrace. I stay off in the corner, the bad thoughts gone for now, feeling something I never have felt before. I lean in when Mom and Dad move toward me, not yet ready for a full hug. They pull me close into a group huddle with my brothers and sister. *I belong!* And I realize *that's* the feeling. For the first time in my life, I have a place, and today, I get to claim it. If belonging can be a feeling, I am filled up with it.

CHAPTER TWENTY-THREE

May 19, 2018

Jodi

Spring 2018

It is May 19, 2018, exactly six years from the day my mother died, and I feel her presence. The date is perfect. I sit in the adoption suite on the bed, waiting for what's next. Someone dropped us here to wait for our children. Just a few minutes later, I hear chatter and the clunking of feet just outside our door. The room fills with thick anticipation and eager sentiments. Garry and I have fought hard for this moment, and we are tired. Worn out, but ready—I am sure of it.

The door bursts open to a tall, blond teenager with a video camera. After her, six children rush in, along with the woman I recognize as Sharon. My eyes focus on each little face, heart pumping wildly. I don't have clear thoughts, so I only say, "Hello!" It feels grossly understated.

Everyone politely smiles, but it is hard for anyone to know what to say. Three kids crowd on top of Garry, and I fall to my knees to welcome the children. Rogie and Angela stand just out of our reach, grinning politely and remaining quiet. As the moment grows, we get to meet each child, one at a time.

After introductions, I hear Andrew bellow out, "Mom! Dad! I want to show you!" Pulling my hand, he drags us to see his room, but all I notice is the word he uses: *Mom.*

This first day we spend at Open Arms, meeting everyone's friends, seeing their rooms, and sharing their food. Within minutes of meeting her, Zoe jumps out of one of the rooms to surprise us with a diaper on her head, dancing and laughing the richest laugh, deep and infectious. Edward and Rogie Nino, who tells us he prefers "just Rogie," attempt to confiscate our phones to watch dance videos and sing along. The gentler, more watchful Robert just wants to be with us, sweet and particular with each of his movements. Andrew gives us a forceful tour of the facility; he is rowdy and quick—and reminds me of William. We observe him on the fifth-floor basketball court, the jungle gym, and the top of his bunk, doing his best to impress us. Unlike our other adoption experiences, these children—my children—yearn for family and unquestionably accept us as Mom and Dad. They don't listen to us very well, but that, too, feels like family. Everyone joins in the commotion, except Angela.

At Open Arms, we meet the dog, the van driver, the "cleaner," and the wonderful cook, Miss Barbara. We eat dinner with Sharon, two of her children, and all six of ours. Throughout our time there, Sharon corrects them and helps them in the intimate ways that only mothers do. My children also call her "Mom," and they sometimes listen to her. Mostly, they sneak away to poke at one another or tattle on small wrongs being done to them. The children are understandably chaotic.

On the first night, we help with pajamas and tuck our six into their orphanage bunks—hopefully for the last time. Garry gathers up our bags from the adoption suite to leave for our hotel. Although most adopting families sleep at Open Arms, we had booked nearby accommodations, hoping to steal some moments alone with our children for bonding. As we linger at the door to leave, Sharon promises me the children can stay at the hotel with us tomorrow night, just as the lights go out and music blasts from the speakers fastened to plaster walls. The song muffles the pandemonium and crying that ensues. I assume that is the point. It is hard to leave them behind—and not just my children.

The next day my six want us to visit Sabik Bay, the beach about three hours away. Taking along seventeen other children, we crowd into large vans and pick up food from the Jolly-bee drive-thru, my kids' favorite restaurant. The uncontained exuberance from having new people, lots of friends, and bags of fast food makes for a humorous ride. At the beach, we swim for hours, attempting to build bonds with our children by jumping into the bay and making sand art, a process that feels much like playing with someone else's kid on a class field trip.

That second day of our visit, the children come stay with us at a local hotel. Having never seen anything like it, they run through the lobby to the elevator, where they press all the buttons. Finally at the mini-suite after stopping on every floor, they take over. They explore the fabrics with their dirty fingers, fight over the remotes, and even sneak small kitchen items into their pockets. Tooth brushing seems to be a new activity for them, and minute by minute, we begin to discover all kinds of habits, quirks, and personalities. After the rush, they fall asleep in the biggest beds they had ever seen—all together.

At the hotel buffet the next morning, the children request to try every type of food and all five kinds of juice. Their hyper movements appear so erratic that people come up to question us. No one is immune from their noise and energy. When I ask the boys to repeat themselves—so I can understand them—they only increase the volume, not realizing that our ability to hear them is not the problem. Their odd accents and partial English require determined listening. To avoid frustrating them, we often just smile in response and usher them from one activity to the next to keep up with the adoption schedule.

Amid the confusion and newness of their surroundings, the children often find fault with one another: "Zoe touched my paper!" "Edward bumped me on purpose!" "Rogie took all the towels!" None of the offenses are egregious enough to warrant the angry retaliations and hours of stomping and hissing that follow. Expressions of shame and anger emerge quickly, effortlessly, and often. Boundaries between the six don't exist, and even the smallest offenses produce hours of brooding and rebuffs.

On day three, Sharon and her crew drive us to the local waterfall where Rogie, Edward, and Andrew show off their cliff-diving skills. Even though it's clearly not safe, we all participate in the fun. Garry and I help Zoe and Robert take their first jumps off a lower cliff, and we begin to win over the younger ones with our light-hearted approach to attachment by joking, giggling, and playing. I take a jump from a higher cliff with Angela, who's afraid to go alone. The jump is completely out of my comfort zone, but I do it anyway. This jump is the first time she lets me hold her hand.

During the next few days at Open Arms, we eat together, feasting on adobo chicken and rice and celebrating with the legendary *halo halo*, a mixed dessert of shaved ice, sweet cream, red and white beans, coconut chunks, gelatin, and assorted lychee fruit, jackfruit, and plantains. I ask Chef Barbara for the recipe. Like the rest of this adoption adventure, the *halo halo* tastes unexpected, peculiar, and sweet.

On our last day in Manila, we sign papers, take photos, and participate in exit interviews at the ICAB office downtown. I don't recall many of the details of these events because I am eager to go home. It is time for these children to escape the unpredictable patterns of orphanage living and discover their unique selves. I yearn for them to meet their brothers and sisters and find a life beyond this place where they can learn the language and love of family. I cannot be sure if they will get it, of course, but I am certain that it's time to start trying.

CHAPTER TWENTY-FOUR

Awfully Good

GARRET

MAY 19, 2018

"Garret, come here!" Tina hollers up at me from the kitchen. It's late at night; I am playing my Switch and don't feel like going downstairs. "Garret! Jolyn!" she calls up again.

Maybe someone is hurt. I promised Mom that I would help. Reluctantly getting up from the floor where I'd been lounging, I wander down to see what's wrong. There is a commotion in the kitchen, and Jolyn beats me to it. The yelling, shrieks, and thumping seem to be coming from Tina's phone.

When I reach Tina, I see them. In the screen of her WhatsApp appear a bunch of Filipino faces, smiling and handsome. "Garret, these are your new brothers and sisters!" Mom says. She introduces me to the crowd, "This is your big brother, Garret."

I try to see them clearly, but it is difficult because they

continue to squirm around the lens and fight over who gets to have the camera closest to their faces. Looking at them makes me dizzy, so I move away from the screen and try to listen to them as I pace the kitchen floor. "Who are you?" I say to the first face.

"I'm Edward!" I hear.

"Hi, Edward, I'm Garret!" I return.

Then I see a little girl screeching and grabbing at the phone on the other end. "Zoe!" is all she says. One by one, my new siblings pass the phone back and forth to one another. It's hard to tell them apart because the children look similar. The older girl must be Angela, since there are only two girls and Zoe already grabbed the phone. Angela is in view but doesn't say anything.

All four boys look the same to me, although some are bigger than others. I meet Rogie, Andrew, and Robert; all simply say, "Hi." They ask me to walk around the house and show them their new home, which I do.

Taking the phone from Tina, I aim the lens ahead and begin the tour. Room by room, I walk around to show them our home, now also theirs. They scream out some phrases, but the words are mostly indecipherable. "Pool," "table," and "big" are three words I can make out, but that's about it. Tiring of the noise and yelling, I end the excursion after about five minutes and pass the phone back to Tina and Jolyn, who continue chatting with my new siblings.

I can hear the new kids all the way back to my room and for several more minutes after I close my bedroom door. I don't think too much about it; actually, they looked cute. Weird and loud, of course, but cute. They'll fit in fine. I return to gaming, trying to tune out the happy shouts still radiating from Tina's speakerphone. It's amazing that six little people could be so noisy from halfway across the globe.

CHAPTER TWENTY-FIVE

Relentless Love

GARRY

Spring 2018

It's time. I push to complete the adoption process in the same manner I would one of my business transactions. I ruffle feathers, bend the procedures, and rebuke a few officials along the way. "I can't help it," I share with Jodi, who dutifully engages in all the appointments with her notetaking and questions while volunteering to counsel other children in the orphanage.

While she offers her services, I offer my opinions and make my intent clear. At first, I offend Sharon by questioning the process, appointments, and house rules. By the end of the week, however, she and I have built an unmistakable rapport. Appreciating my impatience and my ADHD, she makes it clear with a sly smile: "You're the perfect Dad for these children!" In her eyes, I recognize her joy in getting the children placed as well as the deep anguish of knowing she will not see them again.

"We didn't know if they would ever find a family. It's a miracle," she stated at their farewell party, as all the children gathered around to celebrate the adoption of my children. Zoe, Robert, and Andrew climbed onto our laps, as if to claim us, while other littles crowded in to get close. Even though we are not their mom and dad, the others snuggled near to inspect and approve of us.

During the final moments of the celebration, Sharon spoke to the bunch of us, about 100 orphans and various teachers and helpers, reminding the children that families like us are coming for all of them. "Just as you see this miracle for Rogie, Angela, Edward, Andrew, Robert, and Zoe," pointing to me and Jodi, she asserted confidently, "a family is coming for you, too." It was a risky claim and bold statement, and I appreciated it.

Early the next morning, we begin a thirty-six–hour journey home. Along the way, our children bicker, complain, and groan under the anxiety, terror, and mysteries of their new lives. From Manila to Beijing, everyone does fine, with fewer squabbles than anticipated. During the Beijing layover, however, something prompts Rogie to go dark. It might have been fatigue, fear, or being corrected when he taunted his younger brothers. I'm not sure, but he won't budge from the blue airport lounge chair, keeping his head down and not talking.

After several hours of his not responding to any of my questions or requests, I tell Jodi to take the other kids and get on the plane. The flight crew calls a second time for the passengers of Flight 678 to come to the gate for boarding. I have few options as I try to navigate a difficult situation in a foreign country with my stubborn son, who doesn't look like he belongs with me. I can't place hands on him or escort him onto the plane, and I feel certain we'll miss our flight. Resolved, I simply ask him, "Do you really want to allow your brothers and sisters to leave without you?"

At the final call, Rogie does slink over to the plane. The relief I feel is palpable. For the entire flight over the Atlantic, Rogie does not speak and only gets up from his chair once to vomit all over the lady sitting in front of him.

Her angry response both discourages and pierces me deeply. "See what happens when *you* try to do good?" she yells, glaring at us. "Everyone else has to pay the price!"

I understand her anger and apologize as much as I can before the flight attendant whisks her away from us and up to first class. It isn't the first time we've encountered disdain because of our decisions—nor will it be the last.

There are similar untimely and frightening outbursts during our next layover in Newark, this time from Angela. Annoyed at her younger sister—a clear trigger—Angela proceeded to kick Zoe from underneath the table where we sat, waiting for our final flight. When Jodi corrected her, she went on to kick her as well, while screaming out venomous phrases, ending with a high-pitched "hahhhhh" at the end of each.

At this point, "demon-possessed" would not be an exaggerated description of her trauma-charged behavior. The hateful look she gave Jodi is something I will never forget. Stuck in the airport, with all eyes on us—two white parents and six Filipino children—we look bad. All the children are tired, frantic, and, according to Angela, they "hate this family!" I glance over at Jodi, her expression deeply troubled yet resolute.

At these ugly moments, the ones we will hide from doting grandparents and awaiting friends, we wonder why we did it. Not only did we accept this challenge, we fought hard for it. There is no logical reason, of course, even though it makes sense to us. I am not sure whether these kids will make it or if they will ever come to love themselves or us. Whatever the cost, we are choosing to offer them a chance at a full life, a real family, and relentless love. The offer is enough for us.

■ ■ ■ ■ ■

When we arrived home, the six-pack took full advantage of our new home, their own beds, and all the food they wanted. Jodi and I gave frequent hugs, listening ears, and plenty of room for play. Still, our home assumed a higher level of structure than ever before. Mealtimes, bedtimes, personal spaces, and basic hygiene became regimented and disciplined activities filled with instructions and protocols.

While the behavioral standards remained simple, we backed them up with diligent accountability. We attempted to have our eyes everywhere, using video cameras on the top floor to understand the patterns, needs, and squabbles that would later require our arbitration. The original six fell into the new patterns with grace, since the new "rules" were only low-bar expectations like, "Don't steal," "Don't draw on the couch," "Come to dinner when called," and "Shower in the shower." Admittedly, William and Luxmi still required a few of these basic rules as well.

When the six-pack wasn't finding trouble, they spent their time drawing countless pictures, depicting people, places, and emotions they couldn't yet put into words. Edward tried to write words that seemed to indicate that he loved us (there were hearts on them). Robert drew a big brick house with lots of people—presumably us—in front of it. Zoe cut up paper and drew hearts with random letters on each little piece, which we'd later find strewn about the kitchen floor. A growing display of this artwork adorned the wall above my wife's computer desk, placed there to give her a boost of courage to face each day.

The children expressed themselves differently. Instead of drawing, Andrew often danced and sang to the Alexa in our kitchen. Although Alexa never could figure out the song titles he named, he danced to any tune that played. And he gave big hugs. Even Rogie began to hug and smile from time to time. Within a short while, everyone would hug me.

All the children hugged Jodi, except Angela, who obstinately refused. I wasn't sure if she resented Jodi for taking over her caretaking role, or if it was the horrible memories of her unsafe and unstable first mother. Every night, I tucked Angela into bed, saying, "I love you, Angela."

She responded, "I love you, Dad."

Every night, Jodi also tucked her in, saying, "I love you, Angela."

She responded, "'Night, Mom."

Angela fought for her position as the boss among the younger children. I often found her telling them what to do, explaining situations, doing chores, and answering all their questions incorrectly. In this new environment, she did not have the right information.

Jodi and I thanked her for being helpful but told her plainly: "You don't have to do dishes or take care of Zoe. You get to be a kid!" Still, so much of her self-worth came from knowing the plan and directing the day. One day, she even took me on.

Angela had refused to take a shower, so I reminded her that, as her Dad, I got to be the boss.

"NO!" she retorted, "I'm the boss." She wasn't joking.

Game on, I decided. I had been waiting for the right moment to teach my daughter to understand her position in the family. I gently clarified that parents are the leaders. Angela protested violently, running from the living room to the laundry room, sometimes kicking wildly on the floor or—in other moments—crouching in the corner, expressionless. Between her outbursts, I explained the concept of family roles. She kept saying "No," and "I hate this family!" With her force, she knocked down chairs and picture frames from the walls.

Fits like this happened often, but today I chose to engage full force. She knew we loved her, and it was time she understood her position. I carried her to her room while Jodi brought the others outside to swim. We continued the same conversation until her shouting turned to crying.

Again, I repeated to her that I loved her, and I was the boss. She needed to rest, allowing me to carry the burdens of the family. Finally, she wept, then quieted and flashed a look of understanding. We rejoined the family at the pool, and Angela splashed with joy, laughing just as robustly as she had raged.

But Angela's peace didn't stay for long, and we've had numerous such fits since then. Angela's control-anger-fight-cry routine happened at least daily, if not several times a day. Jodi and I continued to impress on her the importance of parents as leaders, protectors, and coaches. We cheered her on, disciplined her, and called her higher.

Together, Jodi and I took turns training, loving, and setting boundaries for our children, sometimes all together or with different children simultaneously. As we created consistent, safe spaces and structure for both the new kids and the original six, we coined a new phrase: full-contact parenting. In the beginning, it didn't make much of a difference. The six were utter disasters, cute and mischievous, crafty and ignorant, loving and cold.

Once—all in the same day—Zoe broke a television, a lamp, and several of her sisters' toys. When they were not fighting, the three younger boys had only one topic of conversation—butts— and often pulled down their pants in front of each other and perfect strangers.

As Dad, it was my job to coach my sons and daughters in various "life lessons." The first was that "You can touch your own penis, but you can't touch anyone else's." That happened one night after I corrected Andrew for poking at his brother's private area, to which he simply responded, "Whose penis can you touch?"

After this lesson came many others: "No farting at the dinner table." "Say please and thank you instead of screaming for food." "Don't make random bopping noises." "Flush the toilet." These simple life lessons became dinnertime favorites. Each night we ate together, a family of fourteen, laughing, teaching, interrupting, singing, and shouting. Jodi stepped into banquet cooking with ease, creating at least two ethnic offerings for every meal. The spreads reminded me of my fraternity parties twenty years earlier.

Much joy came along with these lessons and adventures. Twelve stockings hung over the newly painted fireplace at Christmastime. Jodi commemorated each birthday with uniquely baked cakes of each child's choosing. We hung First Day of School pictures on the walls, and the new children reveled in the fact that they could attend school. Nighttime hugs, books, and I-love-yous became standard operating procedures. The settling routines and new exploits began to quench the sting of their endless moodiness and bickering. The problems usually outweighed the victories most days, but any progress became reason to celebrate.

Still, the codependent personalities of the new six—their

tendency to protect, then blame each other—got old. Their lies, stealing, subtle digs, and underhanded gazes stifled the atmosphere of our home. Each child and their trauma history provoked the others' resentments and needs.

Zoe stole from everyone, yet she also assumed the scapegoat role for her older sister, who blamed her for everything. Edward might hit Robert and Andrew over a toy, but desperately needed them to go upstairs with him because he was afraid to go alone. The younger ones bartered treats in return for approval from the older ones. Jodi and I had to break the need-based patterns of control so that love-inspired interactions might blossom.

We decided to split them up as often as possible. They needed space from each other to learn that we would meet their needs and so would their new siblings, teachers, neighbors, and friends. We had to create trust, and this was where my original six children—with all their strengths and oddities—really shone.

We swapped out Angela from Zoe's room and had her bunk with Shiya, whose obstinance, acceptance, and cluelessness were a surprisingly great fit for her angry, moody, and often naughty new roommate. Zoe moved in with Luxmi, whose ability to live out joy and forgiveness matched perfectly with her new little sister, who laughed hard and broke everything. Luxmi's mercy gave Zoe space to be little.

Jolyn took on the big sister role for all four of these strange, difficult, and eager young women. She jumped into doing hair, choosing cute outfits, and baking with the girls. She seemed chosen for this role and always knew exactly what fun activity would most delight her sisters.

Although Rogie, Edward, Andrew, and Robert roomed together on the top floor of the house, they joined the realm of their older brothers, whose games and wit showed them a new and better way to be cool. Even James took Rogie under his wing, sharing painful tales of his past hurts, as both boys found solace in their parallel histories. While they argued over who had it worse, they were at least communicating on a genuine level.

Edward shared Garret's love of gaming and idolized his serious-minded brother, while Garret relished the genuine admiration from his sibling. William, too, fit into the mix, becoming "a triplet" with Andrew and Robert, who shared his small stature, disruptive curiosity, and love of swimming, bugs, and all things outdoors. Quite unexpectedly, they all started to fit. Never for one moment did the original six children question or doubt welcoming the new six-pack.

This isn't to say times got easy. Wonderful moments of laughter and bonding often turned bad, ending in fits of rage, hurt feelings, and misunderstood intentions. The new six had trouble using language for simple communication, much less to express complex emotions. Angela still resented Jodi and me for being the decision-makers, often trying to bully her younger siblings into following her instead of us. Under duress, Edward's feelings of shame incited frequent blow-ups and shutdowns. Andrew also screamed, mostly to satisfy his incessant need to make noise.

Instead of yelling, Robert and Zoe cried, sometimes out of brokenness, but more often just to get attention or deflect attention away from their mischief. They had endless boo-boos, both real and imagined. Figuring out which tears needed empathy or demanded a rebuke required all my emotional intelligence skills.

Rogie was the only one who did not cause trouble, mostly because he was rarely around. Much like James, he pushed others away and withdrew by taking over the remote or escaping into a world of books. I wondered often if he could hear me.

Just as they did at home, the new kids wreaked havoc at school. Administrators called Jodi daily to complain about at least one of the children; in fact, most every school day ended with some kind of bad news: "Edward threatened to stab his teacher with a pencil because he felt frustrated that he can't read yet." "Zoe stole her classmates' pencils." "Rogie refuses to pick his head off the desk." "Robert threatened to kill himself." "Andrew needs more testing." "Zoe pulled her pants down in lunch line." They hired an extra staff member just for my kids.

It wasn't only their behaviors that created challenges; it was the sheer number of them. Dentist appointments for twelve are hard to book. School physicals for a dozen spans several days. Logistically, every activity has to assume a new structure when you have to do it twelve times: a dozen parent-teacher conferences; twelve school plays; twelve times three field trip forms; two dozen eggs at breakfast; twenty-four socks and shoes. Then there are the endless extras like box-top drives, winter coats, birthday parties, picture days, and school lunches. It all added up to time and money.

My wife starts at 4 a.m. and goes till 9 p.m., often saying, "I might not be a great mom, but I can be organized!" Her ability to balance and fulfill the kids' many roles and needs established reliable patterns that built a firm foundation for trust.

I helped as best as I could, and I wrote the checks for all the bills coming in, which on some occasions took my breath away. The first round of dental care for the six-pack cost $21,000, and that was the discounted price for treating forty-nine different teeth requiring either fillings or extractions. Doctor visits, along with insurance, added up as CDC and other checkups became routine obligations. Weekly trips to Costco took two or three carts and easily cost $1,000.00. We got the corporate membership. Unfortunately, no corporate account covers the medical extras, clothing budgets, teacher appreciation gifts, orthodontic braces, Christmas gifts, and birthday parties.

We did not have a normal household budget—our bills were more in line with running a boutique hotel. Plus, the regular household-quality products deteriorated from activity that was more akin to commercial hotel use than residential living. The cost of running our 11,000 square-foot house was exponential, with the six HVAC units alone costing us $600 per month, not to mention the additional fees for repairing an endless line of newly broken items: countless doorknobs, handrails, faucets, and cabinet doors. At some point during our first year at Stonepile Manor, anything requiring manual rotation literally fell off its hinge from overuse.

Every day numerous items quit working. Televisions stopped turning on, computers crashed, and chair legs broke off, often without warning. Larger household items also became damaged from use and misuse due the persistent needs of twelve kids, including the washer and dryer, the microwave, the water dispenser, and upholstered furniture of any kind. With fourteen people waiting on clean socks, a broken washer classified as a crisis event in my house. Jodi made me pay for the expedited service to have it fixed immediately.

Everything just adds up, and that's when we stay at home! When we do dare to leave the property, I budget at least $150 to do anything. The simplest outings, like a trip to the movies or the zoo, easily hits $200. Even Sunday lunch at McDonald's costs a hundred bucks.

There's no way around it. A dozen kids is a lot of kids, and it all accumulates, both financially and emotionally. As I look forward, I understand the inevitable expenses will only escalate. It's all coming in fast: twelve phones, cars, and college tuitions. I reflect on the impending bills every day. The collateral cost of raising a dozen children cannot be understood until it's lived.

It wasn't that I didn't expect the bills or budget for them, but every time I sit down to pay our monthly credit cards, I'm still astounded at the cost of running my family. Among the sounds of our family's beautiful chaos, laughter, and healing, one voice keeps telling it to me straight: *Keep on working, Big Guy!*

CHAPTER TWENTY-SIX

Making It

GARRET

Summer 2018

"No, really," I plead with my best friend Al, "you have to see it. They're so bad." I am referring to my new brothers and sisters, of course. Al hasn't met them. He gets it though—he also has younger brothers who like to drive him crazy. "My siblings are way more annoying than yours!" I brag.

"I don't think you're supposed to call your family members 'bad,'" retorts Al, who loves to debate me on useless topics. Mom told me it's better to say "sometimes they make bad choices," but, really, they are just bad. As we banter on, my mom pops into my room, gesturing for me to quiet down. Al's ready to hang up anyway, so I end the call and wave goodnight to Mom.

Instead of leaving, Mom hugs me and tells me she loves me. With a wink, she begins the long routine of nighttime check-ins.

Twelve tuck-ins means lots of tooth brushing to check, hair to comb, books to read, and kisses to dole out. After all that comes the inevitable parade of requests for water, Band-Aids, and late-night snuggles for reassurance. I don't need a tuck-in, but I get one anyway.

Following the routine is at least thirty more minutes of commotion. Four of my new brothers live on the floor above me. I often hear thumping as feet jump from bed to floor when they're supposed to be sleeping. The sink often runs, and the younger brothers fight, wrestle, cry, or scream at one another. Usually, one of the boys has taken someone else's item, thrown something across the room, or farted on someone else's bed. Time-outs, more stomping, and occasional yelling ensues. It all depends on the mood of the moment. By 8:00 p.m., Mom and Dad look a complete mess; they fall into bed and are asleep often by 9:00 p.m. I applaud their commitment to the nighttime tuck-in.

My new brothers and sisters have serious issues. I think they're even worse than I was with the fits. Sometimes, Angela rolls on the floor yelling at Mom, "I hate you!" or "No!" repeatedly.

"We get it," I tell her. "You're mad. We all hear you!"

Zoe, Andrew, and Robert also stamp and shout, but they get over their ferocious moods quicker than Angela. The school calls at least once per week about Robert's antics, and Mom leaves work some days to pick him up. Edward already has earned probation for threatening to stab his teacher with a pencil; he had gotten frustrated about not completing his math sheets in time with his classmates. I understood. The agonizing shame of not measuring up makes you do dumb stuff sometimes. At least Edward is honest about it.

That's more than I can say for Rogie, who lies all the time.

After stealing my phone, he had lied about it for three months afterward. The phone doesn't matter, of course, but the dishonesty bothers me because it makes no sense. Rogie lies every day to Mom and Dad about homework, getting so many incompletes that he might not pass sixth grade. His deceitfulness baffles me since he is super smart and very able to do the work. *How stupid!*

Zoe steals and lies too, but she is not as good at it. Zoe's type of lying is to pretend ignorance. "Zoe, do you know where my phone is?" Jolyn will ask.

"What phone?" Zoe will say.

Mom always rephrases it. "Zoe, can you help me find Jolyn's phone? You're a great finder..." she'll say. And Zoe will.

At school, Zoe has stolen so many items from her classmates that Mom empties her bag each night and follows up with her teacher to make sure she returns them.

My parents declared that everyone must keep their own stuff and cannot take anyone else's—even to borrow. "Don't give or take anything from anyone else," Mom says. The barter system must have been big in the Philippines. The six exchange "stuff" for favors, food, and coverage from blame.

After the first few months of sneaking around and conspiring against Mom and Dad, the kids now have strict protocols for what they can and cannot do. Everyone goes to their room at 7:30 for bedtime routines. We eat at 5:30. No one gets out of bed until they are woken for the day. No one touches anything of anyone else, and everyone oversees cleaning up their own things. Oh— and everyone must be kind and "do the right thing."

The meaning of *do the right thing* is debatable. For Rogie, "the right thing" was getting internet access, even if it meant taking my phone. Angela convinced Zoe to give her a new plush puppy dog in exchange for a broken Barbie. It was "the right thing" for Angela, but it wasn't an even swap for poor Zoe. Edward punched Robert in the head for cleaning the toilet when he had to pee. "The right thing" for OCD Robert was cleaning the toilet, but not for Edward, who wet his pants. Mom and Dad insisted that the children understood the "right thing," but I had my doubts.

The good part is that the new kids make the rest of us look great. I do well in comparison, and so do my other sisters and brothers that came before the six. Even James seems better. He recently got his driver's license and a job. He is in his fifth of six years of high school, earning an actual high school diploma and not the Special-Ed non-diploma they tried to push on him a few years ago. And James *is* making it. Sure, he is unpleasantly moody sometimes, but he's more human and much happier. Well, maybe not *happy*, but at least he's not hopeless.

Since the new kids came home, Jolyn also has gotten more fun. I give her a hard time, of course, because she is so normal. She helps little sisters with hair, teaches cheerleading, and tries to take over the kitchen, baking goodies for all. Mom gives her a lot of freedom in the kitchen, which usually results in piles of dirty dishes for Mom and loads of sweets for me.

In fact, food seems to be everywhere now—foods of all different kinds. Mom cooks with Jolyn and Angela after school, and our kitchen is always alive with rice, eggs, noodles, pork, chicken, and sweets. Dad makes me go to the gym for "P.E.," so I don't get fat. I am not winning any awards for my physique, but at six feet tall, I think I look rather good.

Shiya, Luxmi, and William still struggle mightily in school, but with the new six, the teachers don't have time to criticize them. Mom goes in weekly, usually to make sure Shiya stays away from the bullies and William keeps his focus. Luxmi is the only one who might not make it. Her IQ scores came back half as high as mine. *Half.* Mine is high, but her IQ means she doesn't get to graduate—or that's what they told my parents. Knowing my mom, she'll find some program to get Luxmi exactly what she needs.

Even my high school isn't completely terrible. I am enrolled in a dual program online where I earn my high school diploma and associate degree at the same time. Mom helps me structure my workload and edits the dreaded writing assignments, but it's doable. I still get panic attacks, like last week when one of my assignments didn't upload correctly, but I am finding my way. Maybe I'll go away for college, and I want to be smart and successful like Dad. My goal is to make enough money to take care of myself, buy a lot of video games, and help some people out. I think the world is pretty messed up, and I see a lot of things I'd like to fix.

Al and I discuss all the ways to remedy life's problems, but our methodologies differ. Al wins at school, getting high grades and a nearly perfect ACT score. He will attend one of the best universities in the country, ace his doctoral degree, and invent ways to harness bioscience research to save humanity. Seriously, he is that smart.

Although we seem to be the same amount of smart, I don't keep up with his academic accolades. School seems to have been created for the elite. By *elite,* I don't mean rich or clever, because I think we're both. To me, elite means those lucky people whose well-ordered lives seem less messy than mine, whose realities dictate that their futures and paths remain safely marked out for them. They have the emotional capacities to follow the rules, make the most of their opportunities, and avoid the dangers of unpredictability.

I am not elite; I'm too messy, too risky, and just beyond appropriate. Because of that, I'm not sure I can ever measure up to the academic standards in the current collegiate environment. Furthermore, I'm not sure I want to. I am not interested in marketing about saving the planet or embracing multiculturalism. As a 4-H forester and a brother to ten immigrants, I'm already doing both. I don't want to waste hundreds of thousands of dollars to debate the issues of the day, whether it's climate change, gender identity politics, or the ever-changing standards for global political correctness. People with autism aren't P.C. anyway.

No one in my family is *elite* either—at least not anymore. Although Mom and Dad did graduate from Ivy League institutions and make lots of money, they've long since stopped fitting in. I think they used to be elite, but after having all of us, they changed their viewpoints.

They even see good in the progress James has made, even though he is still learning to read and likely will never attend traditional college. At night, James works clearing out banquets at the Embassy Suites; he is their best team member, always showing up on time and willing to work hard. With his salary last week, he bought me a hundred-dollar gift card from GameStop, his way of showing me love—even though he'd never tell me so. I saw Mom's happy tears when she saw James pass me the gift card, an act that means more to her than academic or extracurricular honors.

Mom and Dad always look for the good in the middle of the mess. Although I love to point out their bad behavior, the six do continue to improve. They yield to the corrections and routines, demonstrating resiliency and devotion. Unlike James and me, who tend to withdraw from the world, they have jumped right in. That takes guts.

No matter what happened the day before, the six wake up every day smiling, chatty, and curious. They continue to hug me uncomfortably and look up to me as their game master. It's the same level of engagement they also give any visitors, whom they attack with sloppy hugs and eager stares. They want to be here—with us and with me. I even enjoy Rogie when he's not lying, although now I hide my phone.

We are making it, even though we view "making it" differently than others. In our home, my dad speaks about being a plumber or a CEO or the President with equal exuberance. My parents encourage college if it leads to meaningful work and only if we desire it. They value exercise and health without pressing us to do sports or be on competitive teams. We aim for fierce effort rather than certain victory. When we do win big, we ultimately come back to this humble reality: the world is tough, and we're the lucky ones, even if I do get itchy and bothered sometimes.

Fully aware of our limitations, Mom and Dad have begun to develop our property, creating cabins for anyone who "fails to launch" as they call it. I expect Luxmi will get one of the cabins, yet she still can have a meaningful job and accomplish good things. Had she been left in India, chances are she would have been trafficked, abandoned for a lifetime without love or value. I know 'cause I've seen it.

In my sixteen years on earth, I have been to some bleak places where scores of children stay unfound. I never will forget their faces, pressing their noses against our car window and begging for food, performing for onlookers in hopes of getting some loose change, or lying naked in the small gutters on the side of the road. I have walked with the unadopted others, who never found their place or potential and now remain lost forever.

Luxmi is not lost. She is found, and she's here with us. Even though most people discount her for not being very smart, I know better. She knows she belongs, and that's all that really matters. People discount me too, because I come across as weird with my incessant pacing and awkward social inadequacies. All my siblings, except Jolyn, have similar quirks. Still, no one can predict how much we will surpass our inherent limitations. *And who knows?* We might succeed more than anyone ever imagined—with our oddities, late starts, and all.

In honor of us and their retrofitted definition of success, my parents spent the last year building a new postsecondary institution in Tennessee. Only my parents would look at the lack of educational opportunities available to kids like us and say, "Hey, let's start a college!" Even though people laughed at them and the red tape almost stopped them, they did it.

With our unique perspective on learning strategies and incentives, the rest of my atypical siblings and I shaped my parents' concept of a practical, online, and success-oriented college. It doesn't require standardized testing, high tuition, or lots of prerequisites. Students don't have to impress with lengthy interviews, class ranks, and extracurricular rosters. I think of it as a school created for the anti-elite, for those who are eager to reach their goals, but who don't want to waste any time or money on the stuff that doesn't matter.

Stonepile, as they named it, just received approval from the Tennessee Higher Education Commission and opens its doors in the Fall of 2020, offering an Associate, Bachelor, and Master of Applied Science in Construction Leadership. With his passion for devising tech-savvy construction processes, Dad inaugurated the institution with programs aimed at educating the next generation of leaders for the 1.3-trillion-dollar construction industry.

These first three programs are just the start, as my parents work every day to build areas of study that will place graduates into immediate and meaningful jobs at the top of their chosen fields. Stonepile doesn't attract the elite, yet its goal remains clear: train students in real-world skills and values-based leadership so that they graduate ready to get money and do good.

Oh yes, and they even accept people like me.

CHAPTER TWENTY-SEVEN

Extreme Parenting

JODI

Fall 2018

"Are you taking care of yourself? I am worried for you," says my Dad, visiting us for Thanksgiving.

It's the first Thanksgiving with Rogie, Angela, Edward, Andrew, Robert, and Zoe. My Dad and Linda visit every Thanksgiving, Easter, and the Fourth of July, sharing time with Garry's parents who holiday with us at Halloween, Christmas, and any time in between. Our new house has a grandparents' apartment, which often fills with visitors, relatives, and—always prioritized—grandparents.

"I'm taking care of myself as best I can," I respond, "and I feel better after the surgery." I go on to explain my daily routine, early morning start at work, laundry room tactics, shopping and cooking strategies, and daily problem-solving duties.

"It's not really the physical logistics of parenting a dozen kids that's the hardest part, although that part is quite something," I admit to my Dad.

I am trying to be transparent without worrying him. It's hard to know what to say when people ask me how it's going. What I want to say would take too long or depict the new children in an unfair light. After all, the six are engaged in an epic struggle to emerge from the shell-shocked existence they had known all their lives, up until this year. I see and appreciate them trying hard to be sons and daughters, even when they fail miserably.

What I could say to my dad—what I hold back—is, *these children hate me*! I want to complain about how they take and whine, push and fight. The rant would explain all the ways the kids battle against me in a relentless offensive to prove that I don't really love them. I often wonder whether it will get better, or if I will make it to the end of the day without resenting them. *And will they ever stop yelling?* I think the answer is "yes," but some days, I am not sure.

The children's fits reveal the horrors of their abuse. The stealing shows me they never had enough to eat. Their lies say they do not trust me. Their anger is meant to push me away. I am perpetually inadequate when the children come at me with questions, demands, terrors, and nightmares. But instead of saying all that, I tell Dad, "The children are healing, and it doesn't look good. In fact, the good often looks bad."

My dad and others see the grocery shopping, cooking, dishes, laundry, and chaos of such a large family and worry about me. The question I am asked most often is: *How do you do it?* To this question, I usually joke back, "I'm doing it, but maybe not so well."

That is true, but I'm not referring to the chores. Although it is challenging to do dinner, cleanup, and laundry for twelve, these physical duties seem easy compared to the task of loving them. Loving them is the hard part and often what I get wrong.

"Did you know fourteen people means washing and matching twenty-eight socks a day!" I tell inquisitive onlookers. The socks put it all in perspective for me, and I often contemplate the magnitude of my responsibilities while sitting on my laundry room floor collecting, sorting, and matching all the socks. It's a lot of feet, a lot of people, and a lot of emotional and logistical baggage to carry around each day.

As a mental health counselor, I know healing comes. Full restoration may not be possible, but I believe these children can make it to the other side of their traumas to live a full life, to be able to love and be loved. I have that vision, although I often lose focus in the middle of the day when the school reports that "Robert kicked his reading teacher," or when Angela elbows me in the gut as I restrain her from self-injury.

In those impossible moments, which come more often than I would like, Garry and I carry the heavy realization of how tough it is to change just one life. The relentless trials test my desire to do true good. Standing in the gap as mother—being compared to other, former mothers—dares my heart and wears my soul. Often, I cry; sometimes, I hide in the bathroom for a few minutes, just to be alone or catch my breath. I take early morning walks and drink a lot of coffee. More than anything, I prayerfully tell myself *one day at a time.* Love is a decision, and today, I claim it.

But love doesn't always look good. Love requires boundaries and consequences. It asks my children to live like the people they want to become, not like the ones who hurt them. Love means saying "no" and spying on them to ensure they do the right thing. It gives them special gifts or rich discipline at just the right moment. Love demands that they walk instead of being carried—because they are able. Love inspires them to heal and make their beds. It pushes them to kindness even when they want to be mean. Love calls out the truth: "You're choosing to be a bully." "You're deciding to be mean." "You're better than that." "You're forgiven for that." Love keeps on.

This journey to healing often surprises me. Words and hugs do not make the difference. Many of my kids won't hug me anyway. James has never hugged me, and physical contact with Garret, Shiya, and Angela remains scant and awkward. Words don't work well either. Most of my children joined the family unable to speak English and prefer yelling, crying, and beeping to indicate what they want. Or they just take without saying anything.

Where words and hugs fail, however, I have found other ways to build trust and communicate love. Food has become the most helpful balm in the healing process. I make what they love, serve it on a consistent schedule, and offer it up in a kitchen full of fragrance, light, and acceptance. Every night, we eat at a white pine table that is larger than the bedroom in my first New York City apartment. Scrambling between the buffet and the long benches around the table, the children huddle together around pots of noodles, pounds of rice, and meats of every kind—especially spicy chicken. Garry and I always serve the food onto their plates, never allowing them to grab and go. I have learned to make everything from pot stickers to hot pot pork, adobo chicken to *halo halo*.

In the end, everyone gets to eat what they love! And we do. Early on, the six frantically shoveled food into their mouths even to the point of vomiting. "Slow down. There's always enough," we say repeatedly, putting limitations in place so they can learn that it's true. After twelve months, their rate of consumption has slowed, which shows me they are learning to trust.

Animals also have inspired healing. For the past four years, Garret and Jolyn's involvement in 4-H has made Garry and I reluctant farmers. Starting with chickens, we now have quite the farm, filled with dogs, outdoor cats, birds, fish, and swine. We have eighteen chickens (eight Black Australorps and ten Golden Sex Links), two English shepherds, five outdoor cats, a pond filled with 700 fish, and two mixed-breed market hogs. Countless hours have been spent combing dogs, removing ticks, feeding chickens, looking for lost cats in the woods, herding wild pigs into the barn, and shoveling pounds and pounds of manure. We chase down escaping hogs, wrestle rogue chickens, and create special places for our roaming cat population.

I admit we are not good farmers. Coyotes and raccoons have massacred our chickens, and it took several attempts to secure our pen from nocturnal hunters. Cats have come and gone, often preferring to live in the quiet hills behind our house rather than inside with us. It has taken a year to build that fishpond, which we recently stocked with bass, sunfish, and catfish. And we are losing the battle against the manure offensive; there is just so much of it.

But the effort is worth it. In caring for the animals, the children develop a palpable connection to life. They commit to caring for other living beings, mark the passage of time with their growth, and appropriately mourn losses when they occur. Nestling chickens and running with the shepherds, their eyes sparkle and their words make sense as they engage in the work of the farm.

The outdoor spaces provide them access to wildlife, freedom, and creativity, as well as swimming, biking, and exploring—all of which empower them to process some of their pervasive anxieties and fears. The children still fight and tattle on one another as they play and roam, but they also problem solve, help each other out, and learn the rhythm of family.

School also has provided much-needed structure and time away from one another. Although school days often end up with disastrous reports, each child gets to discover life on their own for those eight hours. The codependent patterns of I need you/I hate you begin to soften as the siblings separate and learn to stand on their own—at least for a while. The new six adore school, proudly showing off their new backpacks and school supplies to one another over and over again. They grin widely when teachers greet them with hugs at the classroom door and never complain about attending. In rare flashes—when the children's minds become clear and newly independent—I can see the good coming.

Until it doesn't. Such is the case with Angela. As the children take steps forward and back each day, she seems stubbornly planted in her place, especially with me. To her own admission, many days she hates me. I know she doesn't hate *me*, but in her manifest self, she hates me every day. In her bitterness toward mothers past, she needs a safe place to let go of her anger, terror, and resentments. I am that safe place, and I hurt.

On those days of disturbance and maternal deficiencies, there is only one thing to do: keep going. That has always been my best skill, anyway—stubbornness. I compel myself to accept the mess and continue to love the best way I know how. My kids don't have to choose me, but they will know that I chose them. Angela might push me away forever, but she knows she is loved. And that's enough for me, most days.

As the one-year anniversary of the adoption draws near, I wonder if I will ever come to know the real Angela, healed enough to give freely and embrace the love that is right in front of her. I understand if she doesn't get there. After all, the world has not proven itself to be a safe place. I accept that as a brutal truth, and I don't try to convince my children otherwise.

Life is messy, unpredictable, crushing, and at times, horrifying. Clever people attempt to understand and explain the bad stuff. Politics attempts to rationalize it by blaming others. Religion throws strategic programs at it. And schools attempt to prepare us for it. Still, nothing can explain, box up, or prepare any of us for the pain, disappointments, and unmet desires that inevitably come to all of us who engage in this phenomenon called life.

The question simply becomes, *what is our place in this complicated process of living*? Should I throw up my hands because I cannot make a difference today, or do I choose to say "yes" to trying anyway? Do I continue to engage in the messiness of life or try to live a more neatly controlled reality? I am tempted to retreat to an easier way, of course, but have made my decision, the choice to stand in the middle of an unsafe world, powerless to dictate results but still endeavoring for good.

With all my mistakes and foolishness, I believe my "yes" matters. It matters to Garret. It matters to James. It matters to Angela, even though the emotional price tag for my commitments continues to rise. In our past ten years, Garry and I have paid our time, money, status, and hearts in full. To date, we have lost church memberships and school admissions, friendships and reputations, bank accounts and career paths. And based on the current outcomes, the return on our investments remains low; still, our saying "yes" matters to those who are with us. It also matters to the others standing next to us in the same risky fight. It's not a secure way to live, I admit. And sometimes, our good just looks bad. Yet, I remain confident of this: if life's success is measured by the moments that matter, we win, every time.

CHAPTER TWENTY-EIGHT

A Good Day

ANGELA

Spring 2019

"Your bill has been paid," I hear the waitress say to Dad. We just have finished eating Sunday lunch at one of three restaurants in town that can fit all of us at the same table.

"What? Who paid it?" Dad asks. His voice sounds puzzled—and loud like always.

"Another table saw your family and wanted to buy you lunch to say, 'thank you.' They left a few minutes ago."

Looking out the window to see if he can spot their car, Dad thanks the waitress, who continues to stare at us.

"Stuff like this happens a lot, actually," I blurt out to her, as she begins to walk away. I always like to have my say.

And it's true. I have been in the United States now for one year. Almost any time we leave the house as a family, people stop and stare at us—sometimes, they even point. Others try to be careful, so we don't see them gawking, but we do. Sometimes, people yell out angry stuff like, "You better teach them to love America!" But mostly people smile and ask if we are a family. It seems obvious that we are. Still, I like to talk to people and tell them the names of all my brothers and sisters.

As we gather our jackets, the same waitress walks over to our table again and pauses. Dragging over the chair from the table next to us, she sits down next to Mom and Dad and whispers, "Tell me your story," as if it's a secret.

Mom's face brightens whenever she's asked this question, and she knows just what to say. I love to hear it again and again: "We have twelve children from all over the world, six from the Philippines, three from China, one from India, and two originals." Dad comments about how noisy, fun, and crazy we all are, and as always, we deny it loudly.

From the look in his eye and smile on his face, I know Dad likes the uproar. Mom strokes my head and brings me over to meet the waitress, taking the time to share our story and the stories of the many children still left behind. I don't understand all of what she says or why she always strokes my head, but I am glad I have a story to tell.

Today is a good day because the bad thoughts don't interrupt me. On hard days, I have angry thoughts that flash across my mind. I see people with terrible faces, and my feelings run away. I have nightmares, too, ones that I remember the next day, which make me sad. The worst dreams have all my brothers and sisters in it, except one. Someone is always missing. The lost person changes, but each time, I wake with the scary, mean, and lonely feelings. I try to put them away, but usually I just can't.

Dad calms my scary thoughts because he is so big and loud that I don't think he'd let anyone steal one of us. He tells me every day, "I love you, and I'm the boss."

I like him being in charge, even though I would never tell him that. He is quick and strong and won't let anyone hurt me. I never had a real dad before, and he is a good one.

I have had other moms, but none like my mom now. She is kind but tough and smart. I cannot trick her very often. She always knows what's happening in our house, and she is the best cook. Sometimes, I make noodles with her, and we talk about all kinds of things.

I have begun to tell Mom my stories. At first, I just told her small parts, like about the dreams. She usually continues cooking while we talk, which makes me feel less nervous. She asks me curious questions. I don't know why, but I feel better after the talks. I think I will tell her more secrets because she'll know what to say. She might know how to make the bad thoughts go away.

Once we arrive home from the restaurant, I pull out two pieces of white paper from the drawer in our kitchen and run to my room. The first, I fold into an envelope, which is where I will put my note. All of us love to draw and have filled the wall of my mom's office with pictures of us, our home, and all the things we get to do here, like pumpkin carving, Christmas tree decorating, horseback riding, taking our chickens to the county fair, swimming in the pond, dancing in the kitchen, and traveling in the big truck. I have drawn hundreds of pictures of my new life, but I have never written a note. Today I write, choosing my words easily and practicing my best handwriting.

Once done, I find Mom in the kitchen—she's wiping down the counters and cleaning up after our rushed Sunday morning. I come up close and lean into her. I could use my arms to give her a real hug, but I can't seem to relax them and keep them gripping my waist instead. As I stay stuck, she drops her rag and wraps her arms around me, holding them there for a while. It's kind of too long, but I like it.

"Here, Mom," I say pulling away from her and handing her the note tucked into my right hand. Then I run back upstairs so I am not there when she reads it:

Dear Mom,

I love you. I really do. You're kind, loving, and fair. I know whenever I need you that you will be straight. You pick me up when I am down. You teach me right from wrong. You back me up and are my best friend. You help me stay strong.

From: Angela Rose Vermaas

CHAPTER TWENTY-NINE

When Good Looks Bad

GARRY

Summer 2019

"Why did you do this?" the producer asks me as we sit in my office, pointing to the children noisily running around outside my door. The media company is here all day, filming what they call a "sizzle reel" that they can use to pitch my family as the topic of a new reality TV show. The children adore visitors, and knowing the visitors have cameras has added a new level of excitement, movement, and volume to my already chaotic home. It's a good question.

"Many years ago, Jodi and I decided to do two things without restrictions or rule books. We decided to get money—as much as we could—in order to do good in any way possible."

My wife adds, "We didn't aim to parent a dozen children, but we found that doing true good takes total engagement in other people's lives. Adoption does that. With adoption, you're 'all in'!"

The producer looks cynical and not at all inspired by our words or the wild cohort of kids in the next room. His doubt about the wisdom of our choices is the exact reason why he's sitting here in my office. "People are interested in this," he admits to me. Our story draws attention because, although helping children seems good, the uncertain outcomes of our choices—along with the obnoxious advocacy efforts and sizable sums of money it takes to make them happen—often look bad to other people.

I don't care if we look greedy, pushy, or reckless. In fact, I don't care *at all*. "My life is perfect," I often tell Jodi, who mostly struggles to share my sentiment. She's not wrong, of course. Our lives overflow with difficulties—both the expected ones of running a big family and business, along with the atypical troubles that accompany a dozen children with unique needs, trauma histories, and personalities.

It's not that I don't recognize the problems or feel their weight, but I am satisfied with the fullness of my life. I set out to reach the goal to get money and do good, and I did it. I am still doing it. And it's perfect.

After the camera crew leaves, the children jump in the pool as they usually do when there's free time and warm weather. Sitting along the edge, chatting with Jodi and drinking a beer, I feel my satisfaction deeply.

Edward jumps on Andrew's head. Zoe pulls down her suit to flash Robert, who yells back at her and then pouts for a few minutes on the steps of the pool. Angela picks a fight with Shiya, and William interrupts us with a myriad of random questions about megalodons. Jolyn practices water gymnastics as Luxmi paddles along with her one good arm. A few minutes later, Garret and

Rogie drop bothersome cannonballs into the pool.

Eventually, they charge over to Jodi looking for snacks. In the distance, I see James drive off to work as Tina pulls in for an afternoon swim with little Anavi.

Leaning back in my chair, I say to Jodi without thinking, "We should get a few more." Shocked, yet smiling, she asks, "Really?" I can't read her tone, but sarcasm seems the most appropriate.

"Our house and hearts have more room!" I go on, knowing it's mostly just a passing thought.

Or is it?

Jodi pauses, and I recognize her thoughts spinning, as if she never has thought about it before now. Her expression clears, becoming the familiar determined face I know and love. "If we ever get more," she says, "I want to find and adopt the lost sister—I heard they called her *Angel*."

The idea is impossible, of course. We have no clue where she might have been taken.

"We don't even know her real name," I say, as if that could deter Jodi. "Let's do it."

THANK YOU FOR READING OUR STORY!

Since publishing this work, much more has happened—including the addition of a 13th child. If you like this book and want to find out more about the fascinating Vermaas family, join our email list and get your very own photo album of the whole gang:

www.getmoneydogood.com/photo-album

Made in the USA
Monee, IL
22 February 2021

61096919R00184